BEYOND EVOLUTIONARY PSYCHOLOGY

The nature/nurture question is an age-old problem. *Beyond Evolutionary Psychology* deals with the relation between culture, evolution, psychology, and emotion, based both in the underlying biology, determined by our evolutionary heritage, and in the interaction of our brain with the physical, ecological, and social environment, based in the key property of brain plasticity. Ellis and Solms show how the brain structures that underlie cognition and behaviour relate to each other through developmental processes guided by primary emotional systems. This makes very clear which brain modules are innate or 'hard-wired', and which are 'soft-wired' or determined through environmental interactions. The key finding is that there can be no innate cognitive modules in the neocortex, as this is not possible on both developmental and genetic grounds; in particular, there can be no innate language acquisition device. This is essential reading for students and scholars of evolutionary psychology and evolutionary biology.

George Ellis is Emeritus Professor in the Mathematics Department at the University of Cape Town, and visiting Professor in the Physics Department, Oxford University. He co-authored *The Large Scale Structure of Space-Time* with Stephen Hawking. He has been awarded the Star of South Africa Medal by President Nelson Mandela, the Order of Mapungubwe by President Thabo Mbeki, and the Templeton Prize. He has many awards, including six honorary doctorates, the latest being awarded by the University of Paris. His latest book is *How Can Physics Underlie the Mind? Top-Down Causation in the Human Context* (2016).

Mark Solms is a psychoanalyst and a professor in neuropsychology. He currently holds the Chair of Neuropsychology at the University of Cape Town and Groote Schuur Hospital and is the President of the South African Psychoanalytical Association. He is also currently Research Chair of the International Psychoanalytical Association and Science Director of the American Psychoanalytic Association. Solms founded the International Neuropsychoanalysis Society (with the late Jaak Panksepp) in 2000 and was a Founding Editor of the journal *Neuropsychoanalysis*. He has published over 350 articles and chapters and seven books, the latest being *The Brain and the Inner World* (2002, translated into 13 languages) and *The Feeling Brain* (2015, his selected papers). He is the lead educator of the free online course *What Is a Mind?* on the platform FutureLearn.

CULTURE AND PSYCHOLOGY

Series Editor

David Matsumoto, *San Francisco State University*

As an increasing number of social scientists come to recognize the pervasive influence of culture on individual human behaviour, it has become imperative for culture to be included as an important variable in all aspects of psychological research, theory, and practice. *Culture and Psychology* is an evolving series of works that brings the study of culture and psychology into a single, unified concept.

Ute Schönpflug, *Cultural Transmission: Psychological, Developmental, Social, and Methodological Aspects*

Evert Van de Vliert, *Climate, Affluence, and Culture*

David Matsumoto and Fons J. R. van de Vijver, *Cross-Cultural Research Methods in Psychology*

Angela K.-y. Leung, Chi-yue Chiu, and Ying-yi Hong, *Cultural Processes: A Social Psychological Perspective*

Romin W. Tafarodi, *Subjectivity in the Twenty-First Century: Psychological, Sociological, and Political Perspectives*

Yair Neuman, *Introduction to Computational Cultural Psychology*

John W. Berry, *Mutual Intercultural Relations*

Ronald Fischer, *Personality, Values, Culture: An Evolutionary Approach*

Beyond Evolutionary Psychology

How and Why Neuropsychological Modules Arise

George Ellis

University of Cape Town

Mark Solms

University of Cape Town

CAMBRIDGE
UNIVERSITY PRESS

CAMBRIDGE
UNIVERSITY PRESS

University Printing House, Cambridge CB2 8BS, United Kingdom

One Liberty Plaza, 20th Floor, New York, NY 10006, USA

477 Williamstown Road, Port Melbourne, VIC 3207, Australia

314–321, 3rd Floor, Plot 3, Splendor Forum, Jasola District Centre, New Delhi – 110025, India

79 Anson Road, #06–04/06, Singapore 079906

Cambridge University Press is part of the University of Cambridge.

It furthers the University's mission by disseminating knowledge in the pursuit of education, learning, and research at the highest international levels of excellence.

www.cambridge.org
Information on this title: www.cambridge.org/9781107053687
DOI: 10.1017/9781107283954

First published 2018

A catalogue record for this publication is available from the British Library.

ISBN 978-1-107-05368-7 Hardback
ISBN 978-1-107-66141-7 Paperback

CONTENTS

List of Figures   *page* vi

List of Plates   viii

Preface   ix

Acknowledgements   xi

1   Introduction   1

2   The Mind and the Brain   16

3   Hierarchy, Modularity, and Development   38

4   Claims of Innate Modularity   59

5   The Mind and Emotions   83

6   A Realistic View of Evolution, Development, and Emotions   104

7   Conclusion   136

Appendix: Language Infinities   174

References   178

Index   195

The colour plate section appears between pages 116 and 117

FIGURES

1.1	The chain of causation	*page* 6
2.1	The triune brain	17
2.2	The hypothalamus	20
2.3	Primary and association cortical areas	22
2.4	The tectum	24
2.5	The hippocampus	26
2.6	The power of illusion	30
2.7	The thalamus	31
2.8	Corticothalamic circuitry	31
2.9	Broca's area and Wernicke's area	33
3.1	Hierarchical structure of the central nervous system	39
3.2	Connections of neurons via synapses	41
3.3	Top-down effects on cell function and gene expression	45
3.4	Neural network model	47
3.5	The chain of developmental causation	51
4.1	Mappings from objects or mental activity to concepts to words	64
4.2	The short route from the genome to cognition	73
4.3	The longer route from the genome to cognition	73
5.1	Periaqueductal grey matter (PAG)	86
5.2	The SEEKING system	90
5.3	The RAGE system	93
5.4	The FEAR system	94
5.5	The PANIC/GRIEF system	97
5.6	The effectiveness of placebos	102
6.1	The interactions between evolution, development, structure, function, and environment (context)	107

7.1 The ancient environment selects developmental systems that
provided desirable outcomes in that context 140
7.2 The way conscious problem-solving routines get embodied in
intuitive problem-solving patterns 149
7.3 Spoken and written languages are different instantiations
of the same expressions representing abstract concepts 158

PLATES

1   The nervous system
2   (a) Cortex structure (left), (b) ascending systems (right)
3   (a) The optic tract, (b) the retinal synaptic connections
4   Some major nuclei of the reticular activating system and PAG
5   Association areas
6   The visual word form area
7   Semantic models: Principal components of voxel-wise semantic models, revealing four important semantic dimensions in the brain
8   Physical domains in the cortex
9   Hierarchical structure of a gene regulatory network
10   (a) Sketch of cortical columns made up of interconnected neurons, (b) Detailed microsketch of cortical columns
11   The nucleus accumbens

PREFACE

A profound question regarding brain/behaviour relationships is this: which aspects are innate, that is, are essentially genetically determined, and which are not? That is, which aspects have an initial structure that is genetically determined but rather loosely prescribed at a detailed level, their detailed nature then being precisely determined through developmental processes as a consequence of learning experiences and interaction with the environment? Major disputes have raged around this question, with many linguists supporting Chomsky's proposals concerning the existence of innate language modules in the brain, and with some evolutionary psychologists recently claiming existence of many other innate cognitive modules, even modules for folk psychology, folk biology, and folk physics. An opposing school, largely composed of 'evo-devo' theorists, have strongly denied these claims.

In our view, this dispute can only be resolved through a more detailed consideration of the specific brain structures that are innate in the above sense, thus avoiding sweeping statements about the brain as a whole, as is the common practice. Such detailed consideration must take seriously both neurophysiology and developmental neurobiology, based in epigenetic processes, instead of simply relying on theoretical speculations about the evolutionary origins of behaviour.

We argue that when this is done, a rather clear picture emerges as to which brain structures are innate, or 'hard-wired', and which are not. That is the topic of this book.

The conclusion is to recognize a number of brain modules that are indeed hard-wired, but these modules exclude the whole of the neocortex. If correct, this book shows that the existence of innate language modules and other innate cognitive modules is not biologically plausible. Rather, we argue that any and all cognitive modules must have essentially developmental origins, based in a genotypic structure that (for example) creates a phenotype that is language-ready but not language-specific. In short, if language functions can be assigned to non-language cortex, as happens, for example, in cases of surgical removal of the left hemisphere in childhood (where the right hemisphere readily takes over the language functions normally assigned to the left) and in congenitally deaf people who acquire sign language (where the visual cortex performs language functions that would normally be assigned to auditory cortex), then there is no such thing as innate language cortex.

Much work is needed to develop the details of this proposal, that is, to identify the specific biological structures and mechanisms that underpin cognition generally, and language specifically. However, we are confident that the framework we outline here will stand the test of time.

ACKNOWLEDGEMENTS

We thank David Matsumoto, Series Editor for Cambridge University Press's *Culture and Psychology* series, for suggesting that a talk given by one of us (GE) in Stellenbosch at the symposium on evolutionary and ecological paradigms in the study of culture at The International Association for Cross-Cultural Psychology 21st Congress (2012) be turned into this book. GE thanks David Kibble for introducing him to Jaak Panksepp's work, the late Leslie Shackleton for jointly running a discussion group on the brain that led to this happy occurrence, and Judith Toronchuk for a creative collaboration that developed details of the idea of Affective Neural Darwinism (AND).

We particularly thank Peter Fries for discussions on the varied views on the nature of Linguistics, in specific Halliday's and Hoey's views, and for notes on Systemic Functional Linguistics that have been incorporated in Chapter 6; Carole Bloch for her helpful insights as regards the section on reading in Chapter 7, and help in drafting that section; and the late Bill Stoeger for collaborating on the work presented in the Appendix. We thank Aimee Dollman for helping with collating illustrations and for indexing work.

1

Introduction

1.1 THE ISSUE

One of the key issues in human biology is the nature/nurture debate: which aspects of our bodies and behaviour are genetically determined, and which are environmentally shaped? As regards the human brain, what innate modules are there in the brain, producing behaviours that are hard-wired rather than learnt through our life experiences (Carruthers et al. 2004)? Or to put the issue another way, where does human knowledge come from (Elman et al. 1998)? Even more fundamentally, what is the nature of human nature (Buller 2005, pp. 420–480)?

Many evolutionary psychologists propose, in reply, that there are a variety of genetically determined brain modules – our evolutionary heritage – which provide innate knowledge from the day we are born: modules for language, folk psychology, folk physics, folk biology, cheater detection, and so on (Chomsky 1965; Tooby and Cosmides, 1992, p. 13; Pinker 1994, pp. 419–427; Cartwright 2000, pp. 193–211; La Cerra and Bingham 2002, pp. 179–187; West-Eberhard 2003, p. 81; Buller 2005, pp. 127–200; Geary 2005; Carruthers et al. 2005, 2006, 2007). A full set of possible cognitive modules is listed by Cartwright (2000, pp. 195–196). Other ways of talking like this are to propose a language instinct (Pinker 1994), or refer to innateness (Carruthers et al. 2005), nativism (Pullum and Scholz 2002), or domain-specific modules (Laland and Brown 2004; Carruthers et al. 2005). These authors propose that key aspects of human knowledge are innate; that is where much cognition comes from and how much human behaviour is determined.

The evidence brought forward in support of these proposals is, on the one hand, the evidence of 'poverty of stimulus' (Carruthers et al. 2005, pp. 6–7) and, on the other, data concerning the behaviour of young children (Carruthers et al. 2005, pp. 8–10). In particular, the poverty of stimulus argument has been strongly supported by Chomsky in the case of language (Chomsky 1965): the developing child does not have sufficient input data to deduce the rules whereby language is constructed. Hence, that knowledge must be innate.

There are a number of problems with this argument. In particular, it is based on a view of language as a rigidly *rule-based* system (Chomsky 1965) – which is not the natural way the mind works. The mind is grounded not so much in rules as in pattern-recognition and prediction (Hawkins 2004; Frith 2007; Friston 2010; Churchland 2013; Clark 2016) based in connectionist principles (Elman et al. 1998). While it can be trained to operate in a rule-based way, that is not the basic way it functions. This applies specifically to language, as can be demonstrated, for example, by documenting how learning to read actually takes place (Bloch 1997) and how reading actually happens in a meaningful context (Flurkey et al. 2008). One can argue that lexis is complexly and systematically structured, and that grammar is an outcome of this lexical structure (Hoey 2005), as evidenced by collocation studies (Biber et al. 2006). Learning actually occurs via Latent Semantic Analysis (Berry et al. 1995; Landauer and Dumais 1997).

Theoretical arguments for the 'poverty of stimulus' proposal pick up on the linguistic view that an infinite number of sentences are possible; therefore, there is no way the required understanding for reading all sentences could be learnt from available stimuli. See Kamorova and Nowak (2005) for a formal 'proof' that is supposed to show that innate language modules exist. This is hopelessly unrealistic; the longest sentences that can occur in the real world are strictly bounded, because you must remember the start of the sentence by the time you reach the end (see Appendix). Furthermore, the poverty of stimulus argument is undermined by empirical assessment of its criteria (Pullum and Scholz 2002). Lastly, it disregards the effects of the intense emotional bond between the infant and its mother (Greenspan 1997; Greenspan and Shanker 2004).

In any case there are a number of problems with all these cognitive innateness proposals, arising in essence from the fact that they do not take physiological and developmental issues seriously enough. Behavioural or brain imaging data may be able to establish that domain-specific modules exist in developed or developing brains, for language for example, but that does not establish that such modules have a genetic origin. Genes determine outcomes to some extent, but a key feature of brain development is plasticity in response to interactions with the environment (West-Eberhard 2003; Fernando and Szathmary 2010). This shapes neural networks at the higher level (Elman et al. 1998) and gene regulatory networks at a lower level (Kandel 2006; Wagner 2011), resulting in a simultaneous evolutionary origin of regulation and form (West-Eberhard 2003). An adequate investigation of the nature/nurture issue must take such biological effects into account; it cannot proceed simply on the basis of behavioural outcome data. That data must be carefully unpicked to analyse what kinds of innate modules it might actually support, when developmental and physiological issues are also taken into account. In particular, we should recognize that cortical modules can be adapted to quite different roles if the sensory input to the cortex in question is rewired (Roe et al. 1992) or if it is damaged (Johnson 2007, pp. 132–137; Chanraud et al. 2013). Perhaps, the most dramatic example of this is the experiment in which Sur and colleagues (Roe et al. 1992; von Melchner et al. 2000) reconfigured newborn ferret brains in such a way that their visual pathways were directed to the cortical region where hearing normally develops; these ferrets developed visual functions in the supposedly auditory parts of their cortex. In other words, they saw the world with brain tissue that was supposedly genetically specialized for hearing sounds. If this can be done for sounds in general, how much more must the principle be true for language sounds in particular?

As regards the behavioural data on infants and young children, this must be carefully related to which specific brain modules the data are supposed to support. In particular, it must distinguish between sensory modules, cognitive modules, and emotional modules. As discussed in the subsequent passages, these form very different categories.

This book sets out a developmentally based view that challenges ideas proposed in the name of evolutionary psychology regarding the genetic origin of neocortical brain modules. It will propose a much narrower, more biologically based set of innate modules underlying development of the brain, which are not in themselves cognitive modules but play a key role in cognitive evolution.

The fundamental point here is that there *are* innate modules in the brain, but they do not perform cognitive functions; they perform affective ones. A growing body of research shows the guiding role of affect (emotions) on both behaviour and cognitive development (see e.g. Greenspan (1997) and Damasio (1994, 1999)). This research suggests that emotion must have played a key role in evolutionary development – it must both have been selected for by evolution and affected evolution. So what then are the genetically determined affective systems that have been selected for? They are the 'primary emotion command systems' investigated in particular depth by Jaak Panksepp (Panksepp 1998; Panksepp and Biven

2012), based in the ascending activation and limbic circuits of the mammalian brain (Kingsley 2000) releasing dopamine, norepinephrine, and many other neuromodulators in the cortex.

These ancient systems have an important role to play in the function and evolutionary development of the human brain. The case will be made that *these affective systems are the innate modules that shape both cognitive development and behaviour* and are the lynchpin between evolution and psychological development. This link is what is missing in standard discussions of evolutionary psychology. The role of this book is to make good the hiatus.

1.2   GUIDING PRINCIPLES

Why should there be modules in the brain in the first place? It is a basic principle of complex systems that the only way to create true complexity is via modular hierarchical structures (Simon 1962; Flood and Carson 1990; Booch 2007). As stated by Nelson in Schlosser and Wagner (2004, p. 17):

> Modularity pervades every level of biological organisation, from proteins to populations, biological units are built of smaller, quasi-autonomous parts. This type of organisation is essential to much of biological function. In particular, modular design enables evolutionary change. To quote Raff, 'It is the property of modularity that allows evolutionary dissociation of the developmental process and thus makes the evolution of development possible.'
>
> (Raff and Sly 2000)

Thus, modularity is a key to evolutionary processes (Simon 1962). But how do evolutionary and developmental processes lead to modularity?

As famously pointed out by Dobzhansky, 'Nothing in Biology Makes Sense Except in the Light of Evolution' (Dobzhansky 1971). However, that is hardly the whole story, as one might believe from some evolutionary psychological writings. It is equally true that nothing in biology makes sense except in the light also, firstly, of epigenetic developmental processes (Gilbert 2006; Gilbert and Epel 2009), secondly, of physiological structure (Rhoades and Pflanzer 1989), and, thirdly, of biological function (Hartwell et al. 1999; Campbell and Reece 2005). These interlocking issues are the foundations on which a sound understanding must be built.

Principle 1: Evolutionary origin: A theory of brain modules must be based in an account of evolutionary processes whereby they could have come into existence.

This will of course be a Darwinian process of natural selection over geological timescales. It is based on survival of the fittest (in some suitable sense). While many genetic variants ('genotypes') may be neutral in the sense of not affecting reproductive survival rates, others are crucial because they lead to behaviours or functions ('phenotypes') that are better adapted to the local physical, ecological, or social environment. It is these better adapted phenotypes that preferentially pass on their genes to succeeding generations and so lead to environmental adaptation (Corning 2005; Ayala 2012). But they must be sufficiently important to compete as survival criteria with all the other biologically compelling issues impinging on animate life, such as the search for food and for safety from predators.

Principle 2: Behaviour/function: A theory of brain modules must include an account of behaviour or function whereby reproductive survival rates are enhanced.

It is a further principle of biology that structure underlies function, and this applies in particular to the brain (Nicholls et al. 2001; Clark et al. 2012). Hence, physiological structures are selected biologically on the basis of the functions that they enable.

Principle 3: Structure/physiology: A theory of brain modules must identify physiological structures whereby behaviour or function that enhances reproductive survival rates is enabled.

The structures that occur come into being by developmental processes (Johnson 2007) based on the information contained in the genotype but adaptively controlled via gene regulatory networks (Wagner 2017) and epigenetic effects (Gilbert and Epel 2009). These change outcomes in an essential way in response to environmental conditions (West-Eberhard 2003) and so are not pre-set developmental programmes (Buller 2005, pp. 123–126, 133–137).

Principle 4: Adaptive development/neural plasticity: A theory of brain modules must identify viable developmental processes whereby the needed physiological structures can be brought into being. These processes involve developmental plasticity in response to the environment; this shapes neural connectivity.

Principles 1–4 are the basis on which we develop our proposals. It is important to note that these principles will apply to all the interlocking scales involved in a living organism. Figure 1.1 represents the basic causal chain we have outlined here.

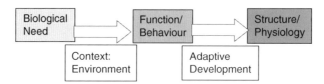

FIGURE 1.1 The chain of causation. The basic needs are survival, involving in particular the continual search for energy (metabolism), and reproduction with inheritance

1.3   PROBLEMS WITH INNATE COGNITIVE MODULES

There are problems with innate cognitive modules in regard to each of these principles.

Principle 1: Evolutionary origin: The issue here is the following: suppose there is some cognitive behaviour that enhances survival prospects, for example an effective understanding of physics or biology. There is no plausible mechanism whereby this behaviour can get written into DNA. Firstly, because developmental issues strongly suggest DNA cannot encode the needed neural network details (see the following). Secondly – supposing we ignore that issue – because it is unlikely that emergence of such modules would lead to sufficient enhancement of survival prospects, in competition with all the other variables that affect survival, as to control which genes get passed on to later generations. Thirdly, because the massive early developmental expansion of human neocortex – beyond what is found in living anthropoid apes (chimps, gorillas, and orangutans) – is largely controlled by a single gene (Florio et al. 2015), which leaves little room for hard-wiring of intrinsic human neocortical functions.

Principle 2: Behaviour/function: The modular argument is often phrased in terms of survival advantage in the context of an environment of evolutionary adaptedness (EEA) (Laland and Brown 2004), usually taken to be an African savannah. But there is not a single relevant environment; what is actually needed is the ability to adapt to whatever environment is encountered. This is stated by La Cerra and Bingham (2002, pp. 186–187) as follows:

> We agree that your brain is composed of neural adaptations that resulted from evolution. but these adaptations did not take the form of well-defined, inherited information processing circuits that were designed to generate predetermined adaptive solutions to Stone Age problems. Rather, they took the form of components of a system that could

construct adaptive information processing networks – individualised circuitries that generated behavioural solutions that precisely fit the specific environmental conditions, bioenergetic needs, personal experiences, and unique life history of an individual.

Principle 3: Structure/physiology: This principle is related to the previous one: if our cognitive processes were based in cortical modules adapted to the EEA, we would not survive for a day in New York or Johannesburg. We need an *adaptive* modular system rather than an *adapted* modular system (Buller 2005, pp. 127–200).

Principle 4: Development/neural plasticity: If we ignore the previous problems and suppose the needed information could get written onto DNA, there is no way it could get read out in developmentally plausible terms. The point is that it is difficult enough seeing how the modules that certainly do need to be hard-wired (the homeostatic brainstem and instinctive limbic systems, the primary sensory and motor systems) can be generated by developmental processes through reading DNA. In these cases (as in the case of c elegans) the networks and synaptic connections are well defined and can be 'hard-wired' by reading DNA with suitable positional indicators guiding the process. But the forest of detailed synaptic connections in cortical columns (Plate 2(a)) is a completely different story. Reading out DNA with precise enough positional information to uniquely specify these connections just does not seem possible.

The conclusion is that we need a process whereby one lays down specific connections in the brain and sensory-motor organs that perform precise predetermined functions and are more or less invariant through life, which in turn prime instinctual learning systems that can respond and adapt to changing local circumstances. The kind of adaptive developmental processes described by West-Eberhard (2003) will do the job nicely. What happens is that random synaptic connections are initially set up, and then on the one hand pruned and on the other hand strengthened or weakened, on the basis of experience.

Thus, 'precise patterns of environmental stimuli to which the developing cortex is exposed play an essential role in shaping brain circuits, and the functional properties of those circuits . . . Environmental inputs to the brain shape the more fine-grained cortical structures by determining the outcome of cell competition' (Buller 2005, p. 133).

This is a process of adaptive selection whereby 'neurons compete with each other for the sort of information processing structure they are going to be, and brain activity, guided by environmental inputs, determines which neurons win this competition, hence which processing roles they end up playing' (Buller 2005, p. 135). This is a form of neural Darwinism, as discussed by Edelman (1989, 1992). At the molecular level, this happens because of top-down control of gene regulatory circuits through the activity of the mind (Kandel 2005, 2006). This process sets up *Adaptive Representational Networks* (ARN) in the cortex (La Carra and Bingham 2002), which are the basis of pattern recognition and prediction through learning (Hawkins 2004; Friston 2010; Churchland 2013).

1.4   HARD-WIRED AND SOFT-WIRED CONNECTIONS

To proceed, it is useful to distinguish between what we will refer to as *hard-wired* and *soft-wired* connections in the brain. Here,

- *hard-wired connections* refer to neurons where genetically based developmental programmes produce a fairly tightly prescribed set of connections to other neurons in a specific domain; they will be affected to some extent by contextual variables, but nevertheless the outcome is connections with a very specific set of predetermined functions. This leads to the kind of innate modularity envisaged by the authors cited above.
- *soft-wired connections* refer to neurons where genetically based developmental programmes produce an initially random set of connections to other neurons in a specific domain, which then get pruned and altered in strength in response to experience so as to produce specific connections that are essentially the product of learning processes, with broad functions that are an outcome of this process (Buller 2005). This is the kind of developmental plasticity described in detail by West-Eberhard (2003).

Given this distinction, hard-wired modules exist in brain areas where specific pre-prescribed functions are required. Such hard-wired connections occur in two contexts:

- *targeted connections* that connect neurons in specific local brain domains to other neurons (specific post-synaptic targets) which are also in specific local brain domains;
- *diffuse systems*, which are the topic of the next section.

The hard-wired targeted connections are (see Plate 1 (see colour plate section)):

1. The spinal cord and peripheral nervous system (Kingsley 2000, pp. 22–30).
2. The autonomic nervous system (Kingsley 2000, pp. 471–487) and cranial nerves (Kingsley 2000, pp. 337–380).
3. The subcortical sensory systems, ultimately leading to the cortex: specifically, the somatosensory system (Kingsley 2000, pp. 165–208), the auditory system (Kingsley 2000, pp. 393–415), and the visual system (Kingsley 2000, pp. 433–465), mostly excluding in each case the associated cortical areas, as well as the gustatory and olfactory systems.
4. The subcortical motor systems, ultimately leading from the cortex: specifically, the spinal mechanisms of motor control (Kingsley 2000, pp. 209–238), descending motor systems (Kingsley 2000, pp. 239–283), and basal ganglia connections (Kingsley 2000, pp. 285–310).
5. Much of the connectivity of the limbic system.

By contrast, soft-wired connections exist where brain plasticity is required in order that flexibility and learning be possible; this is the case in

- all intrinsic cortical areas associated with cognition: the cerebral hemispheres and lobes (Kingsley 2000, pp. 7–15) – which are structured in terms of columns and layers;
- the cerebellum (Kingsley 2000, pp. 311–336);
- some aspects of the limbic system (certainly hippocampus and amygdala).

Outcome 1: *There are no hard-wired cognitive systems within the cortex. There are, however, soft-wired, developmentally shaped cognitive modules arising from interaction between individuals and their social, physical, and ecological environments.*

Neurons in specific layers of the sensory cortices may all have a common property, but that does not amount to the kind of detailed neural network weighting system that is required for coding cognitive information (Churchland 2013).

In more detail, it is crucial that the connections from the primary sensory systems (from the eyes, ears, tongue, nose, skin) be hard-wired through neuronal migration, so that the sensory input ultimately leading to the cortex is directly related to incoming signals – such as the synaptic connections in the retina (Plate 3(b) (see colour plate section)) and from there to the visual cortex (the optic tracts via the lateral geniculate nucleus, Plate 3(a) (see colour plate section)) – must be tightly prescribed, and so must be hard-wired. However, the connections into and within the visual cortex itself (Plate 3(b) (see colour plate section), bottom) can only be soft-wired, according to the above outcome. This is why we have to *learn* to see cortically.

Similarly, the descending cortical motor systems must be connected to muscles via hard-wired subcortical connections, in order that the cerebrum can accurately control our actions. But this must be flexible, so their connections in and from the cortex itself are soft-wired. This is why we have to learn to perform voluntary movements.

As to the cortex itself, this outcome excludes the possibility of language modules, folk physics modules, and so on, on developmental grounds. Such modules could not be pre-wired, even if the needed data could somehow be stored in DNA (or even in gene control networks). The specificity required of the wiring process is simply too high.

1.5 DIFFUSE SYSTEMS AND THE CRUCIAL ROLE OF EMOTION

Our second key point is that a family of diffuse projections from the upper brainstem and limbic system nuclei to the cortex are hard-wired. Here,

- *diffuse connections* refer to neurons that do not link specifically to other neurons in a small domain (no obvious postsynaptic targets are seen) but rather link to widespread cortical and subcortical areas, their function being to modulate synaptic activity across such large areas (Nicholls et al. 2001, p. 282).

The relevant modules here are the so-called *ascending systems* (Plate 2(b) (see colour plate section)) which include

- the *noradrenaline (norepinephrine) system* originating in the locus coeruleus complex (Kingsley 2000, p. 132; Nicholls et al. 2001, p. 283);
- the *dopamine systems* originating mainly in the substantia nigra and ventral tegmental area (Kingsley 2000, p. 132; Nicholls et al. 2001, pp. 284–285);
- the *serotonin system* originating in the raphe nuclei (Kingsley 2000, p. 133; Nicholls et al. 2001, p. 278);
- the *cholinergic system* originating in the basal forebrain nuclei (Nicholls et al. 2001, p. 278);
- the *histamine system* originating in the tuberomamillary nucleus in the hypothalamus (Nicholls et al. 2001, pp. 284–285).

Because these are hard-wired, they must play an important role in brain function and hence in evolution. Indeed, Edelman (1989) has pointed out that these systems play a key role in shaping brain plasticity, so they play an important role in adaptive developmental processes ('neural Darwinism'). But what are their psychological correlates?

Damasio (1994, 1999), Le Doux (1998), Panksepp (1998), and others have pointed out that cognition is not all that happens in the brain: *emotion* plays a key role, both in terms of directing cognitive activity and affecting brain plasticity through the various neuromodulators just mentioned, and others (La Cerr and Bingham 2002, pp. 119–126). So in fact the ascending systems are a key component of the primary affective systems whereby emotions affect brain function across the cortex, including during brain development (Panksepp 1998; Panksepp and Biven 2012). These systems are genetically determined and their basic structure is constant across all individuals (including all mammals, as summarized in depth by Panksepp 1998).

Putting this all together,

Outcome 2: *The ascending systems linking the primordial emotional systems to the cortex are hard-wired and play a key role in adaptive developmental processes that shape behavioural outcomes. Consequently, they must have played a key role in evolutionary processes as well.*

Building on the work of Damasio and Panksepp and others, this makes clear that any attempt to deal with the evolution of the mind purely on the basis of cognition is fundamentally mistaken. We must therefore add to our principles (Section 1.2) a fifth one:

Principle 5: Emotion as well as cognition. A theory of brain modules must take into account how the basic emotion systems proposed by Panksepp (1998) and others, working in conjunction with all-purpose cognitive modules in the cortex, are evolutionarily developed systems that play a key role in brain plasticity.

It will be suggested that these basic emotion systems are the real innate brain modules that shape the brain through developmental plasticity as the individual interacts with their physical, social, and ecological environment, and thereby lead to effective modules for language and other cognitive functions. This is the key insight that will be developed in this book.

1.6   WHAT IS NEW IN THIS BOOK?

This view on the relation between genetic and environmental determination challenges views set out in writings on evolutionary psychology and on

innate cognitive modules, for example by Chomsky, Pinker, Buss, and
Geary (referred to in the aforementioned discussion). It develops from
the work of Panksepp (1998), Edelman (1989, 1992), Damasio (1999),
Stevens and Price (2000), and Greenspan and Shanker (2004). It is consonant with views on evolutionary psychology and modularity by others,
for example Buller (2005), La Cerra and Bingham (2002), and Laland and
Brown (2004), and with views on adaptive development, in particular by
Karmiloff-Smith (1996) and West-Eberhard (1998). Each contains part of
our argument, but not the overall integrated viewpoint set out here. A short
version of the present argument is, however, given in another book written
by one of us (Ellis 2016).

   Many authors have queried the viability of the evolutionary psychology
proposals concerning a variety of innate cortical (cognitive) modules, and
we agree with them. What is new here is the identification of the key role
played by the primary emotional systems in understanding the modular-
ized relation between cognition and brain evolution and development.

   It brings in neurological aspects of the argument, and so gives some
explanation of the neurobiology that underlies the existence and nature of
modules. The whole point is that this is what is being overlooked in much of
the evolutionary psychology literature. Evolution must explain the universal
physiological structuring of aspects of the brain, as discussed briefly in the
preceding paragraphs. These are determined by their functional roles that
have materially enhanced survival prospects. Development must explain
how the brain adjusts to specific local conditions and experiences. And it
can be claimed that the basic emotion systems, functioning via the ascending
neuromodulator and limbic systems, are key in the link between evolution
and development, between the biologically universal and the specific. The
book that comes closest to what we have written on these topics is that by Lee
et al. (2009), which we became aware of only as we were concluding this text.
That book is in broad agreement with what we propose here, but does not
refer to Panksepp's work on primary emotional systems, and does not make
the developmental points as regards the neocortex that we make here.

   This view has implications for various proposals for educational policy
that have been alleged to follow from evolutionary theory, and we briefly
comment on that aspect in the following section.

1.7   SUMMARY OF CHAPTERS

Chapter 2 provides an overview of the structure of the brain, and the relation
between the mind and the brain. It summarizes basic brain macro and micro

structure, and then considers elementary brain functions and their survival value. It then looks at the evolutionary process for life in general, and its relation to the human brain in particular. The evolutionary development of humanity specifically required development of a 'social brain' and hence means of communication between members of society. This may have been the origin of symbolic behaviour and reflexive consciousness.

Chapter 3 considers modularity and its relation to complexity. The brain has many levels of emergence. The chapter deals firstly with the way complexity arises out of modular hierarchical structures, and secondly with issues of evolution and development. Key here is the relation between genetic effects on the one hand and environmental influences on the other when adaptive developmental processes take place. This is particularly important in considering the fundamental concept of brain plasticity, which is the basis of learning and memory, and hence of personal identity.

The relation between causality, emergence, and development in relation to evolution, function, and structure is summarized in Figure 1.1. The implication is that we can run the deductive chain the other way: Structure ➜ Function ➜ Evolutionary path.

Chapter 4 considers claims of innate modularity in general and in relation to cortical cognitive modules in particular. It looks particularly at the claims of language modules by Chomsky and Pinker, and then of other evolutionary psychological modules proposed by Buss, Geary, and others. It considers the type of behavioural evidence advanced for such cortical modules, where there is indeed evidence for functional specificity in particular locations; but this is divorced from biological evidence as to what it is that leads to such specificity. There are many difficulties with hard-wired cognitive modules:

- Information issues: there is not enough genetic information.
- Developmental issues: there is no way to hard-wire them.
- Evolutionary issues: they could not be selected for.

Because of brain plasticity in an uncertain environment, there is no plausible developmental path for the alleged specific innate cortical modules. They arise developmentally during interaction with the environment, rather than directly ('genetically').

Chapter 5 deals with emotion/affect and its important functions: first, as a means of communication, related to facial expressions conveying emotions and so helping facilitate and regulate social interactions. Second, as a guide to behaviour, whereby emotions have a key role in brain function (e.g. as emotional tags attached to memories). Third, emotions function as a guide to development by guiding adaptive development through the processes of neural Darwinism. Here the role of non-local neural connections is crucial in underlying brain plasticity. These emotional systems provide evolutionarily based guidance as to what is immediately important for survival, which then shapes brain plasticity.

The basic affective systems can be identified as psychobiological universals. This set of primary emotional systems occurs in all mammals, including humans. They are hard-wired systems (hence developed in our evolutionary past) that provide rapid guidance as to how to act in any situation. Possible additions to Panksepp's proposed taxonomy of primary emotional systems are considered.

Chapter 6 puts together a realistic view of evolution, development, and emotions. It makes the case that emotional modules are a key link in both psychological function and development, and hence also in evolution: affect shapes intellect through developmental processes with a key causal factor being social experiences. The ascending systems associated with the limbic modules are hard-wired because of the key role they play in function, development, and plasticity; cortical modules are broad-purpose modules that get specialized and shaped through social, physical, and ecological interactions and experiences. The position taken here is that there are no genetically fixed cognitive modules whatever, and in particular no innate language modules that control grammatical structure.

Where, then, do the language regularities come from that Chomsky recognized and categorized as being due to a deep grammar module? On this view they are due to essential syntactic limitations on any language whatever, in order that it be an adequate symbolic system for describing the world around us. They are due to fundamental semiotic constraints on a symbolic representation of our experiences and environment, as explained in detail by Deacon (2003). How then is language learned? Through ongoing experience of the use of language in meaningful contexts (Tomasello 2003), driven by the drive for interaction (Lee et al. 2009), and developing an Embodied Construction Grammar (Feldman 2008), particularly via mother–child bonding and the child's search for meaning in this developing relationship (Greenspan and Shanker 2004). This process is beautifully described in *Chloe's Story* by Carole Bloch (Bloch 1997). Is there a poverty of stimulus, as claimed by Chomsky and others? Certainly not if we take the ongoing, intense mother–child interaction into account (Bloch 1997; Greenspan and Shanker 2004).

Chapter 7 is the Conclusion, giving a summary of our argument, and outlining further possible developments. It considers possible implications for educational policy, as advocated in particular by Geary. As there are no innate folk physics modules, there is no need to unlearn what they may be imposing on our understanding. Rather, educational policy must adapt on the one hand to the exploratory developmental way the brain works, making mistakes on the way to getting a correct understanding, and on the other hand it must take into account the crucial role of affect in the classroom and its effects on learning motivation.

An **Appendix** counters arguments for innate language modules by language theorists that are based on the idea of infinite length sentences.

2

The Mind and the Brain

This chapter provides an overview of the relation between the mind and the brain. It considers basic brain functions and their survival value.

2.1 BRAIN STRUCTURE AND FUNCTION

As always in biology, structure and function are intimately related.

2.1.1 The Basic Structures

The broad nature of the nervous system was outlined in Chapter 1. It consists of networks of neurons connected together by synapses, broadly forming the peripheral nervous system and the central nervous system (CNS) (Plate 1 (see colour plate section)). The latter comprises the spinal cord and three major levels of brain structure. Although an oversimplification, MacLean's (1989) classification of these levels is well known: the reptilian brain, the limbic system, and the neocortex, which are – very broadly speaking – respectively responsible for reflex behaviour, emotional behaviour, and symbolic behaviour (Figure 2.1).

The sheet of tissue called neocortex has a complex convoluted structure with left and right hemispheres, each comprising four lobes, made of layered columns with numerous finely detailed vertical and horizontal synaptic connections (Plate 2(a) (see colour plate section)) embodying individualized learning and personality. It also has recurrent connections between brain regions. The limbic system has many interconnected nuclei such as the hippocampus, amygdala, hypothalamus, septum, accumbens, and so on, with different functions broadly related to emotion and emotional learning.

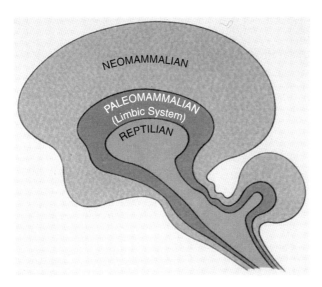

FIGURE 2.1 The triune brain. A broad categorization of the brain into three primary components: the neocortex, limbic system, and reptilian brain

The sensory and motor systems are connected by nerve tracts to the neocortex via relay stations, mainly in the thalamus, that integrate information. They are wired in a precise pattern at the muscle and sensory receptor ends (Plate 3(b) (see colour plate section)) and in the relay nuclei, but in a flexible fashion at the neocortical side. Diffuse projections link limbic system nuclei to the neocortex (Plate 2(b) (see colour plate section)). Various parts of the neocortex such as the visual cortex and motor cortex are, after development, dedicated to specific functions, but this is not written in stone: because of brain plasticity, these regions can be rewired to serve other purposes. This brain plasticity is based in *the ability of cortical neurons to alter their connections with other neurons in terms of both synaptic patterning and synaptic strengths*; and this in turn is based in the way that gene expression in neurons is modulated by the activity of neurotransmitters (Kandel 2006) – an example of epigenetic control through gene regulatory networks.

2.1.2 Affective and Cognitive Structures

In this book, we draw a basic distinction between those parts of the brain that serve affective functions and those that serve cognitive functions. These are crucially different: the cognitive functions analyse what is

happening, recognizing patterns to make predictions of possible outcomes, and presenting alternative action choices for selection. The affective functions assign *values* to the different events, outcomes, and
memories, and give guidance to the cognitive functions as to what should
be the current locus of attention and broadly how to react. The events in
question crucially include endogenous ones, like the need states of the
individual (homeostatic 'drives' like hunger and sleepiness). Without
such affective guidance, the cognitive functions will not cohere and will
fail to achieve biologically imperative goals. This may be demonstrated
through study of individuals with impaired affective functioning (Damasio
1994).

We believe that the 'hard-wired' part of the mind (or brain) is mainly
affective whereas the cognitive part relies primarily on learning. Hence,
we argue that language, a cognitive function, is learnt; there is no
'language instinct'. There is, however, language preparedness: the
human mind is adapted to develop symbolic behaviour in general, and
some form of language in particular, through its ability to assign categorical labels, in hierarchical sets, to patterns of perceptions and emergent concepts in a recursive way. The extent of this ability in humans
separates us from all other animals, and even from the other higher
primates. While some species (specifically, bonobos) have been shown
to have an impressive symbolic ability, it does not extend to full language use with syntax allowing construction of arbitrary semantic
meaning.

The nature of possible languages can vary widely, but they must obey
semiotic constraints that restrict the nature of symbolic systems able to
adequately model and represent the natural, ecological, and social
worlds in which we live. This is plausibly the origin of 'language
universals' across cultures (Deacon 2003), but it must be remembered
that the same constraints apply to numbers and other symbolic systems
too (such as musical notation or road traffic signage). It would be
absurd to claim on this basis that we possess an 'instinct' for each
such system. The evolutionary push to develop language readiness
arises not from innate 'language modules' but rather from the enhanced
survival prospects arising from abstraction and communication, when
living in groups and supporting each other, sharing knowledge, and
planning common ventures. To do this effectively requires the socially
cooperative development of a refined symbolic system allowing the
formulation and sharing of abstract thoughts and plans (Section 2.5).

2.2 BRAIN AND MIND

Shortly we will define what we mean by 'instinct'. But first we must clarify that the affective and cognitive parts of the brain are not the whole of the brain. The brain performs many functions that are neither affective nor cognitive: that is, they are not mental. Consider, for example, the vital functions of heartbeat and breathing. These bodily functions are regulated by the so-called reptilian brain but they are not mental functions. The same applies to the complex processes involved, for example, in the function of walking. The intricate processes that regulate muscle tone in relation to vestibular and proprioceptive variables in order to maintain an upright posture while ambulating over an uneven surface involve an enormous amount of brain power. But these processes are not mental processes. In other words, the mental part of the brain is a subset of the totality of the brain. However, it is easier to understand the mental part of the brain by situating it within the totality of the brain's functions

2.2.1   Inner and Outer Worlds

Very broadly speaking (the way we speak when we want to see the wood for the trees), the brain's major function is to *straddle two worlds*, which we are going to call 'inner' and 'outer' for short. The inner world is the internal milieu of the body, the non-ambulatory (vegetative) or visceral body, also known as the autonomic body. It is called 'autonomic' because it functions automatically, and this provides an important link to the concepts of hardwiring and of instinct, to which we will return in the subsequent passages. The outer world is the environment around us, the 'not me' world. This part of the world is far more complex and unpredictable than the relatively fixed and immutable inner world of the autonomic body. The unpredictability of the outer world provides an important link to the imperative for learning, which is the opposite of instinct and which underpins all cognition. Instincts are hardwired responses to predictable situations of universal significance; learning (and cognition) begins where the predictability ends.

The inner world of the body is regulated neurologically by a series of nuclei located mainly in the upper brainstem, known as body-monitoring nuclei. Some of these nuclei are shown in Figure 2.2.

The most important of them are located in the medial hypothalamus. These are called 'need detectors'. They and all the other body-monitoring nuclei represent the *demands for work* that the body makes upon the brain.

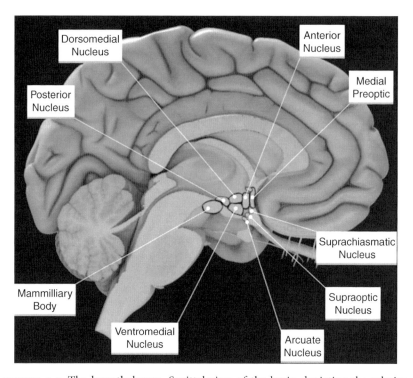

FIGURE 2.2 The hypothalamus. Sagittal view of the brain depicting the relative positions of the major nuclei of the hypothalamus

These demands of the internal body (also known as 'drives') are not represented in the form of sensory images like the external world is; rather, they are measurements of functional *states*. In other words, we do not have little pictures within our brains of how our vegetative body is doing (e.g. we do not literally 'represent' images of the food being processed in the stomach and intestines); rather, our brains *measure* the states of autonomic functions like digestion, respiration, etc., across a variety of scales. These scales of measurement are absolutely vital to the maintenance of life. There are, for example, very narrow ranges of sugar levels, salt levels, water levels, oxygen levels, core-body temperature levels, and so on, that are compatible with life. It is the task of the body-monitoring nuclei to ensure that we remain within those measurement ranges.

In order to do so, the brain (more specifically the part of the brain connected with the outer world, and the ambulatory body which is under its control) must perform work.

This is why body-monitoring nuclei project onto the ascending consciousness-generating structures of the brain shown in Plate 4 (see colour plate section). These latter structures are known collectively as the 'extended reticulo-thalamic activating system' (ERTAS). The ERTAS generates what is classically called the *level* of consciousness, 'arousal' or 'wakefulness', but the level is actually better described as the *state* of consciousness (Mesulam 2000) for the reason that 'level' implies a purely quantitative dimension. This dimension of consciousness is not purely quantitative; it entails multiple qualitative states. In short, it *feels* like something to be awake (Merker 2007; Solms and Pankepp 2012).

This is the point at which brain functioning becomes mental functioning. The upper brainstem structures of the ERTAS onto which the body-monitoring nuclei project generate consciousness, and thereby attribute *valence* to internal bodily states. According to at least one prominent theory (Damasio 2010), this is what consciousness is *for*; it enables the organism to monitor its own bodily status within a biological scale of values – in terms of which it is 'good' to survive and reproduce and 'bad' not to do so. These values control the whole of evolution. Thus, it feels good to eat when you are hungry and to drink when you are thirsty, etc., and it feels bad not to do so. In this way, pleasurable and unpleasurable feelings (known as 'affects') drive the organism's behaviour. Hunger and thirst are good examples of drives. Anyone who has ever felt hungry or thirsty will, we hope, know why we say it is absurd to think of them in purely quantitative terms. It is of the essence of such drives (also known as 'homeostatic affects') that you feel them. And the different drives feel different; the conscious *quality* of hunger is different from that of thirst (and sleepiness and sexual arousal, etc.).

Internal bodily needs (drive demands) can ultimately only be met through *behaviour*: that is, through interaction with 'not me' objects in the outside world. This is why the ERTAS (located mainly in the upper brainstem) activates the forebrain. Although it is not *only* the upper brainstem that underpins affective mental functions, before we can complete our description of the affective brain, we must now turn to the forebrain and thereby turn to the cognitive side of the equation – to the part of the brain that interacts with the external world.

Whereas the internal milieu of the body is monitored by deep brainstem and diencephalic (mainly hypothalamic) nuclei, and generates *subjective* states, the external 'object' world is monitored by the sense organs. In this respect, the sense organs are roughly the external equivalents of the internal body-monitoring nuclei. Whereas the latter project mainly to the

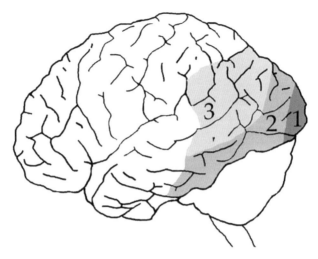

ERTAS, sense organs send their information – via subcortical (mainly thalamic) relays – to the primary cortical projection areas, which are illustrated in Figure 2.3.

The qualities of consciousness attaching to the activation of these brain regions are those of our classical sensory modalities: vision, hearing, somatic sensation (colloquially called 'touch'), taste, and smell. Collectively these are known as the modalities of *perception*, although they would be more properly described as the modalities of *external* perception, for, as we have seen, the internal world has a modality of perception of its own, namely affect. Affect differs from the classical perceptual modalities not only in terms of its particular qualia (feelings like hunger and thirst versus 'feelings' of sight, sound, taste, etc.) but also in terms of its locus of origin; whereas the classical senses represent the state of *objects* in the outside world as detected by the specialist sensory receptor organs distributed over the surface of the body, affect represents the inner state of the *subject*. Later we will learn of another important distinction between affective and perceptual consciousness, too.

For now the important point to make is that *cognition* derives from the external, perceptual form of consciousness. More correctly put, it derives from *representations* which are in turn derived from perception. Representations are learnt. (That is what the 're' in representation means.) Although we experience the object world as unmediated here-and-now perception, in fact it is always filtered through previous experience, through learning. It is re-presented. Hence Edelman's felicitous phrase, 'the remembered present' (Edelman 2001). For example, you do not have an image of your mother until you have seen her (many times), and learned to distinguish her from other women, and women from men, and people from other living things, and so on. The same applies to everything you encounter in the world. But we are exquisitely capable of acquiring such representations, such 'patterns', by the million. This is because the cortex, with its random access memory space (Solms and Panksepp 2012), is a pattern-recognition machine (Carpenter and Grossberg 1988). Because 'neurons that fire together wire together' (Hebb 1949), the cortex is capable of storing an enormous variety of such patterns, but it will only *actually* acquire representations of those patterns it actually encounters. That is to say, the weighting of synaptic connections between neurons is *activity-dependent* (or, to say the same thing psychologically, *experience-dependent*). That is why it is even possible to train the visual cortex of a cat to see (i.e. to recognize) only verticals and not horizontals, by depriving it of the experience of horizontals (Stryker et al. 1978). For such cats, horizontals simply do not exist; they do not *see* them. This is an excellent example of how we perceive only what we have learnt to perceive, and of how our perceptions are in fact *learnt* representations.

Representational patterns, unlike affects, are literal maps (of the patterns of activity in our external receptor organs) which we experience as images that can be pictured in our heads. They are 'mental solids'. When we said in the aforementioned discussion that the function of the brain is to straddle the internal and external worlds, we went on to explain that the internal aspect becomes mental in the form of subjective *states*: 'affect'. Now we have added that the external aspect becomes mental in the form of perceptual *representations*, which, as we have known since Hume and Locke (if not long before), give rise to all that we call *ideas*: 'cognition'.

Before concluding this section, we must emphasize that the external object world is not represented *only* in the cortex. We said above that sense organs send their information – via subcortical (mainly thalamic) relays – to the primary cortical projection areas, which were illustrated in Figure 2.3. Now we must add that they also send information to some subcortical regions.

Perhaps the most important of these is the tectum (Figure 2.4), which is more ancient than the cortex. The tectum contains maps of the sensory surfaces of the body just like the cortex does, but these are much simpler and cruder, more rough-and-ready representations than the precise and detailed images that are generated in the cortex; and they are not capable of becoming conscious. The most famous instance of tectal perception is

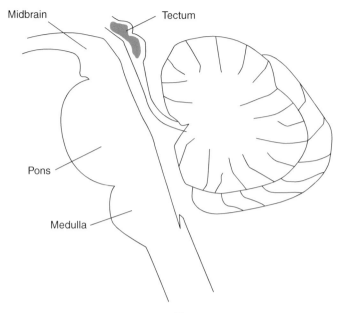

FIGURE 2.4 The tectum

provided by the example of 'blindsight', wherein patients who cannot see consciously – i.e. who are blind – due to visual cortical damage can nevertheless identify the presence and location of visual stimuli (Weiskrantz 1997). These patients see unconsciously by virtue of the visual information that is sent from the retina to the tectum, not the information that is sent via the thalamus to the (in these cases, damaged) visual cortex.

2.3   LEARNING

The primary cortical zones shown in Figure 2.3 project mainly to *association cortex*, which comes in two grades, namely unimodal and heteromodal, as illustrated in Plate 5 (see colour plate section). These are the neocortical brain regions for the representational functions introduced in the aforementioned discussion. ('Neocortex' means new cortex, i.e. phylogenetically young cortex; we will discuss the old cortex next.)

As already stated, the representations in question are literally *maps* (images, pictures) of *patterns of activity* in the receptor surfaces of the external sensory organs. In association cortex, these primary patterns are combined and recombined into ever higher syntheses, which – like the primary patterns – are retained for future reference. The syntheses become progressively less concrete (less perceptual) and more abstract (more 'cognitive') the further removed they are from the sensory periphery – i.e. the further they are removed from the primary cortical zones (Figure 2.3) – and they thereby entrain unimodal and then heteromodal association cortex (Plate 5 (see colour plate section)). These representations, as we know, are the raw material of cognition.

Cognition does not merely involve manipulations of concrete perceptual images; it also involves the manipulation of abstractions – of concepts versus percepts, that is labels of categories of images. Concepts are not only higher order representations than percepts (more abstract, further removed from the sensory periphery); they also include a broad class of representations that we call 'symbolic' (Deacon 1997). Symbolic representations stand for (re-represent) both percepts and concepts. The best-known such symbols are words, but language is far from being the only symbolic code that the brain is capable of using. We have already mentioned, for example, numbers, musical notes, road signs, etc. Each of these symbolic codes has a system of rules attached to them, which govern how the individual representations are manipulated. It is our contention, argued in other chapters, that *all of these cognitive representations* (including, perhaps especially, the symbolic codes and rules) *are acquired through learning.* We are no more born with innate grammatical rules than we are born with innate rules of the road. Nevertheless, because of the constraints of reality, it is no surprise that the national rules of the road throughout the world bear a strong resemblance to each other.

To return to the fundamentals of learning: We obviously do not retain representations of each and every moment of sensory experience. There must be some principle of *selection*, whereby we 'decide' which patterns of sensation, and combinations of such patterns, we should retain for future use. In cognitive science this selective process is known as *consolidation.* Consolidation – which involves not only selection but also ongoing updating of previous selections in the light of new experience – occurs over stages, starting with 'synaptic' consolidation at the transition between short-term (working memory) and long-term memory and ending in 'systems' consolidation, which involves multiple long-term memory systems. The representational forms of long-term memory include episodic memory, semantic memory, and priming, which are progressively less conscious (in the phenomenological sense of the explicit presence of the *subject* of consciousness). The representational forms of memory are also called 'declarative', in that the subject of consciousness can declare

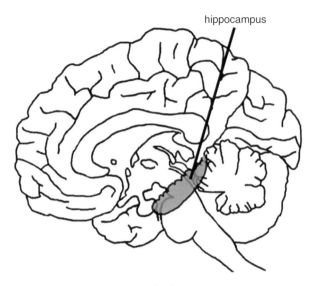

FIGURE 2.5 The hippocampus

awareness of the mental images to others (or to itself). This latter term is usually reserved for humans, since reflective declaration of one's mental contents relies upon re-representing them *and then communicating them* in a symbolic form.

The transition through the stages of systems consolidation seems to involve a progressive uncoupling of cortical representations from the hippocampus (Squire et al. 1984). Thus, 'subjective presence' or sentience in cognition involves hippocampal activation (Tanaka et al. 2014). The hippocampus (Figure 2.5) is part of the phylogenetically ancient cortex known as 'archicortex' ('old cortex'). It is no accident that this part of the cortex is included in most definitions of the limbic system, the emotional brain, to which we will return next. The next most ancient type of cortical structure is called 'corticoid' (i.e. it is transitional between cortex and subcortical nuclei). Corticoid tissues include the amygdala and the substantia innominata, which are older parts of the limbic system, and therefore more explicitly emotional than the hippocampus.

Before discussing these lower structures in detail (Chapter 4), we must point out that the involvement of these affective structures in the cognitive process of consolidation is pivotal; their involvement is central to the selective (biological) imperative which underpins all learning.

The deepest memory systems are entirely unconscious, and are located mainly in the basal ganglia. The long-term memories consolidated at this level are automatized, which means incapable of conscious reconsolidation (they are 'non-declarative').

At this point we must make clear the obvious principle that learning is not an end in itself; the organism only engages with the external world because that is where the objects of its internal bodily needs are to be found, and it learns (on the basis of experience) only in order to retain a record of what does and does not work there, in terms of the biological scale of values already mentioned. In other words, the organism learns about the world in order to improve its chances of survival and reproductive success: that is, it learns in order to (better) meet its internal needs in the external world. This is the biological purpose of all cognition, and that is why learning in general – and consolidation in particular – *is guided by affective valence.* In short, the selection of cognitive representations involves the survival of the fittest representations. That is why the ongoing process of representational selection (synaptic pruning, Wolpert 2002) is also known as 'neural Darwinism' (Edelman 1989). However, one must note here that the mammal brain is a social brain (Dunbar 2003, 2014); so its needs are not just physical; they are social as well. This is because physical survival is predictably enhanced by in-group survival. Thus, learning involves learning about each of the physical, biological/ecological, and social worlds we inhabit, all of which are important for survival and reproductive success.

We have mentioned already that not all forms of long-term memory are representational or 'declarative'. The corticoid structures just mentioned, especially the amygdala, form part of the memory system for emotional learning, which is described as 'non-declarative'. Thus, each newly formed memory has attached to it an emotional tag, which is retrieved when the recent memory is retrieved, and gives us guidance as to how to respond to the situation, in particular assessing if it is likely to be a hazardous or fruitful situation. This is an automatic response which we cannot control, though we can try to control how we respond to it. The same applies to procedural memory and associative reflexes.

2.4   INSTINCT, AUTOMATIZATION, AND INTUITION

Instincts are fixed patterns of behaviour in animals in response to certain stimuli – that is, they are hard-wired reactions to specific situations, which tend to lead to survival and reproductive success. They are embodied in connections in the so-called reptilian and emotional brain resulting in fixed action patterns, and don't have to be learnt. These are thus examples of *innate CNS modules*.

Before we proceed, it is important to distinguish some terms which are frequently conflated, namely instinct, drive, affect, and emotion. A 'drive' is a measure of a demand made upon the mind to perform work, by dint of a deviation (or approaching deviation) from the range compatible with life in respect of a vital bodily function. An 'instinct' is a hard-wired response pattern to predictable situations of universal biological significance. These situations might be both internal and external. Thus, whereas drives always arise from the internal homeostatic systems of the autonomic body, instincts can derive from external survival situations such as separation from the mother (attachment instinct, which also serves drives like hunger) or attack by a predator (fear instinct). Both drives and instincts give rise to 'affects' (e.g. hunger versus fear).

Here (following Panksepp 1998) we differentiate between these two broad categories by referring to 'homeostatic' versus 'emotional' affects. Whereas homeostatic affects arise from states of internal bodily needs (drives), emotional affects arise from environmental situations (instincts). What makes them instinctual is the fact that they trigger hard-wired, stereotypical behavioural responses: for example, in the case of fear, freezing, or fleeing. Homeostatic and emotional affects do not, however, exhaust the varieties of affect. We (following Panksepp 1998) also recognize 'sensory' affects, examples of which are pain, disgust, and surprise. These entail simple, reflexive responses to predictable sensory stimuli. They are, as it were, the external equivalents of internal, homeostatic affects. What unites all these varieties of affect is the fact that *they are innate*. They are hard-wired or built in, and they trigger *unconditioned* behavioural responses. That is, they are not learned. You do not learn what to do when approaching a cliff-face (or when you are hungry, or when you have swallowed rotten meat, etc); this is because you cannot afford to learn these things. However, not all affects are innate. There are also learnt affects. These are hybrids between the innate forms which are acquired through experience of reality in all of its unpredictable complexity. There are therefore also affect/cognition hybrids. Most learnt affects are 'social' emotions, but not all social emotions are learnt. Good examples of learnt social emotions are shame and guilt. Guilt, for instance, combines the innate emotion of attachment bonding with that of rage, which can contradict each other in relation to particular objects (e.g. frustration with the mother). It is clear that such hybrid affects – guilt, shame, envy, etc. – entail complex learning, including declarative memory.

However, learnt responses can become just as automatized (subcortica-lized) as innate ones. This happens when they – like the responses triggered by innate affects – come to embody absolutely reliable predictions. Many problems which are solved by trial and error learning, such as playing the piano and riding a bicycle, become absolutely solved after many episodes of declarative learning, and then the solutions (the predictions as to what to do, through *conditioned* pattern recognition) become automatized as non-declarative action programmes, which run unconsciously when needed. In our view, *language acquisition functions like this*. Although it is automa-tized, it is learnt; it is not an instinct.

The best-known non-declarative memory system is called 'procedural' learning, which is the form of learning we have just described. But there are other non-declarative systems too, the most important one for our pur-poses being 'emotional' learning. This form of learning entails the attach-ment of innate affective responses to novel stimuli. For example, although the fear response is innate, and cliff-faces and approaching predators are hard-wired stimuli which trigger it, we can also *learn* to associate fear with, for example, electric sockets and headmasters.

This leads in more complex cases to intuition: the fast unconscious assessment of a situation and crystallization of an action plan (Myers 2003; Kahneman 2011), which is non-declarative, although it can later be rationalized if necessary: that is, one can if necessary work out after the event what kind of declarative thought would have led to the decision made.

Intuitive assessments will automatically have an emotional element in them which will be based in the (conscious) affective signals associated with the unconscious cognitive processing. They could also have elements of skills learned, such as the intuition of a brain surgeon, a fighter pilot, a ballet dancer, which are deployed much faster than they could be in the case of rational decision-making. These are thus not innate traits, and are not the result of innate brain modules.

2.5   SENSES, THE THALAMUS, AND PREDICTION

In understanding the overall function of the brain, it is crucial to realize that it does not just take in sensory data and analyse what is implied by the incoming light, sound, touch, taste: rather, the brain is essentially an organ of *prediction* (Hawkins 2004), and what appear to be sensory perceptions are actually the brain's construction of a representation of reality on the basis of what it expects to be there (Frith 2007; Kandel 2012). This mode of

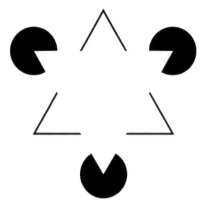

FIGURE 2.6 The power of illusion. There are no triangles in this picture. The mind fills them in, on the basis of its expectations of how vision works to comprehend physical objects

functioning is most apparent in the case of optical illusions (Purves 2010), as, for example, in visual illusions such as Figure 2.6.

The same process is at work, for example, when listening to someone speak, or when reading a passage of writing. The mind creates an ongoing picture of the world on the basis of its expectations due to past data and events, continually corrected on the basis of those parts of the incoming data that do not fit with its expectations. Thus – in particular – written language is not read in a bottom-up way, syllable by syllable, being integrated to give an overall picture. Rather, it is read in a holistic contextual way, skipping much of what is written and replacing what is there with equivalent words that fulfil the same purpose (Goodman et al. 2016). This is quite different than interpreting what is there on the basis of a set of strict grammatical rules, whether learnt or innate. The brain is not fundamentally operating in a rule-based way, as envisaged by many linguists: it is essentially a contextual pattern recognition and prediction device. Data on how people actually read texts confirm this view (Goodman et al. 2016), just as do studies of how people react in a gestalt way to art (Kandel 2012).

The way this works in physiological terms is that the thalamus (Figure 2.7) acts as a relay station between the sensory systems and the neocortex, thereby playing a central role in ongoing cortical functioning (Alitto and Usrey 2003; Sherman 2016), modulating responses to incoming data in the light of expectations.

Its function is shown in Figure 2.8.

As stated by Cudeiro and Sillito (2006):

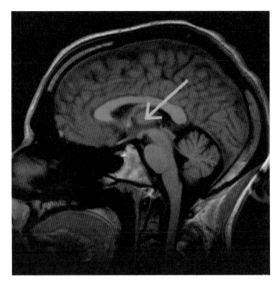

FIGURE 2.7 The thalamus

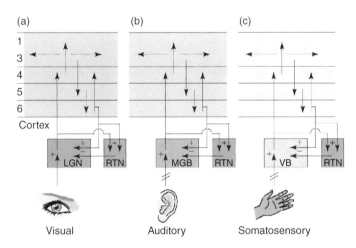

FIGURE 2.8 Corticothalamic circuitry. From Alitto and Usrey (2003).
Published with permission from Elsevier

Although once regarded as a simple sensory relay on the way to the
cortex, it is increasingly apparent that the thalamus has a role in the
ongoing moment-by-moment processing of sensory input and in cognition. This involves extensive corticofugal feedback connections and the

interplay of these with the local thalamic circuitry and the other converging inputs. [. . .] Cortical feedback mediated by ionotropic and metabotropic glutamate receptors, and effects mediated by the neuromodulator nitric oxide, all have a role in integrating the thalamic mechanism into the cortical circuit. The essential point is that the perspective of higher-level sensory mechanisms shifts and modulates the thalamic circuitry in ways that optimize abstraction of a meaningful representation of the external world.

Clearly, at least some of the thalamus is hard-wired. It may well embody image recognition networks that may recognize, say, the broad outline of a face or a snake. However, because of the multiple downward connections from the neocortex to the thalamus, its responses to incoming data are modulated in respect of our current expectations. Another possibility – perhaps more likely – is that hard-wired patterns in image recognition are inscribed at the tectal (upper brainstem) level. The tectum, too, is subject to top-down cortical influence.

2.6   FUNCTIONAL DOMAINS

Various brain areas have been identified as being related to specific cognitive functions, for example motor functions and sensory functions (such as the primary auditory cortex).

According to Friederici (2011), networks involving the temporal cortex and the inferior frontal cortex – with a clear left lateralization – were shown to support syntactic processes, whereas less lateralized temporo-frontal networks subserve semantic processes. The anterior temporal cortex is involved in semantic and syntactic processes. Syntactic and semantic ambiguities involve the posterior temporal cortex, as this is where context comes in. Different studies indicate that the processing of syntactically complex sentences recruits Broca's area (Figure 2.9). The data point towards a language processing system which recruits different subregions in the perisylvian default language network as needed.

None of these regions represent a language acquisition device of the kind envisaged by Chomksy. Nevertheless, one can ask why the same regions are used for language processing in different brains, if this function is not genetically determined. We will make just two points here.

Firstly, Matyja and Dolega (2015) remark on the growing evidence against the possibility of mapping singular cognitive functions onto narrowly circumscribed brain regions (Price and Friston 2007). The existence of pluripotency (the participation of a particular region in carrying out

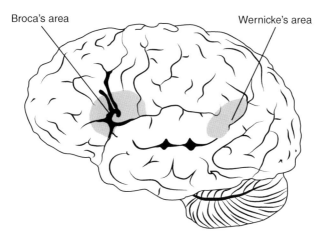

FIGURE 2.9 Broca's area and Wernicke's area

more than one cognitive function) and degeneracy (different regions 'taking over' the performance of a particular function after a given brain area is damaged or disabled) supports the idea of a network-based view where massive neural redeployment takes place: a particular brain region can realize different cognitive functions by participating in different functional networks at different times. Thus, the evidence for language processing in specific regions is real enough, but does not mean that this is all that those domains do. They are not hard-wired for that specific purpose, but can be recruited for that purpose when context-dependent population-level computations take place in the prefrontal cortex (Mante et al. 2013). Indeed, it is known that in cortical and subcortical areas, the formation of cell assemblies critically depends on neuronal oscillations, which can precisely control the timing of spiking activity. Precise spike timing through the coordination and synchronization of neuronal assemblies is an efficient and flexible coding mechanism for sensory and cognitive processing (Dejean et al. 2016).

Secondly, the Visual Wordform Area (VWFA) is described by Dehaene and Cohen (2011) as follows:

> Reading systematically activates the left lateral occipitotemporal sulcus, at a site known as the visual word form area (VWFA). This site is reproducible across individuals/scripts, attuned to reading-specific processes, and partially selective for written strings relative to other categories such as line drawings. Lesions affecting the VWFA cause pure alexia, a selective deficit in word recognition. These findings must be

reconciled with the fact that human genome evolution cannot have been influenced by such a recent and culturally variable activity as reading. Capitalizing on recent functional magnetic resonance imaging experiments, we provide strong corroborating evidence for the hypothesis that reading acquisition partially recycles a cortical territory evolved for object and face recognition, the prior properties of which influenced the form of writing systems.

This area is illustrated in Plate 6 (see colour plate section).

Now the same issue arises in this case: why should this area be the same in all human brains, given that this location cannot be ascribed to any evolutionary/genetic influence, because writing only emerged about 5,400 years ago – far too short for Darwinian evolution to have shaped our genome for reading (Dehaene and Dehaene-Lambertz 2016). The answer seems to be that functionally specific regions develop in their characteristic locations because of pre-existing differences in the *extrinsic connectivity* of that region to the rest of the brain (Saygin et al. 2016). These results suggest that early connectivity instructs the functional development of the VWFA, possibly reflecting a general mechanism of cortical development. And if that applies to the VWFA, there is no reason why it should not apply to the areas devoted to spoken language also.

It has been suggested that extrinsic connections play a key role in directing brain development, instructing the functional development of cortical regions by determining the information that each region receives. Osher et al. (2015) support this view, giving strong evidence for a precise and fine-grained relationship between connectivity and function in the human brain, and raising the possibility that early developing connectivity patterns may determine later functional organization. This is of course not the same as saying it determines specific cognitive content. Thus, for example, Devlin et al. (2006) in commenting on the role of the posterior fusiform gyrus in reading state:

> These findings conflict with the notion of stored visual word forms and instead suggest that this region acts as an interface between visual form information and higher-order stimulus properties such as its associated sound and meaning. Importantly, this function is not specific to reading, but is also engaged when processing any meaningful visual stimulus.

However, what one does find is fascinatingly consistent semantic maps that tile the human cerebral cortex (Huth et al. 2016), see Plate 7 (see colour plate section).

To some degree, this might represent the kinds of folk modules discussed by Geary et al., not because they are innate, but rather due to the
consistent operation of developmental processes subject to experiences
that are universal to all humans as they interact with the environment.

Secondly, while much of this is compelling and very illuminating work,
it is not clear that it adequately captures the predictive contextual nature of
perception (Frith 2007; Purves 2010; Kandel 2012), and in particular the
predictive contextual way that language works in both oral and written
form (Goodman et al. 2016). One can only study these aspects of language
adequately by examining genuine communication events occurring in a
meaningful context, rather than just some specific aspect of meaningful
communication, as is all too often the case. One must be cautious about
many of the models proposed for language and cortical function (Bennett
and Hacker 2006).

Harris and Mrsic-Flogel (2013), however, start to capture this holistic
aspect:

> The sensory cortex contains a wide array of neuronal types, which are
> connected together into complex but partially stereotyped circuits.
> Sensory stimuli trigger cascades of electrical activity through these
> circuits, causing specific features of sensory scenes to be encoded in
> the firing patterns of cortical populations. Recent research is beginning
> to reveal how the connectivity of individual neurons relates to the
> sensory features they encode, how differences in the connectivity pat-
> terns of different cortical cell classes enable them to encode information
> using different strategies, and how feedback connections from higher-
> order cortex allow sensory information to be integrated with behavioural
> context.

2.7   THE BRAIN AND EVOLUTION

The evolutionary development of humans, and specifically of the brain,
follows from the same principles that underlie all evolutionary development: in a nutshell, reproduction with variation followed by selection of
the fittest, resulting in highly effective adaptation to a specific physical and
ecological environment. As the social brain develops, this includes adaptation to the social environment also. However, this is not the simplistic 'one
gene – one outcome' process suggested in many popular books and articles.
It is a highly complex phenotype to genotype mapping resulting not so
much in specific structures but rather in developmental systems, based in

underlying evolution of gene regulatory networks, signal transduction networks, metabolic networks, and the necessary proteins. We will comment on these aspects further in Chapter 7.

As far as primate (including human) species are concerned, what was required specifically was the development of a 'social brain' and hence means of communication between members of society, allowing passing of knowledge from generation to generation, communal social action such as planned group hunting, and the development of technology. The need for such communication may have been the origin of symbolic behaviour and reflexive consciousness, which separate us humans from the great apes, but the chain of cause and effect may have run the other way. It is still unclear precisely what the neural difference is between us and them that allows symbolic behaviour and the development of language, apart from our greater prefrontal connectivity and vocal development allowing us to speak (Christiansen and Kirby 2005). But these may be a consequence rather than a driver of whatever it was that enabled us to develop tool usage and technology as well as symbolism and language (Hauser et al. 2014). Thus, drivers of our unique abilities required the following:

- Physiological developments such as an enlarged prefrontal connectivity and specialized vocal apparatus; these are genetically determined.
- Improved energy sources, including meat and fish, perhaps helped by the development of fire, enabling better digestion of cooked food; these are socially determined, but may then result in genetic selection.
- Development of a social brain (Dunbar 2014), enabling all the benefits of communal living, in particular improved safety and the possibility of accumulation of knowledge and development of technology; this is based at least partly in the development of (not specifically human) hard-wired affective systems that drive the desire to live in groups and the regulation of conflict, as discussed in Chapter 5.
- Development of the capacity for symbolic thought (Deacon 1997) through specifics of the way cortical connections are wired at the micro level. Thus, one needs patterns of connections that allow logical operations such as OR, AND, and XOR (Marcus 2003) and hence understanding of abstract relations (Churchland 2013), as well as the labelling of patterns of cortical firings (Hawkins 2004) in a recursive way. This might need some specific genetic alteration, but none such has yet been identified.

Taken together these amount to gene/culture co-evolution (Richerson and Boyd 2005) in a social context (Donald 2000, 2001), with emotional systems playing the key role in language development (Greenspan and Shanker 2004) and culture leading to the development of written as well as spoken language.

The kind of project that needs to be enjoined is indicated in a study of the language-ready brain by Boeckx and Benítez-Burraco (2014). They state:

> Our core hypothesis is that the emergence of our species-specific language-ready brain ought to be understood in light of the developmental changes expressed at the levels of brain morphology and neural connectivity that occurred in our species after the split from Neanderthals–Denisovans and that gave us a more globular braincase configuration. In addition to changes at the cortical level, we hypothesize that the anatomical shift that led to globularity also entailed significant changes at the subcortical level. We claim that the functional consequences of such changes must also be taken into account to gain a fuller understanding of our linguistic capacity. Here we focus on the thalamus, which we argue is central to language and human cognition, as it modulates fronto-parietal activity. With this new neurobiological perspective in place, we examine its possible molecular basis. We construct a candidate gene set whose members are involved in the development and connectivity of the thalamus, in the evolution of the human head, and are known to give rise to language-associated cognitive disorders.

This focus on the thalamus fits in with what we suggested above, and with Harris and Mrsic-Flogel (2013), notwithstanding the fact that the tectum is more 'hard-wired' than the thalamus. However, there is also a need for characterizing how labelling takes place in cortical columns; and this requires specific kinds of cortical connections (Hawkins 2004). These columns cannot be hard-wired, as discussed previously, but they can be soft-wired to have the required kinds of neurons and associated patterns of initially random connections that can then be refined to give the detailed wiring needed for specific cognitive tasks. For our purposes it is sufficient that the required genotypes for this to occur have been developed through prehistorical evolutionary processes; we do not need to enter the lively debate on which aspects were the formative drivers and which the followers.

3

Hierarchy, Modularity, and Development

This chapter lays foundations for what follows by considering why modules can be expected to occur in living systems in general, and in the brain in particular, and how they are related to developmental processes.

3.1 MODULAR HIERARCHICAL STRUCTURE: LEVELS AND EMERGENCE

The brain has many levels of emergence (Churchland and Sejnowski 1988; Scott 1995; Craver 2007, pp. 164–195); see Figure 3.1, where higher levels are made up of reconstituted lower-level modules. There are also many cortical domains that might be called modules (Johnson 2007, p. 33; Kandel et al. 2013). Here we consider the way complexity arises out of modular hierarchical structures, and the way the central nervous system (CNS) structure is specified through developmental biological processes.

Hierarchy and modularity are crucial to complexity, as pointed out inter alia by Simon (1962, 1992), Schlosser and Wagner (2004), Booch (2007), and Ellis (2016). Modularity occurs in terms of both structure and function (Schlosser and Wagner 2004, pp. 521–541).

Hierarchy: The basic way of creating complex objects out of simple entities is to link together many basic entities that function in a quasi-independent way ('modules'), so creating a higher level of function and structure, and then repeating this process at each level, hence forming a hierarchy (Schlosser and Wagner 2004, p. 5). According to Wimsatt (1994),

> levels of organization are a deep, non-arbitrary, and extremely important feature of the ontological architecture of our natural world, and almost certainly of any world which could produce, and be inhabited or understood by, intelligent beings.

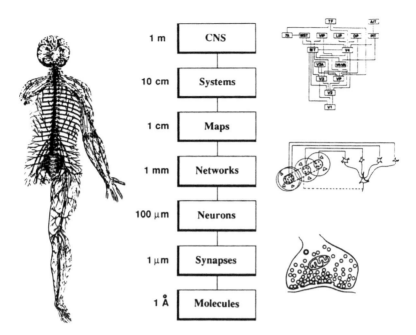

FIGURE 3.1 Hierarchical structure of the central nervous system. On the left: the nervous system as a whole. On the right: a synapse (bottom), network model of ganglion cells (middle), and a subset of the visual cortex (top) (from Churchland and Sejnowski 1988). Reproduced with permission

Essentially, one divides up a complex higher-level task (say running away from a predator) into a set of lower-level tasks (say moving feet one after the other), which in turn are divided up into even lower-level tasks (moving muscles in a coordinated way) based in even lower-level processes (oxygen- and sugar-based metabolism) and so on down to the molecular, atomic, and particle levels. (All this is based in controlled electron flows in dendrites, axons, and muscle tissue.)

Levels: Linking the units together with directed links representing causal relationships between the elements creates a system (Flood and Carson 1990; Craver 2007, pp. 109–114) or equivalently a network (Junker and Schreiber 2008; Sporns 2011): in mathematical terms, a graph. This results in the ubiquity of hierarchical functional networks in biology (Junker and Schreiber 2008), for example (Wagner 2014) gene regulatory networks (Plate 9 (see colour plate section)), metabolic networks, and signalling networks.

This functional hierarchy in turn (remember Figure 1.1) leads to hierarchical physical structure (an implementation hierarchy) in the human body and its CNS (Figure 3.1), with a modular network structure at each level in the hierarchy, based in biomolecules and cells. There is a corresponding hierarchy of academic subjects that tackle the different emergent levels of structure and function (Scott 1995, pp. 161–173; Ellis 2016).

Modular units: By joining the same lower-level units together in different ways, one can create higher-level emergent systems with radically different function (Schlosser and Wagner 2004, p. 520). This is one of the prime reasons that networks are so important in evolutionary biology. Evolution can operate by modifying either the modules or their interconnectivity (Wagner 2011).

Atoms: The key modules in physics are atoms – all matter is made of atoms. These are made up of electrons and atomic nuclei, which are made up of protons and neutrons, which in turn are made of quarks. Atoms bonded to each other make crystals or molecules; in particular, they can form the biomolecules such as carbohydrates, lipids, proteins, and nucleic acids that underlie life.

Cells: The key modules in biology are cells – all life is based in cells; they are the basic unit of life (Campbell and Reece 2005). Cells are made up of nuclei, mitochondria, ribosomes, and so on, each being modules in their own right, in turn made up of biomolecules (lower-level modules) of many kinds. In particular, the key modules in the brain are neurons: cells specialized for signal transmission, joined to other neurons via synapses (Figure 3.2). Connections of many cells through synapses create activity-dependent networks that can carry out pattern recognition, prediction, and so on.

All the major cortical brain areas are made up of networks of neurons, structured in layered columns (Plate 10 (see colour plate section)), but the different areas have different functions (Plate 8 (see colour plate section)). The structure as a whole is hierarchically organized in physical terms (Scot 1995; Craver 2007, pp. 170–195), corresponding to a hierarchical structuring of function: electron flows underlie molecular and genetic interactions, these in turn underlying neuronal and synaptic signal processing, pattern recognition in neural networks, management of motor movements and sensory input analysis, individual consciousness, and social interactions.

Emergence: The higher levels that come into being through the combination of lower-level elements (modules) have their own higher-level laws of behaviour that are largely independent of the lower-level underpinnings, even though they arise out of them. Thus, the Hodgkin–Huxley law for action potential propagation in axons is independent of particle physics (Scott 1995), although it relies on the properties of sodium and potassium

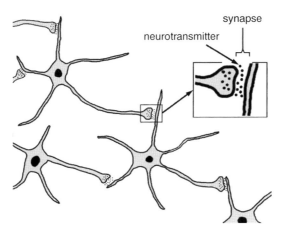

FIGURE 3.2 Connections of neurons via synapses. They may be excitatory or inhibitory

ion channels; the pattern recognition and prediction properties of neural networks (Bishop 1999; Hawkins 2004; Friston 2010) are independent of the detailed structure of synapses, although they rely on synaptic summation and threshold properties; and so on. Indeed, usually any specific higher-level function can be realized by many different lower-level structures, which is the principle of multiple realizability (see Ellis 2016; Brakel 2013). Details of the module's internal structure don't matter, as long as it does what is needed in terms of network function (Section 3.2).

Each higher level is as real as each lower level (Noble 2012), even though it is composed of smaller units. One can relate each level to its lower-level components, and may be able to see how these underlie the higher-level function, but we can understand this function in terms of effective laws of behaviour at its own level independent of the lower-level realization.

3.2 MODULAR HIERARCHICAL STRUCTURES: MODULARITY

Modules, discussed in detail by West-Eberhard (2003, pp. 56–88) and Schlosser and Wagner (2004), can also be called 'components' or 'parts' (Craver 2007, pp. 128–133). To qualify as a module, a part of a larger entity must have a separable function (Schlosser and Wagner 2004, p. 6) and must have inner workings that are hidden from external view (information hiding). Modules can be combined together in a form of structure or organization to form networks (Craver 2007, pp. 134–139), and can be imbedded in higher-order modules in hierarchical fashion (Schlosser and Wagner 2004, p. 5). Recurrent use of modules leads to hierarchy and emergence of higher levels of structure and function out of lower levels.

Modules, abstraction, and information hiding: Booch, following Simon (1992), has usefully described the essential issues as follows (Booch 2007): A hierarchy represents a decomposition of the problem into constituent parts and of processes into sub-processes, the different parts being specialized to handle each of these sub-problems, with each sub-process requiring less data and more restricted operations than the problem as a whole. Modular units with abstraction, encapsulation, and inheritance handle each of these sub-processes.

Modules can be modified and adapted to fulfil new functions, enabling great flexibility as complex structures adapt to a changing environment. Modules at a particular level are identified by tighter binding, higher speeds of internal interaction, and higher energies than those at the next higher level in the hierarchy; indeed, it is this tighter binding that identifies them as modules. The high-frequency dynamics of the internal structures of components (relating internal variables) contrasts with the low-frequency dynamics of interactions amongst components (relating external variables). Combinations of many high-frequency lower-level interactions result in lower-frequency, higher-level actions. (Brain synaptic interactions at millisecond level underlie conscious processes at the level of a tenth of a second.)

The success of hierarchical structuring depends on implementing modules to handle lower-level processes and on the integration of these modules into a higher-level structure (e.g. atoms comprising molecules and cells comprising a brain). This structuring enables the modification of modules and reuse for other purposes, and also enables fine-tuning the internal structure of modules without affecting the large-scale dynamics. It also makes the dynamics understandable: each module has a function that can be understood and integrated with the functions of other modules.

Abstraction: A key feature in logical hierarchies is that compound objects (combinations of modules) can be named and treated as single units by appropriate labelling. This leads to the power of abstract symbolism, symbolic representation, and recursion. An abstraction denotes the essential characteristics of a module that distinguish it from all other kinds of objects. It focuses on the outside view of the module, and so serves to separate its essential behaviour from its implementation; it emphasizes some of the system's details or properties, while suppressing many others. Any physical representation of an abstract hierarchy must have an addressing system enabling access to specific information: this is enabled by labelling ('naming' or indexing).

Information is continually thrown away by billions of bits when one replaces the internal description with this external view. This is what enables modules to generate higher-level structure, and is essential to the emergence of higher-level behaviour because all the billions of micro-alternatives can neither be examined nor be controlled. All that we need to know is how it functions when viewed from outside as a 'black box' with reliable behaviour.

Encapsulation occurs when the internal workings are hidden from the outside, so internal procedures can be treated as black-box abstractions. No part of any complex system should depend on the internal details of any other part – system functionality only specifies each component's function, leaving it to the object to decide how to do it. There are multiple ways the module's functions can be carried out internally; it does not matter which one is used (Schlosser and Wagner 2004, pp. 524–527).

Information hiding: Local variables that control the internal dynamics are invisible from outside: access to the internal variables is only through carefully controlled interfaces. In biology, this is handled by containing reactions within containers such as membranes and cell walls that allow limited access to the outside environment. Thus, information hiding is a key feature of complexity.

Inheritance (replication with modification) occurs when specialized modules (forming a sub-class) preserve most or all of the functions of the super-class, but with extra specialization or further properties built in. This corresponds to fine-tuning the modules to handle more specialized problems. For example, ectodermal cells are specialized during development to form neurons. This is a key feature in both development and evolution.

Modules and reusability: Modules with hidden internal workings and clearly structured interfaces can be reused in many different ways in networks, allowing new higher-level functions to emerge from the same lower-level components. This plays a key role in evolutionary development, which often takes place not by modifying the modules, for example modifying biomolecules such as nucleic acids or proteins (Wagner 2011, pp. 47–67), but by modifying the network in which they function, for example modifying metabolic or genotype networks (Wagner 2011, pp. 18–46).

Modules in biology include (see also West-Eberhard 2003, pp. 60–67)

- proteins, genes, selector genes (Wagner 2014),
- metabolic networks (Wagner 2014),
- gene regulatory networks (West-Eberhard 2003, p. 78; Schlosser and Wagner 2004, p. 5),
- signalling cascades (Schlosser and Wagner 2004, p. 5),
- cell types (Schlosser and Wagner 2004, p. 6),
- organs (Schlosser and Wagner 2004, p. 6),
- entire organisms (Schlosser and Wagner 2004, p. 6).

Modules in the brain: The lower levels are the same as in all biology (atoms, biomolecules, regulatory and metabolic networks, cells, and so on) (see Figure 3.1). At the systems level,

- The major CNS parts can be regarded as modules: the spinal cord, medulla oblongata, pons, cerebellum, midbrain, diencephalon, basal ganglia, and cerebral hemispheres (Kandel et al. 2013, pp. 8, 319–322).
- Neurons in the brain and spinal cord are clustered into discrete cellular groups called nuclei, which are interconnected to form functional systems (Kandel et al. 2013, pp. 331–333, 337).
- Affective tendencies are anatomically localized in nuclei in the limbic system, and associated peptidergic modulators (Kandel et al. 2013, pp. 14–15, 986–994).
- Major modulatory systems in the brain stem with long projections can be defined by their single neurotransmitters (Kandel et al. 2013, pp. 889–895). These are the ascending systems.
- Each somatic submodality (e.g. touch, pain, and position sense) is processed in a distinct subsystem from the periphery to the brain (Kandel et al. 2013, p. 341).
- Local regions of the cerebral cortex are specialized for sensory, motor, or associational functions (Kandel et al. 2013, pp. 914, 325, 337).

3.3   INTERLEVEL RELATIONS

Multilevel explanations are necessary in relation to biological systems (Craver 2007, pp. 9–16). There are interlevel constraints (Campbell 1974; Peacocke 1989; Craver 2007, pp. 248–255), and interlevel integration occurs (Craver 2007, pp. 256–267); hence, lower-level structures are adapted to higher-level functions. Thus, causality is not one way: it flows up and down the hierarchy of complexity (Ellis et al. 2012; Ellis 2016). Interactions between modules create higher-order effective variables and laws, but

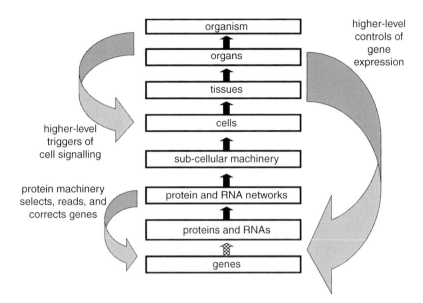

FIGURE 3.3 Top-down effects on cell function and gene expression (from Noble 2012). The ecological and social environment feeds into this hierarchy from above

higher-order variables may not be coarse-grained lower variables: they can be essentially higher-level functions, but can act down to lower levels by setting parameters and by altering gene regulation (Noble 2008), specifically through selector genes (Schlosser and Wagner 2004, pp. 19–31).

Thus, the functioning of lower-level modules (e.g. genes) depends on the higher-level context. They function autonomously in response to signals received from their environment (e.g. selector genes), which inform them of higher-level needs. The effect of genes is therefore context sensitive: top-down action takes place through epigenetic effects to control which gene gets switched on when and where (Schlosser and Wagner 2004, p. 31; Gilbert and Epel 2009).

Note here that top-down influence is a generic interlevel effect: each higher level is the immediate environment for the next lower level, and can alter its functioning by setting its context. Hence, it is not only the global environment that acts down in this way to influence lower levels by providing ecological niches (not shown in Figure 3.3): each level can act on each level below, generally through the intermediate levels.

Top-down developmental effects: A broad principle in top-down control in modular hierarchies is that there should be maximal decentralization of control (Beer 1972): the central system should give broad guidance as to what is needed but allow maximal local autonomy as to how this is carried out. Thus, one should specify what is wanted through suitable interfaces, and allow the detail to be developed locally. This is very clear in the case of computer programming, where one calls subroutines or methods with suitable parameters passed to them to determine how they function (Booch 2007), and they then do the work needed in their own way. In particular, this underlies the key role of selector genes (Schlosser and Wagner 2004, pp. 18–26), which are in effect precisely such parameters passed to modules (the genome) and shaping its outcomes. Because they themselves can get selected for via other selector genes, they naturally generate hierarchies, which are the biologically crucial units. Thus, what get selected for in evolutionary terms are gene regulation networks, not individual genes (Wagner 2011).

Top-down evolutionary effects: Because there are top-down effects affecting development, and evolutionary selection depends on what kinds of outcomes developmental processes produce, there are necessarily top-down effects in evolution (Ellis 2016). Organisms adapt to their environment, which shapes their physiology to some degree (e.g. we have lungs to breathe oxygen because we live on a planet with an oxygen-filled atmosphere), and if it changes (e.g. due to global warming) they had better adapt to the change in order to survive. Past environments have therefore shaped aspects of present-day organisms (Figure 1.1). West-Eberhard states this as follows:

> The universal environmental responsiveness of organisms, alongside genes, influences individual development and organic evolution, and this realization compels us to re-examine the major themes of evolutionary biology in a new light.
>
> (West-Eberhard 2003, p. vii)

We explore how this intertwining of developmental plasticity and evolution affects brain structure and function in this book.

3.4   NETWORKS, INFORMATION PROCESSING, AND FUNCTIONAL PLASTICITY

Neural networks, that is neurons connected to each other through dendrites and axons via synapses with varying strengths, underlie the basic brain processes of pattern recognition and prediction (Hawkins 2004; Churchland 2013). Recognizing this gives rise to the connectionist view of brain structure (Elman et al. 1998, pp. 47–106), popularized under the name

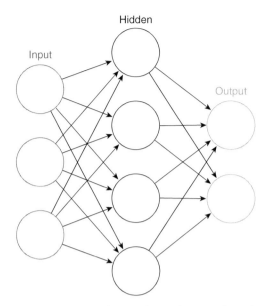

FIGURE 3.4 Neural network model. A directed network with weighted links (Wikimedia)

'Synaptic Self' (LeDoux 2002) or 'The Connectome' (Seung 2012), emphasizing how we each are what we are because of the specific wiring in our brain, which changes throughout our life.

Network connectivity and weights: Networks for cognition (Sporns 2011, pp. 179–206) are layered networks (Figure 3.3), whose essential features are captured in a simple three-layer neural network diagram (Figure 3.4). Its properties are determined by the connectivity between the neurons in the different layers (in this case, each neuron is connected to every neuron in the neighbouring layers) and the weights of each link. These are determined by a training process whereby the weights get adjusted until the network does sufficiently well in some task, for example recognizing the letters of the alphabet. If the weights are from then on unchanged, it will reliably recognize the letters, as can be demonstrated by computer simulations ('Artificial Neural Networks').

In the case of the brain, the weights and even the connections are updated all the time in response to experience. There will be many more hidden layers and connections, but at a very broad level it will still be like Figure 3.4, with sensory input neurons (on the left), numerous layer of interneurons (in the middle), and output motor neurons (on the right). The network can carry out pattern recognition, generalization, and prediction activities (Hawkins 2004; Churchland 2013), and in particular can store memories (Kandel 2006). Its details embody our individuality (LeDoux 2002; Seung 2012).

Neural Network (NN) Principle: It is the detailed connections and weights in a neural network that carry the information stored in the network and shape its functioning.

There are a vast number of possibilities because there are so many neurons (about 10^{11}) and synapses (about 10^{14}) in the brain. According to Kandel et al. (2000, p. 19),

> One of the key organisational principles of the brain is that nerve cells with basically similar properties can nevertheless produce quite different actions because of the way they are connected with each other and with sensory receptors and muscle.

This is the great advantage of modular structures, as discussed above.

Hierarchy in the brain: All this happens in a hierarchical way (Churchland and Sejnowski 1988; Scott 1995; Craver 2007; Friston 2008). Functional systems are hierarchically organized (Kandel et al. 2000, p. 324; Meunier et al. 2010; Jeon 2014) and a general principle of brain information processing is that it is carried out in a hierarchical fashion (Kandel et al. 2000, p. 338). Information processing takes place at each level, redescribed in different terms at lower levels, as in the case of digital computers. It is interactions all the way down (Elman et al. 1998, pp. 319–356). This physical structure allows representation of logical information and has a modular hierarchical structure, and so allows recursion. It can carry out logical operations if it allows a branching {IF (X) THEN (Y) ELSE (Z)} structure; and this is indeed supported at the molecular level by the lock-and-key mechanism of biomolecular binding (Binder and Ellis 2016), as well as at the synaptic level by the additivity and threshold mechanisms (Kandel et al. 2013).

Thus, just as in the case of digital computers, physical modules can underlie the existence of functional or cognitive modules. However, there may be interacting networks that change from time to time as functional networks form and dissolve, perhaps by temporary oscillatory binding, and information storage is distributed:

> Our experience of knowledge as a seamless orderly and cross-referenced database is the product of integration of multiple representations in the brain in many distinct anatomical sites, each concerned with only one

aspect of the concept that came to mind. Thus there is no general semantic store: semantic knowledge is not stored in a single region.

(Kandel et al. 2013, p. 1236)

How are neural network connections and weight determined? Neural networks can have fixed functions, when they represent innate knowledge (Johnson 2005, pp. 8–9), or can have adaptive functions, when their plasticity supports learning (Karmiloff-Smith 1996; La Cerra and Bingham 1998; LeDoux 2002; Buller 2005). In the first case the network structure and link strengths are largely determined genetically; in the second case their foundations are laid genetically, but their details are determined epigenetically by adaptive developmental processes as the brain interacts with its physical and social environment.

Fixed function networks: In this case the network connection pattern and weights are essentially fixed and realize a fixed motor pattern, or pattern analysis function, for example (in vision) edge detection, motion detection, or colour detection. These fixed connections will have been determined through developmental processes based in genetic information read in the developmental context as the embryo develops to an adult. These are innate modules.

Plastic Networks: Plasticity is the ability of the brain to adapt to different operating conditions as the physical, ecological, and social environment changes, and to alter its structure so that it will respond appropriately to specific environments in the future ('learning'). This ability at the macro level is based in plasticity at the micro level in terms of altered cortical connections (Kandel 2006; Cardoso et al. 2015), in turn enabled by adaptive developmental networks at the genetic and molecular levels. Thus, it is based in neural network physical plasticity: the network connection pattern and weights are adjusted as perception, thought, and action take place in response to interactions with the outside world. It is an ongoing process: we learn all the time as we interact with the environment. This is a top-down process from the cortical level engaged with thoughts to the underlying level of micro connections (Kandel 2005).

Functional plasticity at the macro level occurs (Gigerenzer 2000), allowing learning and adaptation (Harford 2011), arising out of plasticity at the micro level (Buller 2005). This involves molecular mechanisms for habituation, sensitization, and classical conditioning (Kandel et al. 2000, pp. 1247–1257), and explicit memory involves long-term potentiation in the hippocampus (Kandel et al. 2000, pp. 1259–1272). Brain plasticity even allows changes in the role of cortical modules:

> The brain is an extraordinarily plastic biological system that is in a state of dynamic equilibrium with the external world. Even its basic connections are being constantly updated in response to changing sensory demands ... To a surprising extent, one module can even take over the function of another. Far from being wired up according to rigid, prenatal genetic blueprints, the brain's wiring is highly malleable.
>
> (Ramachandran 2011, p. 17)

Thus, the visual cortex, motor cortex, and so on are indeed adapted to special functions, but this is not due to the nature of their neurons, which seem structurally the same as all other cortical regions. What makes them what they are is the connectivity *to* them from outside the cortex, rather than any intrinsic structural difference (although different neuronal types may come to dominate according to the function established as developmental processes determine cell fates).

This leads to the question: why do organisms interact with their environments? The answer is: in order to survive and reproduce. All interest in and learning about the world is ultimately governed by this biological imperative, which in turn gives rise to a biological *value* system. In other words, we learn to avoid the ('bad') things that reduce our chances of surviving and reproducing and we learn to seek out the ('good') things that do the opposite. This raises a further question: how are such values, which govern learning, realized within the brain? The answer is: through 'the *feeling* of what happens' (Damasio 1999). Good things feel good, and bad things feel bad, in a variety of ways. These feelings guide all learning. If the brain did not have a system of values, how would it make choices between competing alternatives; in other words, how would it learn? We will return to this absolutely central point later. For now we are merely laying down the basic principle: learning (during development) ultimately serves biological purposes, and is therefore governed by *affective* processes. Affect underpins cognition.

3.5   BRAIN DEVELOPMENT AND PLASTICITY

The generic need for existence of a modular hierarchical structure in order to attain complexity (Section 3.2) does not prejudice views on how those structures arise. Modules will indeed arise via developmental processes utilizing genetic information, but they are not necessarily modules embodying innate cognitive information. They may be fixed behaviour modules, as in the case of reflex arcs, or they may be adaptive

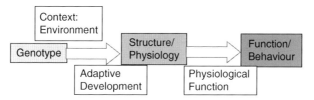

FIGURE 3.5 The chain of developmental causation. Genes are read in an adaptive way in a specific environmental context to produce structure that then enables the desired function

developmental modules (West-Eberhard 2003; Schlosser and Wagner 2004, pp. 519–541; Buller 2005, pp. 127–144), as in the case of the cortical lobes.

Development is discussed in depth by Wolpert (2002), West-Eberhard (2003, pp. 89–138), and Gilbert (2006). It is in a sense the inverse of the evolutionary process (Figure 1.1); see Figure 3.5. Developmental processes create the structure of living beings from a single cell (Wolpert 2002; Gilbert 2006), inter alia leading to the structure of the brain through a combination of genetic and environmental effects (Elman et al. 1998; Nicholls et al. 2001, pp. 479–523; Johnson 2005). Overall,

> Ontogenetic development is an active process through which biological structure is constructed afresh in each individual by means of complex and variable interactions between genes and their environments. The information is not in the genes but emerges from the constructive interaction between the genes and their environment.
>
> (Johnson 2005, p. 2)

Development processes and the brain: This applies in particular to the development of the brain:

> Perhaps the most amazing physical feature of the nervous system is the specificity of its connections. This specificity arises from several developmental processes, including the generation of the appropriate numbers and types of neurons, their migration to appropriate nuclei or laminae, and the guidance of their axons to appropriate target areas. In addition synapse formation is itself a selective process.
>
> (Kandel et al. 2013, p. 1105)

Neurons are generated in a proliferation zone, and then migrate to the destinations where they will be employed in the brain (Wolpert 2002, p. 411; Johnson 2005, p. 22); they then have to make their synaptic connections through outgrowth of axons. This latter step is where *contextual relationships will alter outcomes*. The process is different in different brain regions. It involves the following:

- **Induction and patterning of the nervous system** (Kandel et al. 2013, pp. 1020–1040), involving cell differentiation by inductive signals and patterning of relevant regions (the neural plate, ventral neural tube, dorsal neural tube, hindbrain, midbrain, and developing forebrain). The diversification of cell types is orchestrated by a relatively small number of inducing factors that control programmes of gene differentiation in target cells (Kandel et al. 2013, p. 1038). However, patterns in many regions of the cortex are determined by local cues such as the inputs they receive (Kandel et al. 2013, p. 1037).
- **Generation of nerve cells through a process of signalling between adjacent cells in the proneural region**, differentiating between glial cells and neurons, with neuronal fate partly determined by the timing of cell differentiation (Kandel et al. 2013, pp. 1041–1062). Factors essential for cell survival are provided by the target of the neuron (death of neurons is a normal occurrence during embryonic development).
- **The guidance of axons to their targets in pathway like those connecting the retina to the brain** involves recognition of environmental cues by growing axons (Kandel et al. 2013, pp. 1063–1086), breaking the long journey into manageable legs. The axons possess extremely specific receptors to recognize and interpret these chemical cues. The growth cone at the end of the axon guides axonal pathfinding (Nicholls et al. 2001, pp. 497–498; Wolpert 2002, p. 395) through extensions called filopedia, and guidance by guidepost cells (Nicholls et al. 2001, pp. 500–502). This is influenced by the contacts the filopodia make with other cells (Wolpert 2002, pp. 395–397).
- **The formation and regeneration of synapses:** When the target is specific, after axons have reached their targets synapses will form (Kandel et al. 2013, pp. 1087–1114), and this completes hard-wiring of the relevant section of the nervous system, for example the neuromuscular junction, which requires retrograde signals from the muscle to the nerve.

This last step of making rather specific synaptic connections occurs in pathways such as those from the spinal cord to ganglion cells, and when sensory axons contact specific motor neurons in the spinal cord. But it does not apply to the networks in the cortex itself. These are set in an adaptive way.

The cortex: In the case of the cortex, an initial set of connections is set up and then selectively pruned (Johnson 2005, pp. 169–171). This process involves generation of neurons outside the cortex that then migrate up to their positions in the cortex (Nicholls et al. 2001, pp. 483–484; Johnson 2005, pp. 32–40). Neuronal locations in the cortex depend on timing, and this is what determines the laminar structure of the cortex (Nicholls et al. 2001, pp. 491–493). This broad structure is innate:

> The laminar structure of the cortex rather results from local cellular and molecular interactions, rather than it being shaped as a result of thalamic and sensory input.
>
> (Johnson 2005, p. 37)

This structure enables the basic functions of pattern recognition, generalization, and memory; it is then refined to suit specific cognitive needs related to individual (experience-dependent) histories, which is how specific cognitive representations arise. As stated by Johnson (2005, pp. 33–34),

> It is possible that while the basic architecture of the cortex is innate (basic circuitry, learning rules, type and number of cells, etc), the detailed patterns of (dendritic and synaptic) connectivity are dependent on experience. In such a case we may say that while the network imposes architectural constraints on the representations that emerge within it, there are no innate representations.

It is important to note that *there are no innate representations*. Indeed, this has to be the case because whatever initial set of connections is set up, this is then altered by a number of mechanisms.

Sensory experience and the fine tuning of synaptic connections: Activity-dependent refinement of connections is a general feature of circuits in the CNS, both during development and in adult life (Changeaux et al. 1973; Kandel et al. 2013, pp. 1115–1130):

> The pathfinding of axons to their appropriate target cells within the nervous system and the formation of specific connections with those targets are controlled in a large part by molecular programs that are genetically determined, independent of activity or experience. Such molecular cues are not however always sufficient to establish the final pattern of synaptic connections. The precise matching of presynaptic neurons to postsynaptic targets depends at least in part on patterned neural activity evoked by sensory input. Activity dependent fine tuning of neural circuitry is not

limited to early development. Neural circuits are adaptable even in the mature individual. Indeed modification of synaptic connections is thought to be the physiological basis of learning.

(Kandel et al 2013, p. 1115)

This is shown, for example, by the way the brains of London taxi drivers are altered by their learning of all the streets in London (Maguire et al. 2006). However, this principle is best illustrated by the experiments described in Chapter 1, whereby Sur and colleagues (Roe et al. 1992; von Melchner et al. 2000) redirected the visual pathway in ferrets (the cortical *target* of which is normally genetically determined) and in this way they changed auditory cortex into visual cortex. In other words, visual cortex *learns* how to see (Sur and Rubenstein 2005); *cortical functions are not genetically determined.* The final connectivity of cortex depends upon the patterned neural activity that is evoked in it by sensory inputs; the fine connectivity is not intrinsic to cortex. Cortex may thus be described as 'random access memory space' (Solms and Panksepp 2012).

After axons reach their target areas, three processes refine the pattern of synaptic connections:

- **Neuronal cell death** results from competitive interactions during development (Nicholls et al. 2001, pp. 516–520).
- **Pruning of connections** (Chechik et al. 1999; Nicholls et al. 2001, pp. 517–520; Craik and Bialystok 2006; Low and Cheng 2006) takes place in response to experience. Activity plays a role in synapse elimination.
- **Synaptic weights are adaptively adjusted** in response to experience (Kandel 2006).

Cortical plasticity in development is summarized by Johnson as follows (Johnson 2005, pp. 40–44):

The nature of information entering a region of cortex may be important in ensuring the maintenance and further progression of differentiation. Furthermore, neural activity driven by inputs may be able to change the function and detailed neuro-anatomy of a region.

This is shown to be the case by studies of critical periods in development, for example in the auditory and visual systems (Nicholls et al. 2001, pp. 549–572). Development of visual perception requires sensory experience. The structure of ocular dominance columns in the primary visual cortex can be demonstrated to depend on use of the eyes as monkeys and kittens develop and use their eyes to see, when external input is essential for full development to take place (Wolpert 2002, pp. 409–411); inter alia this involves learning to recognize objects. Whatever initial genetic structuring might be there is changed and shaped by experience with the world. These areas are much less plastic after the critical period is over. Critical periods in development occur for normal vision and hearing, and for normal social behaviour (Nicholls et al. 2001, pp. 549–572; Kandel et al. 2013, pp. 1127–1128).

3.6   DEVELOPMENTAL ORIGIN OF BRAIN MODULES

A summary of the basic process of brain development is given by Wolpert (2002, p. 404):

> When axons reach their targets they make specialized connection – synapses-which are essential for signalling between neurons and their target cells. Formation of synapses in the correct pattern is a basic requirement of any developing nervous system. The connections may be made with other nerve cells, with muscles, and also with certain glandular tissues ... Setting up the organization of a complex nervous system in vertebrates involves refining an initially rather imprecise organization by extensive programmed cell death ... too many neurons are produced initially, and only those that make appropriate connections survive. A special feature of nervous system development is that fine-tuning of synaptic connections depends on the interaction of the organism with its environment and the consequent neuronal activity. This is particularly true of the vertebrate visual system, where sensory input from the retina in a period immediately after birth modifies synaptic connections so that the animal can perceive fine detail.
>
> (Wolpert 2002, pp. 404–405)

This developmental process results in existence of brain modules, because modules do indeed exist in the brain, as famously argued by Fodor (1983). In general terms,

> In the mature CNS a type of modularity is found that is unique to the CNS. This type of module is functional and forms the basis for information processing. Functional modules can process information relatively independently of each other and are typically composed of separate nerve cell aggregates (brain nuclei or regions) that are connected to each other in a highly ordered fashion by specific fibre tracts. Exchange of information is high within modules and low between modules.
>
> (Schlosser and Wagner 2004, pp. 158–159)

Neuronal connections: To consider which CNS modules are innate, and in which sense, let us define the following classes of neuronal connections

N1: Patterned connections: These are axons ending in synaptic connections that have a specific pattern that performs a pre-determined information processing function in a target area. An example is the retinal synaptic connections in Plate 3(b) (see colour plate section), where the details need not be the same in each individual person, and indeed do not matter, but the pattern is the same in all individuals and allows reliable visual processing such as line detection, edge detection, colour detection, and so on.

N2: Diffuse connections: These are synaptic endings of axons that have no specific post-synaptic target; rather, they are connections to a cortical area, and their function is to modulate – that is, *valence* – synaptic activity simultaneously in a widespread area of the nervous system (Nicholls et al. 2001, p. 282). This occurs in the cortical ascending systems (Plate 2(b) (see colour plate section)).

N3: Specific connections: These are synaptic connections (Figure 4.3), between specific axons and specific dendrites (Plate 2(a) (see colour plate section)), whose detailed network structure and link strengths embody our individual knowledge and memories (Section 3.4). This detailed structuring is crucial to our individual behaviour. This occurs particularly in the cortex, but also in areas such as the cerebellum.

N4: Domain links: These are links between specific groups of neurons, such as the optic tract, shown in Plate 3(a) (see colour plate section), and the ascending systems, shown in Plate 2(b) (see colour plate section), conveying information between them. Their connections to each of the two linked domains may be patterned, diffuse, or specific.

Innate modules: So which kinds of innate modules exist in the nervous system? This was already discussed in Section 1.4. The basic claim we now make is that, for developmental reasons, connections of types N1, N2, and N4 can be innately specified, but N3 cannot. This leads to the claims of Section 1.4.

In more detail:

N1: Patterned connections: The domain concerned receives contextual instructions, based on genetic information together with its location in the brain, to set up a basic pattern of connections that will serve the needed purpose. Local developmental processes set up a pattern of connections that have the required kind of connectivity to fulfil that purpose. Individual neuronal connections are not specified genetically but the pattern of development that will lead to them is. There will be variations in detail from person to person but the basic structure and function will be universal and can be regarded as genetically determined. This will apply to the optic nerve connections to the retina, motor neuron connections to muscle, and so on. This also applies to the location of the cortical targets of these systems.

N2: Diffuse connections: The axons are instructed developmentally to spread diffusely through the target area and then to form synapses that have no specific post-synaptic targets. The key case in which this occurs is the ascending systems linking nuclei in the limbic system to the cortex. The connections are genetically structured to enable non-local influences on cortex functioning via biogenic amines (Nicholls et al. 2001, pp. 282–286). These structures are universal, although again the details will differ from individual to individual.

N3: Specific connections: These domains are structured by the above-mentioned developmental processes to have a layered columnar structure, with *random* synaptic connections formed between axons and dendrites. This structure is then shaped by the above-mentioned ongoing developmental processes to have specific cognitive content as the individual interacts with the physical, ecological, and social environment. This interaction is what determines the detailed connectivity in these regions. The genetic formation of the layered columns makes possible the pattern recognition, generalization, and prediction interactions that facilitate this, but does not determine the specific unique detail of the connections, as in Plate 10 (see colour plate section). The kinds of developmental processes that take place, as discussed above, cannot possibly specify uniquely this level of detail. This conclusion is supported by all the available empirical evidence.

N4: Domain links: These developmentally guided links between specific groups of neurons are formed on the basis of genetic information read in the context of contextual cues. Motor neurons from the spinal cord make muscle-specific connections (Wolpert 2002, pp. 397–398), through environmental cues and stepping stones along the way (Wolpert 2002, pp. 398–399). Neurons from the retina make ordered connections on the tectum to form a retino-tectal map (Wolpert 2002, pp. 401–403). In each case the target is specified developmentally; the detailed connections on the cortical sides will necessarily be plastic (type N3), for that is the nature of the cortex, whereas the detailed connection on the other side (muscle or sensory neurons) will be patterned (Type N1) unless they are one of the ascending systems, when they will be diffuse (type N2).

In summary, we propose developmental connectionism has the following character:

Thesis: CNS development produces one of four possible modular outcomes in each region:

M1: Structured microconnections (Plate 3 (see colour plate section)) that perform preset logical operations, for example the link to the visual cortex (edge detection, motion detection, colour detection).

M2: Diffuse microconnections which influence specific areas rather than specific other neurons.

M3: Random microconnections (Plate 1 (see colour plate section)) which then get refined to perform learnt operations and rules and hold specific memories, for example the cortical columns.

M4: Specific macroconnections of one domain to another: for example, the ascending systems and the optical pathway connecting the retina to the visual cortex (Kandel et al. 2013, pp. 1063–1068).

As to the cortex itself, the situation is as follows (Johnson 2005, p. 17):

> Neurobiological and brain imaging studies indicate that the cerebral cortex probably does not possess innate representations. Rather, early in life large scale regions of the cortex have approximate biases that make them best suited to supporting particular types of computation. The fairly consistent structure-function relations observed in the cortex of normal human adults appear to be the consequence of multiple constraints both intrinsic and extrinsic to the organism, rather than of detailed genetic specification.

That is, cortical connectivity is of type M3, with input connections via links of type M4.

Innate cognitive modules: These developmental considerations lead to the following conclusion:

> **Corollary: No cortical cognitive modules:** It is developmentally impossible for the cortex to be genetically wired with detailed, specific cognitive information: the necessary processes to do so simply do not exist. Any such cognitive modules are developed through adaptive experience.

We recall that, as stated above, adaption is based upon biological values.

However, genetic information does indeed guide the way the cortex develops detailed connections, as discussed in the following chapters. Each of the four systems listed in the above **Thesis** is there because it plays a key role in survival and reproductive success and hence in evolution. We explore this in the next chapter.

4

Claims of Innate Modularity

This chapter considers claims of innate modularity in the mind in general (Fodor 1983, 1985; Carruthers et al. 2005, 2006, 2007) and in relation to cognitive modules in particular. It looks at the claims of language modules by Chomsky (1965) and Pinker (1994), and of other modules proposed by evolutionary psychologists (Barkow et al. 1992; Buss 1994; Barrett et al. 2002; Pinker 2002; Buss 2005; Dunbar et al. 2005), for example folk physics and folk psychology modules (Geary 2005) and a number module (Butterworth 1999). It considers the type of behavioural evidence advanced for cortical modules, where there is indeed evidence for functional specificity in particular cortical locations (Chapter 2), but concludes that because of the nature of CNS plasticity and development, as discussed in Chapter 3, this evidence does not suffice to justify claims of existence of *innate* cognitive modules. However, there are a variety of other brain modules that are indeed innate, as mentioned in Chapter 3, in particular the sensory systems (Fodor 1983) and ascending systems (see Chapter 3), whose relation to the development of cognitive modules is discussed in the following chapters.

4.1 BRAIN, BEHAVIOUR, AND BIOLOGY: DIFFERENT VIEWPOINTS

There are a number of different views on the relation between brain and behaviour on the one side and human biology on the other (Pinker 2002). The early battles between comparative psychology (promoting behaviourism) and ethology (Cartwright 2000, pp. 4–16) gave way to a battle between evolutionary theorists, emphasizing evolutionary origins, and cultural anthropologists, emphasizing the crucial role of culture (Cartwright 2000, pp. 16–25). Then followed the rise of sociobiology, applying evolutionary theory to the social behaviour of animals and humans, and evolutionary psychology, focusing on the adaptive mental mechanisms possessed by humans that were supposedly laid down in the distant past (Cartwright 2000, pp. 25–29).

There are, however, still many students of human behaviour who focus only on culture and the humanities (Pinker 2002, pp. 22–27; Kagan 2009) and consequently ignore biology and our evolutionary past in favour of social constructivism. This view has been labelled the *Standard Social Science Model* or SSSM (Barkow et al. 1992, pp 24–42; Cartwright 2000, p. 194), which assumes the mental organization of adults is determined solely by culture. This book argues that model does not make sense: both culture and our evolutionary history are clearly relevant.

Rival current evolution-based theories are discussed in a comparative way in Laland and Brown (2004) and Gangestad and Simpson (2007) as follows:[1]

- *Human sociobiology* (Laland and Brown 2004, pp. 70–108; Gangestad and Simpson 2007, pp. 4–5)
- *Human behavioural ecology* (Laland and Brown 2004, pp. 109–151; Gangestad and Simpson 2007, pp. 5–6)
- *Evolutionary psychology* (Laland and Brown 2004, pp. 153–196; Buss 2005; Gangestad and Simpson 2007, pp. 6–8)
- *Gene-culture coevolution* (Laland and Brown 2004, pp. 241–286; Gangestad and Simpson 2007, pp. 8–10)

Laland and Brown comment that evolutionary psychology (Barkow et al. 1992; Buss 2005) is currently the most popular theory (Laland and Brown 2004, p. 290), with its commitment to innate cognitive modules; this is labelled 'nativism'. La Cerra and Bingham describe the basic logic as follows (La Cerra and Bingham 2002, pp. 179, 183):

> The basic EP idea was beguilingly simple: if the body is a collection of adaptations produced by natural selection, then perhaps the same proposition applies to our brains and our minds. If there are specialised bodily organs   like hearts that pump blood and livers that remove toxins – perhaps there are also specialised mental organs. And just as adaptations like hearts and livers and beaks were locked into an organisms evolutionary toolkit, written into its genome,

---

[1] We omit a section on Memetics (Laland and Brown 2004, pp. 197–239) as we do not regard this as a serious contender in terms of being a theory of any of brain evolution, function, or development.

perhaps mental organs were too … in the view of evolutionary psychologists, nature's solution to the frame problem was the creation of an enormous confederation of information processing programs, or instincts that generated pre-specified solutions to a range of adaptive problems.

This idea is oddly reminiscent of nineteenth-century Faculty Psychology, the heir to Phrenology, which claimed that the cerebrum consisted in a number of innate sub-organs – each containing a mental power or 'faculty' – while conceding that these a priori faculties could not be identified via bumps on the head.

Simpson et al. state the issue of innate modularity as follows (Carruthers et al. 2005, p. 5):

> Nativists are inclined to see the mind as the product of a relatively large number of innately specified, relatively complex, domain specific structures and processes. Their empiricist counterparts incline towards the view that much less of the mind exists prior to worldly experience, and that the processes that operate on this experience are of a much more domain general nature. In other words, empiricists favour an initial cognitive architecture that is largely content free, and in which general-purpose learning mechanisms operate on the input form the senses so as to build up the contents of the mind from the cognizer's experience of the world. Nativists, in contrast, favour an architecture that is both more detailed and more content laden, containing for example faculties or principles of inference that are specifically designed for the acquisition and performance of particular cognitive tasks. This is what the nativist/empiricist debate is really about.

Barkow, Cosmides, and Tooby phrase the evolutionary issues as follows (Barkow et al. 1992, p. 5):

- There is a universal human nature, but this universality exists primarily at the level of evolved psychological mechanisms, not of expressed cultural behaviours.
- These evolved mechanisms are adaptations, constructed by natural selection over evolutionary time.
- The evolved structure of the human mind is adapted to the way of life of Pleistocene hunter gatherers, and not necessarily to our modern circumstances.

On this basis, Tooby and Cosmides propose an *Integrated Causal Model* (ICM) with the following properties (Barkow et al. 1992, p. 24):

1. The human mind consists of a set of evolved information processing systems instantiated in the human nervous system.
2. These mechanisms and the developmental programmes that produce them are adaptations, produced by natural selection over evolutionary times in ancestral environments.
3. Many of these mechanisms are functionally specialized to produce behaviour that solves particular adaptive problems, such as mate selection, language acquisition, family relations, and cooperation.
4. To be functionally specialized, many of these mechanisms must be richly structured in a content-specific way.
5. Content-specific information processing mechanisms generate some of the particular content of human culture, including certain behaviours, artefacts, and linguistically transmitted representations.
6. The cultural content generated by these and other mechanisms is the present state to be adopted or modified by psychological mechanisms situated in other members of the population.
7. This sets up epidemiological and historical level population processes.
8. These processes are located in particular ecological, economic, demographic, and intergroup social contexts or environments.

We agree with much of this, but there are crucial issues with which we disagree: specifically items 4 and 5. Many of the issues that arise relate to the question of what is assumed to be included in the concept 'information processing systems' mentioned in item 1. As we will see next, it is crucial that they include *emotional* information processing systems; but the evolutionary psychology literature usually assumes they are the kind of systems envisioned in 'cognitive science': that is, they are modules related only to logico-grammatical information processing, often referred to as 'computations'.

The modest proposal (Fodor 1983, 1985; Carruthers et al. 2005, pp. 69–70) refers to innate cognitive modules common to all people, with only superficial intergroup variation, namely the specialized input and output modular systems to the cortex. Their properties are as follows:

- Proprietary transducers
- Shallow outputs
- Fast in relation to other systems
- Mandatory in their operations
- Encapsulated from the remainder of cognition
- Have internal processes that are inaccessible to the rest of cognition
- Are innate or innately channelled to some significant degree

- Are liable to specific patterns of breakdown
- Develop according to paced and distinctively arranged sequences of growth.

However, the central/conceptual cognitive processes of belief forma-tion, reasoning, and decision-making, based in the cortex, are taken to be amodular or holistic in character (Fodor 1983, 2000).

The greedy proposals: The stronger proposals are for a large variety of domain-specific innate mental modules (Barkow et al. 1992; Buss 2005; Geary 2005; Carruthers et al. 2005, 2006, 2007), again common to all people with only superficial intergroup variation (Cartwright 2000, p. 194). Many such domain-specific mental modules have been claimed to exist, particu-larly a language module, number module, and cheater detection module. Because they relate to cognitive function, they are necessary claims of innate cortical modules.

We will first deal with language modules, as this proposal was the first and is the most well developed (Chomsky 1965, 1995; Pinker 1994; Carruthers et al. 2005, pp. 149, 156–297, 2006, pp. 133–148, 2007, pp. 233–292), and then we will comment on the others.

It is crucial to note here what 'innate' is taken to mean. Samuels (in Carruthers et al. 2007) analyses the concept in depth and states (Carruthers et al. 2007, p. 26):

> For the purposes of explaining how INNATE functions in cognitive science, the primitiveness condition is central. For what empiricists and other non-nativists invariably claim, and nativists deny, is that the acqui-sition of a given structure can be explained in terms of an inventory of psychological processes: perception, induction, deduction, conditioning, statistical learning, and so on (Segal in Carruthers et al. 2006, p. 90). In contrast, the nativist maintains that some alternative, non-psychological explanation will be required, one that is couched, for example, in the language of genetics, molecular biology, or neurobiology.

Thus, in the end it is a classic reductionist argument, in the vein of Crick (1994).

4.2 LANGUAGE MODULES: CHOMSKY AND PINKER

The initial major claim was made with regard to language (Chomsky 1965), with proposed innate cognitive modules embodying a 'language instinct' (Pinker 1994). According to Pinker (1994, p. 22):

Chomsky called attention to two fundamental facts. First, virtually every sentence that a person utters or understands is a brand new combination of words, appearing for the first time in the history of the universe. Therefore language cannot be a repertoire of responses; the brain must contain a recipe or program that can build an unlimited set of sentences out of a finite set of words ... The second fundamental fact is that children develop these complex grammars rapidly and without formal instruction and grow up to give consistent interpretations to novel sentence constructions that they have never before encountered. Therefore, he argued, children must be equipped with a plan common to the grammars of all languages, a Universal Grammar, that tells them how to distil the syntactic patterns out of the speech of their parents.

This is envisaged as being realized via an innate cognitive module embodying the Universal Grammar (UG). Specific language grammars correspond to particular settings of parameters that are free in the UG, and children learn their specific language by learning which parameter settings correspond to their particular language. Thus, grammar is largely innate, apart from a limited number of parameters that are fixed by experience (Baker 2001), the evidence that syntax is largely innate being that it is universal in the human species in the sense that all languages conform to the UG (Carruthers et al. 2007, p. 240).

According to Pinker (Christiansen and Kirby 2005, p. 17), the most significant aspect of the language faculty is that it makes information transfer possible. There are two primary principles behind this ability: the mental lexicon and grammar.

1. **The mental lexicon** is a finite memorized list of words, where a word is an arbitrary sign: a connection between a signal and a concept shared by members of the community.

This is illustrated in Figure 4.1
But this is not the whole story. Lexical priming studies show one does not just learn a list of words but also associations between words,

FIGURE 4.1 Mappings from objects or mental activity to concepts to words (Pinker in Christiansen and Kirby 2005, p. 17; Maynard Smith and Szathmáry 2007, p. 284)

or lexical co-occurrences, called *collocations* (Hoey 2005, p. 2). This is the property of language whereby two or more words appear more frequently in each other's company in a statistically reliable way, giving word patterns that are expected to occur. According to Hoey (2005, p. 13), 'Every word is primed for use in discourse as a result of cumulative effects of an individual's encounters with the word". And every word is primed to occur with particular other words; these are its collocates; every word is primed to occur with particular semantic sets; these are its semantic associations; and so on. This is well demonstrated by numerous corpus linguistics studies (Biber et al. 2006). These associations are built into a complex series of contextually dependent mappings between thought, language, and reality (Deacon 1997; Fauconnier 1997), where words are hierarchically classed into categories (Maynard Smith and Szathmáry 2007, p. 284). Thus, there is much more to the lexicon than just isolated words.

Pinker (in Christiansen and Kirby 2005, p. 17) identifies the second major principle behind language as grammar: we combine words into phrases, sentences, paragraphs, and so on, which present a hierarchical structure in a linear order. Thus:

2. **Grammar:** The principle behind grammar is the hierarchical combination of words according to logical rules that allow recursion.

Pinker states:

Inside every language user's head is a finite algorithm with the ability to generate an infinite number of potential sentences, each of which corresponds to a distinct thought. For example our knowledge of English incorporates rules that say 'A sentence may be comprised of a noun phrase (subject) and a verb phrase (object)' and 'A verb phrase may be composed of a verb phrase, a noun phrase (object), and a sentence (complement)'.

But this is a computational metaphor, based in the nature of digital computer languages, for what happens in the human brain. It is not what actually happens. The real process in the brain is that the neural networks in our cortex recognize patterns, predict possible outcomes, and generalize in a holistic way that is not rule-based (Elman et al. 1998; Hawkins 2004; Frith 2007; Kandel 2012; Churchland 2013). This process can be approximated by rules, and one can learn those rules; but when we speak or listen, we do not generically do so in a rule-based way, as envisaged by most linguists.

This can be illustrated by the following example given by Maynard Smith and Szathmáry (2007, p. 281): consider the two sentences,

How do you know who he saw? (1)

Who do you know how he saw? (2)

Every speaker of English knows that (1) is grammatical and (2) is not. But what is the rule that makes this true? You have to introduce the idea of a null element after the word 'saw' in (2) which marks the place from which the object of *saw*, now represented as *who*, has been moved (Maynard Smith and Szathmáry 2007, p. 289). But a constraint on movement states a *who*-word cannot be moved across a space occupied by *how*. Knowing this, we know that (2) is ungrammatical.

This example shows the tortuous lengths one has to go to fit the patterns of language used in daily life into a set of rules that are claimed to capture those patterns. One thing we can say for certain is that virtually all English users recognize the difference in acceptability between (1) and (2) without any knowledge of these formal linguistic rules. They holistically recognize the patterns they hear in relation to previous patterns of words they have heard and the present situational context, *just as in the case of the other sensory perceptions* (Frith 2007; Kandel 2012). Indeed, even mathematicians do not work in a rule-based way, despite it being the most rigorous of logical systems the human mind has devised. Feferman, commenting on Godel's incompleteness theorem (Feferman 2006), states it this way:

> Formal systems are an idealized model of mathematical reasoning; in practice, mathematicians don't use strictly limited formal languages in which to carry out their reasoning and don't appeal explicitly to axioms or rules of inference to justify their arguments. But the work on formalization showed that mathematical reasoning as it is actually carried out can be faithfully represented in suitable formal systems.

We can regard Chomsky's programme as an analogous formalization project in the case of language; it is not a characterization of modes of language usage.

However, there is one rule-based aspect of grammar that is specifically worth mentioning: its structure allows analysis of issues and problems in terms of the branching 'IF X THEN Y ELSE Z' logic, where X is some condition and Y and Z are alternative possibilities. This structure is the basis of logical argumentation and is what underlies all computational strategies. Together with the possibility of recursion, it is a key feature allowing the use of language in productive ways. Clearly the neural network structure of the brain can operate so as to instantiate such rules and hence allow logical arguments. It embodies a threshold function that channels subsequent event processing. This occurs commonly in biological contexts (Binder and Ellis 2016).

It is highly plausible that the syntactical structures of grammar were first developed as the syntax of actions involved in tool use (an *action grammar*), involving recursion and branching according to circumstances, and the patterns were then adapted for sentence construction (Maynard Smith and Szathmáry 2007, pp. 293–296). This fits in with the idea of the embodied mind (Lakoff and Johnson 1980a; Clark 2016) and embodied construction grammars (Bergen and Chang 2003; Feldman 2008), taking place in the context of conceptual frames. In computational terms, it can be realized via Latent Semantic Analysis, or LSA (Landauer and Dumais 1997; Landauer et al. 1998), a theory for extracting and representing the meaning of words, which shows that a great deal of what is conveyed by a text can be extracted by using linear algebra; but as stated above, the brain does not naturally work by computations, and grammar is more likely represented by Deep Learning Neural Networks (Schmidhuber 2015; Amodei et al. 2016).

In summary, the Chomsky view is based in the idea of grammar as a logical set of rules that control language, rather than as a set of usage patterns that can be approximated by a set of logical rules, which we believe is the real situation. Thus, in our view there is no Universal Grammar waiting in our heads for parameters to be set as we interact with our family in early life, as proposed by Chomsky; indeed, such a pre-existing cognitive module could not exist because of the developmental constraints discussed in Chapter 3. Lieberman (1984, 2000, 2006) puts the view that the general constraints of evolutionary biology and genetic data argue against any version of Chomsky's 'Universal Grammar', including its most recent version, the 'narrow faculty of language'. He argues that language is a learned skill, rather than an innate instinct. The human capacity for language is based on a 'functional language system' (FLS), distributed across many subsystems of the brain, many of which link directly to the subcortical basal ganglia (Hurford 2001). Instead of the innate modules Chomsky proposes, there are interconnected cortical columns that can recognize collocations and generalize from them, not by using any set or rules, but by using holistic neural network properties (Elman et al. 1998) in something like a Deep Learning Network (Schmidhuber 2015). We will deal with the poverty of stimulus and other arguments in relation to language in Chapters 6 and 7.

4.3   OTHER PROPOSED INNATE COGNITIVE MODULES

A great many further innate mental modules have been proposed (Barkow et al. 1992; Pinker 1994; Cartwright 2000, pp. 195–198; Geary 2005, pp. 127–161; Carruthers et al. 2005, 2006, 2007); indeed, Carruthers refers to 'Massive Modularity' (Carruthers et al. 2005, p. 71; 2006, p. 181). Geary (2005, p. 129) gives a table of modules assumed to exist around the broad areas of folk psychology, folk biology, and folk physics; this is summarized by Cartwright (2000, pp. 195–198). The view is that instead of containing a single reasoning faculty that can adapt to any problem, it may be better to think of a cluster of mechanisms designed to cope with particular ('domain-specific') problems that we commonly encountered in the EAA. Innate modules are here taken to be pre-wired, and the purpose of development is simply to enable the calibration of these modules to local social, biological, and physical conditions by setting suitable start-up conditions.

It is the alleged domain specificity of such modules that is at issue. Particular modules suggested are as follows:

1. **A visual perception module** (Carruthers et al. 2005, pp. 37–51) involving prior assumption that objects are rigid and convex, and that motion is relatively slow, allowing for object cognition in infancy (Carruthers et al. 2005, pp. 37–38). These claims have been hotly contested (Haith 1998). However, it is possible that some elements of object perception are encoded in the pre- or sub-cortical parts of the visual system, which is consistent with our view and needs careful consideration.

2. **A face recognition module** (Carruthers et al. 2005, pp. 51, 58; 2006, p. 160). This probably exists, because face recognition is a crucial survival ability, and the same remarks apply: any basic face recognition facility is probably hard-wired in pre- or sub-cortical areas along with edge detection, motion detection, and so on.

3. **An instinct for detecting facial attractiveness** has been alleged based on symmetry. This is supposed to show genetic fitness and so will be selected for (La Cerra and Bingham 1998, pp. 191–198). After discussing symmetry detection in bees, La Cerra and Bingham comment:

   detecting symmetry is not a property that a mate selection module evolved to solve. Rather it's a general capacity of your intelligence system . . . There are no evolved 'mate preference' systems, no evolved 'taste preferences' in our mind. The preferences you have cultivated are as unique as your sense of yourself. They are the creation of a unique intelligence system that belongs to only you.

There is no solid evidence for such an innate module.

4. **Theory of mind module** (Carruthers et al. 2005, pp. 38–39, 239–253) – anticipating the reactions and emotional states of others. This ability is certainly there at young ages, but developmentally motivated concerns make them seem rather unlikely to be cortical (Carruthers et al. 2005, p. 39). This ability will certainly develop through social interaction, driven by the innate sub-cortical affective systems, such as the PLAY system, which will be described in Chapter 7.

5. **Folk psychology modules:** Geary (2005, pp. 131–139, 159–160, 308–309) and Carruthers et al. (2006, pp. 135–145, 228; 2007, pp. 98–103) propose a whole suite of modules related to individual and group psychology, including theory of mind, pragmatic inferences, emotion detectors, intentionality detectors, eye-direction detectors, action parsers, and imitation systems.

Poverty of stimulus arguments are brought in support, but are weak (Carruthers et al. 2007, p. 100). Young children may be supposed to learn these vital functions in a developmental way. Perhaps, the most likely of these is imitation, which might perhaps be related to the existence of mirror neurons. There certainly are mechanisms which generate and locate mirror neurons in the cortex. But that is not the same as a functional module of the kind envisaged by Caruthers et al.

6. **Cheater detection module:** This is a particularly popular one because of evolutionary psychology theory, proposing an innate means by which to detect cheats (Cosmides 1989; Geary 2005, pp. 180–182). There is no reason why this could not evolve through experience and social interaction. Indeed, strong social pressures come into play in such cases, and activate the secondary (social emotions), which do indeed strongly influence behaviour.

7. **'Folk physics'** modules (Geary 2005, pp. 148–153, 225–226). Systems supporting movement are crucial, but in humans voluntary movement is learnt. Tool use is suggested to be a part of folk physics, which seems a mislabelling, and certainly could not be an innate module. These developed abilities may or may not be modular, but insofar as they are cortical, they are not likely to be innate; they reflect our experience and are based on other crucial (innate) sensory-motor and affective capacities.

8. '**Folk biology**' modules (Geary 2005, pp. 144–148, 225–226; Carruthers et al. 2005, pp. 143–149; 2006, pp. 161–162) have been claimed for identifying flora and fauna, forming a folk biology system. This is claimed on the basis of universalities across cultures. However, the same remarks apply as in the case of folk physics, except perhaps for a few very specific cases: it may be that there is built into the midbrain visual system an ability to recognize dangerous animals such as snakes, sending signals directly to instinctual and other primary emotion systems in order to initiate a suitable reaction. If not sub-cortical, these abilities are probably pre-cortical, as in the other visual abilities mentioned above, such as proto-face recognition.

9. A **number module** encoding innate arithmetic (Butterworth 1999; Devlin 2000; Lakoff and Núñez 2000; Carruthers et al. 2005, pp. 216–238; 2006, pp. 12–132; 2007, pp. 109–148). There is of course a number ability, even in some animals; but this is closely related to physical experience and may be related to language. Lakoff and Núñez summarize evidence alleged to show that very small infants – down to three or four days old – can discriminate between collections of two or three items and by four and a half months a baby can 'tell' that one plus one is two (Lakoff and Núñez 2000, pp. 15–19). We confess to scepticism: at three or four days old a baby can scarcely see. They claim the results for six months show an ability to conceptualize abstract numbers, whereas what the results really have to do with is an ability to determine that some kind of change has taken place. In brief, they are detecting *patterns and changes in patterns*. Devlin (2000) comments on this evidence that a number sense exists already at the age of two and is related to object conservation. But then he states what we believe is a plausible position on page 241:

> Besides showing that syntax is the main faculty of the brain that separates adult human being from infants and apes, the case of Joseph – and others like it – also shows that syntax is not entirely genetic. Human beings are born with a potential for syntax, that makes it easy, natural, and instinctive for them to acquire syntax at an early age. But it takes exposure to language to trigger the development of syntax in each young brain. In that sense, we learn how to think abstractly and how to communicate using grammatical language.

He then continues to discuss how, like language, mathematics is a special form of off-line thinking (a feature emphasized by Bickerton (2001)), and indeed probably depends on the same features of the brain that give us language. Indeed, as proposed by Vygotsky (1962), it may be that all purposeful abstract thought is an internalization of physical action.

10. **'Folk sociology'** modules, detecting an Ingroup and Outgroup, and with mechanisms for cooperative engagement with kin and non-kin (Carruthers et al. 2006, pp. 162–163). This is based in observations of how primates learn. It seems to be based in the premise that primate behaviour is all innate. But they too can learn developmentally, especially on the basis of innate affective systems of the kind that we discuss in Chapter 7.

11. **Natural pedagogy** (Gergely in Carruthers et al. 2007, pp. 173–198). The hypothesis is that

    'the "relevance blindness" of the juvenile's available observational learning mechanisms rendered the newly emerging hominim technological cultural skills cognitively opaque to the naïve observational learner. This created a learning problem stemming from the ensuing uncertainty about what to learn and what not to learn from what is observed . . . this may have led to the evolution of a new type of relevance guided social mechanism of mutual design (i.e. natural pedagogy)'. (Carruthers et al. 2007, p. 177)

This is a hypothesis about the nature of cultural evolution and learning abilities, related to imitation and mirror neurons. It is claimed to be based in two inbuilt functional assumptions: basic epistemic trust and others as reliable sources of shared knowledge (Carruthers et al. 2007, p. 197). These are not the same as an innate cognitive module, and may well be presumed to originate mainly socially.

12. **Ethical modules** (de Waal 1996; Carruthers et al. 2005, pp. 19, 338–370; 2007, p. 101; Hauser 2006; Haidt and Kesebir 2010). This relates to a very old theme: do we begin life with a default personality; are we born evil or born good (Hauser 2006, p. 163)? Evidence is related to the existence of universality of traits such as empathy and sympathy, particularly when they appear early in development, and is largely based on primate behaviour but to some degree on observing young children. Hauser states the basic issue this way (Hauser 2006, p. 153):

    If there are moral universals, then there must be capacities that all normally developing humans share. There are at least three ways this might play out, using parallels to language. On one end of the spectrum is a nativist position that puts precise moral norms in the newborn child's head. She is born knowing that killing is wrong, helping is good, . . . On the opposite end of the spectrum is the view that our moral faculty lacks content but starts off with a device that can acquire moral norms. With this view there are no rules and no content, only general processes for acquiring what nurture hand us. In the middle is the view that we are born with abstract rules or principles, with nurture entering the picture to set the parameters and guide us towards particular moral systems.

There is, however, a fourth position that is more plausible than any of the above: adapt the third option by replacing 'abstract rules or principles' (which would be based in the cortex) by 'innate emotion systems' (which would be based in the limbic system and below). Then it all works. This is, we believe, consistent with de Waal's position, who strongly resists the gene-centric view of all animal behaviour, and the biologizing of morality (de Waal 1996, pp. 10–19). He proposes that primates seek the company of individuals with whom profitable partnerships are possible rather than following the evolutionary biology idea of pitting the interests of one individual against those of another (de Waal 1996, p. 27). He sees reciprocal altruism (Trivers 1971) as essential to morality (de Waal 1996, pp. 135–136); but this is a social and behavioural trait. Even if it is based in underlying biological aspects such as mirror neurons and innate basic or social emotions, it is not equivalent to a cognitive module.

This is a brief summary of a very large literature. These proposals are all claims for cortical modules, except possibly for item 2 and part of item 5, and so they all run into the developmental problems identified in Chapter 3.

In addition, there are suggested to be

13. **Innate emotional systems** (Panksepp 1998; Carruthers et al. 2005, pp. 19, 305–337), realized in the limbic system and upper brainstem;
14. **Sensory input and motor output systems** (Fodor 1983, 1985), which might include aspects of items 2 and 8 above.

We recognize items 13 and 14 as indeed being innate (hard wired) CNS modules, but they are not *cognitive* modules, that is, they are not cortical units. This is what we explore further in the subsequent passages.

4.4   ARGUMENTS FOR INNATE MODULES

The following arguments have been given for the existence of innate mental modules:

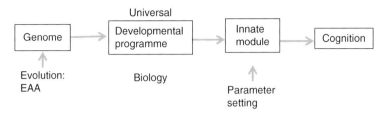

FIGURE 4.2 The short route from the genome to cognition

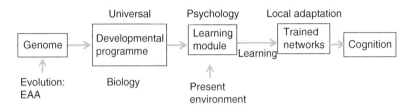

FIGURE 4.3 The longer route from the genome to cognition

1. *Uniformity and predictability of human cognition* (Carruthers et al. 2005, pp. 8–11)

Basic uniformity is certainly there, and surely results from developmental processes based in our genetic inheritance. But the issue is how direct the link is from the genome to the behavioural patterns. Two views are possible: a more direct link (Figure 4.2) and a less direct one (Figure 4.3). The first proposal is fine for fixed action patterns and instinctual responses, but lacks the learning ability, based in underlying plasticity, that characterizes cortical networks. An argument for uniformity and predictability of human cognition must also recognize its variability and adaptation to local circumstances. Any proposal for innate cognitive modules has difficulty handling this tightrope. The second approach has a sound biological foundation, based in ontogenetic development of neural networks (Elman et al. 1998, pp. 106–171).

2. *Evolutionary biology in general* (Carruthers et al. 2005, pp. 71; 2006, pp. 182–183)

This is the view that evolution of new systems or structures works by 'bolting on' new special purpose items to the existing repertoire: 'they will have been designed for a specific purpose, and are therefore likely to display all or many of the properties of central modules'. They will be assembled in a modular way, as clarified by Simon (1962, 1992). However, the assumption that this works as in Figure 4.2 rather than Figure 4.3 is not justified. Modularity of structure is indeed necessary for complexity to arise and function, and there must indeed be some degree of evolutionary explanation of our inner cognitive endowment (Carruthers et al. 2005, p. 12); this does not imply it has to be a directly genetically specified structure.

3. *Evolutionary psychology arguments regarding emergence of cognitive mechanisms*

A general-purpose problem-solver could not evolve because it would be outcompeted by specialist mechanisms (Carruthers et al. 2005, p. 72). This would be true if there was only one 'general-purpose' problem-solver, but there are several innate affective 'tools for living', as we will argue in Chapter 7. It would also be true if we always lived in identical environments. The whole point of brain plasticity, learning, and adaptability is that it can cope with new environments as they are encountered. An animal with a brain characterized by domain-specific modules can only cope with very particular environments and would not last long. This argument does apply to the reptilian brain but not to the cortex.

4. *Mind must be modular because holistic processes are computationally intractable*

This argument is presented in Carruthers et al. (2005, pp. 107–120; 2006, pp. 183–191). Holistic ('gestalt') processes do indeed occur in the mind (Kandel 2012). This is presumably an argument against top-down causation in the brain, which does indeed occur (Ellis 2016). In any case this is an argument for modularity (with which we agree) but not for *innate* modularity.

This is related to the next issue:

5. *The frame problem* (Carruthers et al. 2005, pp. 109, 117–118), or problem of relevance

How can a device determine in a computationally tractable manner which operations, options, or items of information are relevant to the cognitive task at hand? To solve this requires a relevance theory (Carruthers et al. 2005, p. 67). The relevance theory is provided by our emotional systems (Damasio 1994, 1999). This will be developed in Chapter 7.

6. *Poverty of stimulus arguments* (Carruthers et al. 2005, pp. 6–8; 2006, pp. 134–137; 2007, pp. 90–105)

This argument has been made particularly in the case of language (Chomsky 1965, 1995; Pinker 1994), and is discussed in all evolutionary psychology presentations. But in the first place it is undermined by data from deep learning networks (Amodei et al. 2016), and secondly it completely fails to comprehend the essential issue of motivation, as discussed by Greenspan and Shanker (2004). We return to this issue, too, in Chapter 7.

More generally, this is essentially the same as claims for innate modules made on the basis of behavioural evidence in children (Carruthers et al. 2005, pp. 9, 37, 254–271), which purport to show they can carry out cognitive tasks long before they could have learned them. This claim is highly contentious, and has been met with strong disconfirmation (Haith 1998; see Carruthers et al. 2005, p. 38). Thus, for example, in the case of vision, Haith says 'we have calculated that 3.5 month olds have had 800 hours of waking time, that is 48,000 minutes and almost 3 million seconds, during which they have made 3 to 6 million eye movements, plenty of opportunity to benefit from visual experience' (Haith 1998). In many cases there is an extremely optimistic interpretation of a baby's movements in relation to their supposed cognitive determinants, at a time when it has not yet even learned to distinguish its own body from the environment around. In any case any such claims need to be carefully analysed as to whether they relate to cortical or pre- or sub-cortical aspects of the brain. In the latter case, they may well be true. Finally,

7. *Cortical functional specificity*

There is indeed evidence for functional specificity in particular locations, but this is divorced from biological evidence as to what it is that leads to such specificity. This evidence does not distinguish between Figures 4.2 and 4.3. And in any case, evidence of extreme plasticity – in particular the famous case of the rewired ferrets – shows that brain adaptation can override such allegedly innate structures.

4.5 DIFFICULTIES WITH INNATE CORTICAL MODULES

On the other hand, there are many difficulties with hard-wired cognitive modules, closely related to claims of genetic origins and structuring. The claim is, for example (Pinker in Christiansen and Kirby 2005, p. 33), 'there should be genes that have as one of their distinctive effects the development of normal human language abilities'. This is undoubtedly true. There should be. The issue is whether they code for domain-specific information-laden modules, as in Figure 4.2, or for developmental programmes leading to brain plasticity and a learning ability that then develops specific domain abilities through social interactions and experience, as in Figure 4.3, perhaps localized in specific parts of the cortex.

There are many problems with the proposal of innate cortical modules encoding domain-specific information. In particular, there are

- **Information issues:** there is not enough genetic information to allow this to happen, given the small number of specifically human genes in the human genome (Stone 2015, pp. 194–195). The modules could not be coded for in genetic terms (Godfrey Smith in Carruthers et al. 2007, pp. 55–68). This applies especially to genes for specifically human cortical development (Florio et al. 2015).
- **Developmental issues:** there is no way to hard-wire the requisite detailed cortical connections through developmental processes. This is explained in Chapter 3 (and see Carruthers et al. 2005, pp. 23–33). Indeed, Geary's own description of cortex development (Geary 2005, pp. 95–97) makes this clear: there is no way the processes he describes could be capable of leading to the detailed kind of neural network connectivity at the synaptic level that encodes precise cognitive information (cf. Elman et al. 1998; Hawkins 2004; Churchland 2013). Epigenetics will not resolve this problem: where or how could this information be stored?
- **Evolutionary issues**: the required genes could not be selected for (Chapter 4), despite the Baldwin effect (Carruthers et al. 2006, pp. 91–111). Given the challenge that grammar is more complex than it needs to be to fulfil the communication and thought needs of a hunter-gatherer lifestyle, Pinker in Christiansen and S Kirby (2005, p. 25) defends the idea that features like recursion in language give a small selection advantage (say 1 per cent) so that 'the evolution of grammar presents no paradox'. This seems dubious (where does that one per cent come from?), but in any case, who could seriously claim that survival rates are affected so significantly by the difference between sentences (1) and (2) above that this difference gets set into genes and built into a UG module in the cortex?
- **How can a massively modular mind be flexible and context sensitive** (Carruthers et al. 2005, pp. 15, 53–67)? How can innate pre-specification be compatible with learning (Carruthers et al. 2005, pp. 34–52)? Fodor (2000) calls this the 'abduction problem' (Carruthers et al. 2005, p. 15). Development arises from higher-level processes that are not claimed to be innate (they are psychological

in nature) and that overwrite the core knowledge (Carruthers et al. 2005, p. 40). Thus, there is a major tension between innate modules and developmental plasticity (Carruthers et al. 2005, pp. 38–40, 53–68, 122).

- **How can a massively modular mind explain both cultural diversity and stability** (Carruthers et al. 2006, pp. 155–156)? Nativist views preclude developmental flexibility (Carruthers et al. 2005, pp. 37–40) and are seen as minimizing change during development (Haith 1998).

Rather than a massively modular innate mind, what is needed is development of simple heuristic capacity via an 'adaptive toolbox' (Carruthers et al. 2006, pp. 165–193). The adaptive toolbox consists of (Gigerenzer and Selten 2002):

1. A collection of elements – such as search rules, stopping rules, and decision rules for constructing the heuristics.
2. Core mental capacities that building blocks exploit – such as recognition memory, depth perception, frequency monitoring, object tracking, and the ability to imitate.
3. A specific group of heuristics rather than a general-purpose decision-making algorithm. These heuristics are fast, frugal, and computationally cheap, but are less consistent, coherent, and general.

Then it is not true that if cognitive processes are to be tractably realized, the mind must be constructed out of networks of processing systems that are encapsulated in the narrow-scope sense of modularity (Carruthers et al. 2006, p. 197).

Regarding language in particular (Cartwright 2000, pp. 202–211; Jablonka and Lamb 2006, pp. 216, 218, 299–306) and the Chomsky programme: there is a long and highly contested debate on the nature of linguistics, inter alia involving Austin, Bruner, Chomsky, Derrrida, Firth, Goffman, Harris, Jakobson, Labov, Orwell, Sepir, Skinner, Whorf, and Witgenstein (see Joseph at al. 2001), and its relation to evolution and particularly to the Chomsky programme, involving inter alia Savage-Rumbaugh, Pinker, Bloom, Gould, Lieberman, Deacon, Thomasello, Bickerton, Jackendorff, Hauser, and Fitch (see Kenneally 2008). The view put here is that:

1. Chomsky's project is based in a **rule-based view of language usage**, rather than a pattern-based view. But the mind works most naturally by pattern recognition (Hawkins 2004; Churchland 2013), not by rules, although it can *learn* to work by rules, and will generalize

from patterns to rules that approximately capture what is happening. The extraordinary complexity of the rule system devised to approximate what actually happens in language usage simply does not correspond to how we are taught or how we think. It is based on a computational analogy – 'the brain as a computer' – that is in many ways inappropriate. (Lieberman commented on how we always use the latest technology as a model for the brain: see Liebermann 1984; that is why we use a computational analogy at present.)

2. There are **many alternative and more plausible approaches** to linguistics: in particular, embodied construction grammar (Feldman 2008) and lexical priming and collocations (Hoey 2005) as demonstrated by corpus linguistics (Biber et al. 2006). These are cognitively based in underlying domain mappings (Deacon 1997; Faouconnier 1997) and in biological terms are based in Deep Learning Networks (Amodei et al. 2016).

3. **Universality:** The prime evidence for the view that syntax is largely innate is that it is universal in the human species (Carruthers et al. 2007, p. 240). But this universality plausibly derives from the unavoidable rules of iconicity (Deacon 2003), and indeed it is inevitable in any efficient iconic system. This efficient patterning was inexorably discovered socially by humans over the passage of time once the pre-requisites for language were built into cortical structures, as well as the biological requisites for speech production.

4. These **cortical pre-requisites** are the ability to assign labels ('names') to patterns of neural activations, which are how the brain represents reality (Churchland 2013). This can be done by suitable neural network connections (Elman et al. 1998, pp. 125–129; Hawkins 2004). Crucially important here is the extending of this labelling ability to the ability to assign labels to patterns of labels, which allows recursion to take place. This probably required downward projections in the layered cortical structures that get specialized for symbolism, and may well have developed from the grammar of actions (Maynard Smith and Szathmáry 2007, pp. 281–308), which also involves recursion, and is supported by the fact that the subcortical basal ganglia play a critical role both in adaptive motor acts and in speech (Liebermann 2006).

5. The issue of **poverty of stimulus** in relation to language will be dealt with in Chapter 7, after dealing with the issue of emotions in relation to cognition in Chapter 6. In brief, the essential point that has been missed by most linguistic theorists is the emotional drive that makes

infants desperately want to communicate with the dominant care-givers in their lives. That is what makes all the difference (Greenspan 1997; Greenspan and Shanker 2004). As stated by Bruner, 'What may be innate about language acquisition is not linguistic innateness, but some special features of human action that permit language to be decoded by the uses to which it is put' (Bruner 1975, p. 2, quoted by Joseph et al. 2001, p. 171). The child learns language by using it (Joseph et al. 2001, pp. 176–182).

6. **Infinity issue and language modules:** Chomsky (1995, pp. 6–7) stated, 'The class of sentences with which we can operate fluently and without difficulty is so vast that for all practical purposes . . . we can regard it as infinite' (quoted in Joseph et al. 2001, p. 122). The major problem here is that in the hands of linguistic theorists, the vital 'for all practical purposes' has got omitted, and it has become dogma that natural language allows actually infinite sentences (Komarova and Nowak 2005). An analysis based on a mathematical theorem (Gold's Theorem) is then alleged to definitively prove the existence of innate language modules embodying a Universal Grammar.

This analysis has no relation to biological reality, and to suppose you can argue from such mathematical principles to what has occurred in living systems is a category error. It is simply impossible in real-world language to have infinite sentences, because you must remember the start of the sentence by the time you reach the end (see the Appendix for detail). Komarova and Nowak have forgotten that the purpose of language is both to think and to communicate a message from one person to another. Given the famous limits of short-term memory (Miller 1956), the maximum useful number of levels of recursion in a sentence is seven; this corresponds to the limits of assignment of intentions to others in Theories of Mind. The analysis given by Komarova and Nowak is a demonstration of how wrong you can go if you ignore psychological and biological reality in favour of abstract mathematically based argumentation that does not apply to the real world at hand.

A realistic view is provided by Bruner (1975, 1983), based on thousands of hours of observations of infants learning to speak rather than on theoretical considerations. He emphasizes (Bruner 1983, pp. 119–120, quoted in Joseph et al. 2001, p. 171):

> Infants learning language are not academic grammarians inferring rules abstractly and independently of use . . . Whatever else language is, it is a systematic way of communicating to others, of affecting their and our

own behaviour, of sharing attention ... Let us not be dazzled by the grammarians questions. Pragmatic ones are just as dazzling, and just as mysterious. How indeed do we ever learn to get things done with words?

This is the dimension missing in the Chomsky approach. What children need is not Chomsky's Language Acquisition Device (LAD) but on the one hand a brain ready for language (Item 4. above), as explored particularly by Tomasello (1999, 2003), and on the other lots of interaction with significant others (Bruner 1983; Greenspan and Shanker 2004). The infant brain will recognize the patterns and then generalize towards rules that capture the patterns (plurals, past tenses, and so on) (see Lee et al. (2009)), because this is what neural networks can do, handling both the regular forms and exceptions (Elman et al. 1998, pp. 130–147).

Liebermann presents evidence that argues against any form of UG – children instead appear to learn most aspects of language using the general processes employed in learning to walk or to play the violin (Liebermann 2006). As stated by Sampson (2005), 'Children are good at learning languages, because people are good at learning anything that life throws at us – not because we have fixed structures of knowledge built in'. But in order that this is possible, it is crucial that our cortical neural network structures are built so as to allow labelling of patterns of cortical excitations, and labelling of patterns of such labels. This is the cortical language-readiness requirement we all share. It is probably realized via Deep Neural Networks (Hannun et al. 2014).

4.6   THE ALTERNATIVE VIEW

Because of brain plasticity in an uncertain environment, there is no plausible developmental path for alleged specific innate cortical modules. They arise developmentally during interaction with the environment, rather than directly 'genetically'.

There are many discussions of these issues that agree with the position outlined here; see Elman et al. (1998, pp. 371–390), Liebermann (2000, 2006), La Cerra and Bingham (2002, pp. 179–190), Laland and Brown (2004, pp. 176–195), Buller (2005, pp. 127–200), and Sampson (2005). One main critique of evolutionary psychology is that advances in developmental neurobiology indicate that brain cortical development is not characterized by precise genetic programming (Gangestad and Simpson 2007, p. 13). Instead, interactions with the physical and social world shape development of such neural areas. The basic adaptation of higher neural regions is plasticity: the ability to adapt to the specific world in which one develops (Buller 2005; Gangestad and Simpson 2007, p. 13). Sterelny (Carruthers et al. 2006, p. 229) proposes that a behavioural competence that might seem to be the signature of an innate module can be produced by a highly structured development environment. At the behavioural level, Bayesian inference is an effective domain general learning mechanism (Carruthers et al. 2007, pp. 209–213) that seems to apply in the human brain.

Clark Barrett states it this way:

> The folk view of innateness as hard wired must be revised in the case of cognitive modules. Modules are not preformed but rather are constructed by evolved developmental systems that use local real-time information to do so, resulting in modules that can vary along some dimensions yet retain certain features in common.
>
>   (Carruthers et al. 2006, p. 199)

While Sperber and Hirchfield state:

> 'Most modules in the mature human cognitive system are generated by innate learning modules through an epigenetic process and hence are not innate but do have an innate basis'.
>
>   (Carruthers et al. 2006, p. 157)

La Cerra and Bingham comment (2002, p. 186):

> We agree that your brain is composed of neural adaptations that resulted from evolution (and the mind, remember, is a product of the activity of the brain). But these adaptations did not take the form of well-defined inherited information processing circuits that were designed to generate predetermined adaptive solutions to Stone Age problems. Rather they took the form of components of a system that could construct adaptive information processing networks – individualised circuitry that generated behavioural solutions that precisely fit the specific environmental conditions, bioenergetics needs, personal experiences, and unique life history of an individual.

Hence, our overall **thesis:**

Evolutionary psychology claims of innate cognitive modules result from focusing on the outcomes rather than the adaptive developmental processes that lead to these outcomes. Evolutionary processes will have favoured cognitive modules with great adaptive flexibility rather than with fixed cognitive content.

For example, in the case of vision, hard-wiring occurs in the connections leading to and below the visual cortex, not in the visual cortex itself. The basic structure of cortical circuits (the cognitive aspect of vision) forms without any visual experience, and then subsequently is environmentally tuned (Carruthers et al. 2005, p. 511).

There is, however, a key issue that remains: how do developed cortical domains know which kinds of problem they needed to solve? This is the *frame issue* referred to above: it is a matter of processing the most relevant inputs available (Carruthers et al. 2005, pp. 63–67). But how is that determined?

One might claim that the greater the cognitive benefit yielded by the processing of an input, the greater its relevance; or that 'genes may affect developmental outcomes by leading people to be sensitive to particular information in the world' (Gangestad and Simpson 2007, p. 14). Indeed, it is our thesis that this is so and that that crucial information is provided by the genetically determined primary *emotional* systems (see Chapter 7). Reading all the literature referred to above will confirm that, because of the strong influence of cognitive psychology, it is almost all phrased in terms of the evolutionary development of *cognitive* modules. This is true even in the case of developmental psychology (Karmiloff-Smith 1996, pp. 117–138), which talks about theory of mind but not theory of emotion – even though emotion plays such an important role in life in general and in development in particular. The missing dimension is the evolutionary effect of emotion and of affective modules. That is what we pursue next.

5

The Mind and Emotions

This chapter deals with emotion/affect and its important functions: first, as a means of communication, related to facial expressions conveying emotions and so helping to facilitate and regulate social interactions. Second, as a guide to behaviour, whereby emotions have a key role in brain function. For example, there are emotional tags attached to all episodic memories. Third, emotion functions as a guide to development by mediating adaptation through the processes of neural Darwinism described in Chapter 2. Here the role of non-local neural connections is crucial in underlying brain plasticity. The emotional systems provide evolutionarily based guidance as to what is immediately important for survival and reproductive success, but this then shapes brain plasticity. This chapter also deals with some basic affective systems identified as human universals: the set of primary emotion systems found in all mammals, including humans. These are hard-wired systems (hence developed in our evolutionary past) that provide rapid guidance as to how to act in situations of universal biological significance. Possible additions to this set of proposed primary affective systems are also considered.

5.1 MAMMALS

Where, then, should we start; which non-human animals are sufficiently close relatives to provide the necessary context? We suggest that we begin with the biological class to which we belong – namely that of mammals – which diverged from the other lines roughly 200 million years ago. What distinguishes mammals, perhaps above all, is the fact that they suckle their young. This is made possible by the anatomical fact that they possess mammary glands. Mammary glands are wonderful things, but they are not the only distinguishing anatomical feature of mammals. The features we would prefer to focus on are those that have the greatest impact on mammalian behaviour and mental life. We think this is the aspect of being human (or being a mammal) that concerns us most. We all know what humans and other mammals look like from the outside; this is not what concerns us here. What concerns us more is what makes us tick, from the inside; what makes us human *beings*.

The distinguishing mental and behavioural characteristics of animals are inscribed anatomically and physiologically in their brains. This is true even if the brain and nervous system are ultimately inextricable from other bodily systems. Thus, for example, although mammalian suckling evolved in tandem with changes in the mammalian endocrine and reproductive systems, suckling itself (the inclination to suckle and knowing how to suckle) is mediated by the brain. This, then, is the aspect of mammalian anatomy and physiology that we shall focus on: the brain mechanisms that mediate the being of a mammal.

5.1.1   Instincts

Before doing so, however, we want to set out two basic assumptions. Firstly, we are not going to revisit the tiresome debates surrounding the mind–body relation. We take it for granted that the structure and functions of the mammalian brain mediate mammalian behaviour and mental life. This assumption applies to all behaviour and mental life. But, secondly, we want to focus here particularly on the brain structures and functions that mediate the instinctual tendencies of mammals. For a reminder of our views on the mind–brain relation, and our definition of the terms 'instinct', 'emotion', 'affect' and 'drive', please refer back to Chapter 2.

We focus on instincts because they are the aspects of complex mental life and behaviour that are most stereotyped. There are other complex cognitions and behaviours that are stereotyped too, such as the learnt skills and habits we discussed in Chapter 2, but these are not hard-wired. Crucial to our argument is the view that language is a learnt skill; it is not an instinct.

Of course, mammals are shaped by other things too – differences in the individual endowment and environment – but these differences influence a pre-existing 'default' plan; and it is the hard-wired default plan that inter-ests us here. The default plan of mammalian behaviour and mental life is determined by the mere fact of being a mammal. Mammals do not learn to suckle (for example); they just do it. They are *constituted* that way. This innate part of what it is to be a particular type of animal is a common denominator that applies to the type as a whole. It is therefore the most essential part of what makes them (us) tick – and the part that we shall take as our starting point.

What, then, are instincts and where do they come from?

Instincts are inborn behavioural and mental tendencies. They are inborn for the reason that they are fundamental to the reproductive fitness of a particular type of animal. To put it differently, animals that behave in particular ways that increase their chances of surviving to reproduce (increase their reproductive fitness) will for that very reason pass on the genes that incline them to behave in that way; and those that are inclined to behave differently will not pass on their genes, or will be less likely to. This is called natural selection. Thus, the genes that predispose animals to act in ways that enhance their reproductive fitness are passed down from generation to generation. They are evolutionarily conserved. A type of animal is thereby 'bred' to behave and feel in particular ways. These are the instincts of that type of animal.

5.1.2 Values

Of paramount importance in all this, in our view, is the fact that by dint of the existence of instincts, an inborn system of values underpins the way in which all animals behave. The most basic of these values is the very principle that it is 'good' to survive and reproduce. This principle is not preordained; it simply follows, blindly but directly, from the facts of natural selection, as outlined in Chapter 2. We are therefore, by default, in consequence of the fundamental biological fact of natural selection, inherently inclined to do and feel those things that enhance our reproductive fitness.

One should note here, however, that these proto-values are not the same as ethical values, which bring into play all the kinds of issues discussed in moral philosophy over the past 2,000 years. It is not necessarily *morally* right that one struggles to survive at the cost of all those around; if this was the case, society would not be the cooperative venture we aspire to, nor would the great figures of history be willing to die for abstract causes ('Dulce et Dulcorum est Pro Patria Mori') or for the sake of others. Having noted this issue, we will not pursue it further here. We will only add the observation that we do not actually live in the cooperative human world we aspire to; this is in large part because our moral ideals are so easily undermined by our instincts.

5.2 FEELINGS

We turn now to the manner in which the *biological* system of values embodied in our instincts is communicated to each individual animal. It is communicated through feelings. As a general rule, when an animal behaves in accordance with its instincts (i.e. when it acts in ways that enhance its chances of surviving to reproduce), it feels 'good'; when it does not, it feels 'bad'. This seems to be what feelings are for. They motivate us to act in accordance with our instincts (see Damasio 1999).

This, in a sense, defines the most basic instinct of all; we are compelled to act in ways that make us feel good, and to avoid things that make us feel bad. Freud (1911) called this the 'pleasure principle', but it is by no means an exclusively Freudian idea. All animals patently seek pleasure and avoid unpleasure.

This, the most basic motivational principle, evolved long before mammals did. We know this from the fact that the brain region that mediates this basic form of hedonic consciousness – crude, undifferentiated feelings of pleasure and unpleasure – namely the periaqueductal grey (PAG), evolved long before mammals differentiated from the other classes of vertebrate. In fact, the PAG is conserved in all vertebrates. It is therefore at least 525 million years old. This ancient structure can still be found today, in you and me (Figure 5.1), for the very reason that it proved to be so fundamental for our survival and reproductive success.

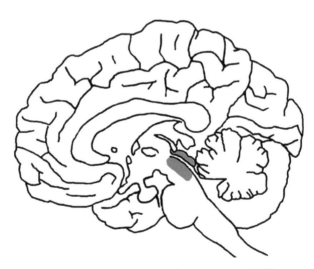

FIGURE 5.1 Periaqueductal grey matter (PAG)

It has a columnar structure, with the dorsal (back) columns generating profoundly unpleasant feelings and the ventral (front) ones generating what can only be called orgasmic delight. Important to mention, but perhaps needless to say, is the fact that the columns that generate these primitive feelings are closely connected with other cell groups that generate primitive movements. In this way pleasurable feelings are connected with compulsory 'approach' behaviours and unpleasurable ones with compulsive 'withdrawal'. This tight connection between instincts and emotions and stereotyped behaviours ensures that we act in accordance with our innate biological values.

But the simple dichotomy between good and bad feelings (and their associated behaviours) cannot possibly do justice to the complexity of the world. Thus, for the same reason that the pleasure principle itself evolved in the first place, more subtle and elaborated instinctual mechanisms developed subsequently. As far as mammals are concerned, seven such instincts have been identified to date (if we follow the taxonomy of Panksepp (1998)).[1] These are not exclusive to mammals (we share some of them with birds, for example) but they do apply to *all* mammals, us included. They are our common ancestral inheritance. We should be grateful for this inheritance, because without it we would not exist at all. The phylogenetic lines that selected the genes that inclined our ancestors to behave and feel in these ways are the reason that we humans evolved. For this same reason, all seven of the basic mammalian instincts that we are about to describe are still conserved in the human brain today. Instincts, once they have evolved, are very hard to shake off; they are profoundly conservative things.

These seven instincts are, as already conveyed, approximately 200 million years old. For reasons that should be self-evident, they are all anatomically connected with the PAG; they are all in a sense rostral (upward) extensions and elaborations of the PAG.

5.2.1 Seeking

The first and perhaps most important of the seven mammalian instincts is given different names by different scientists. Rolls (1999), for example calls

---

[1] Other taxonomies exist, e.g. that of Ekman (Ekman and Friesen 1971; Ekman 1992), which is based on universal facial expressions. Panksepp's taxonomy is based on universal behavioural responses to electrical stimulation of specific deep brain circuits. It is important to note that Panksepp recognizes all the basic emotions described by Ekman; he just classifies them differently. Here we focus only on those that Panksepp describes as 'instinctual' or 'emotional'. Panksepp classifies some of Ekman's basic emotions (e.g. disgust) as 'sensory' affects and he classifies other affects (e.g. hunger) as 'homeostatic'. See Chapter 2 for definitions.

it the 'reward' system, while Panksepp (1998) calls it the SEEKING system, and Berridge (1996) calls it the 'wanting' system. (Panksepp uses capitals to distinguish these brain systems from the colloquial meanings of the same terms.) Anatomically, the reward/SEEKING/wanting system overlaps strongly with the medial forebrain bundle (Plate 11 (see colour plate section)). Its origin is the ventral tegmental area (VTA) and its major terminus is the shell of the nucleus accumbens, in the ventral striatum (basal ganglia), but it also projects to several other brain regions. Chemically, its command neurotransmitter is dopamine, acting on D2 type receptors.

We will follow Panksepp's terminology here, but the common denominator underlying the range of different names for this system conveys the essential quality of what it does for the animal. It compels it to engage with the environment in response to appetitive needs. This is why it has also been called a 'foraging' instinct. It is obvious how fundamentally important this instinct is, because everything that we need – biologically speaking – is to be found in the world around us. The fact that we cannot satisfy our own needs and have to find the objects of our desire in the world outside of our selves (and consequently engage in struggle, competition, and risk, etc.) is one of the most fundamental facts of life. If it were not for the existence of the SEEKING instinct, which enthuses us with energy, curiosity, and optimistic expectations, we would never learn this basic lesson ('go forth and multiply'). We would expire in the narcissistic haze of entitlement that characterizes the intrauterine environment, which is the only maturational phase during which our vital needs are met without effort.

Typical mammalian SEEKING behaviours are foraging and similar generalized exploratory activities. (Imagine a dog in an open field.) An interesting and important fact about the SEEKING system is its primary 'objectless' quality. It does not drive the animal to seek specific objects in response to specific needs. No matter what the currently active needs may be (as detected by the homeostatic 'need detector' nuclei in the medial hypothalamus) the SEEKING system responds in the same way: it motivates the animal to go out and explore, to look for something – anything – interesting and nice. It propels the animal to investigate the world and engage with it, in the firm belief that whatever it needs or wants, it is 'out there'. Crucially here, as with all instincts, it is the *feeling* that does the motivating. Accordingly, the type of feeling that triggers the exploratory and interactive behaviour of SEEKING is energized, expectant optimism, or exuberant, curious interest. If and when the animal does then – accidentally, as it were – find what it needs, it *learns* that relief of a particular urge (consummation of a particular appetite) is causally linked with the particular object that it came upon. The SEEKING system (in conjunction with the systems to be described next) therefore leads to the establishment of causal connections and the formation of *predictions*. This is the prototype for all learning. It is profoundly noteworthy that learning is motivated by feelings; it doesn't just happen.

For this reason, the SEEKING instinct is closely tied to meaning-making; it could also be described as an epistemophilic instinct. Meaning-making and intentionality are absolutely fundamental properties of the mind. It is perhaps not surprising, therefore, to discover that over-activation of the SEEKING system produces mental illness: gambling and superstition and psychotic symptoms like hallucinations and delusions (excessive meaning-making and overly loose prediction; i.e. finding causal connections where none exist; see Kapur 2003).

Amphetamines and cocaine stimulate the SEEKING system very directly. Anyone who is familiar with the over-energized, irritatingly enthusiastic 'cruising' behaviour of someone who has snorted cocaine at a party will know from personal experience what the SEEKING system does. It is also not surprising to learn that this system is heavily implicated in almost all forms of addiction (see Volkow et al. 2009). This system is a fundamental vehicle of craving. (An understanding of the instinctual mechanisms of the human brain holds many important lessons for psychiatry.)

The primordial or proto-values that the SEEKING system generates are something like the following: it is 'good' to go forth, explore, interact, engage with the world, to investigate, to work, to find meaning in the world. It is 'bad' to be inert, lazy, and apathetic. The meaning-making process just described (i.e. linking specific needs with specific objects and thereby learning how to meet one's needs in the world, the meaning of things and events in the world, and inferring their hidden causes) is obviously pivotal to all learning. It is in fact the *driving force* behind learning. This demonstrates how instincts, which are stereotyped and inflexible things, nevertheless underpin open-ended, flexible cognitive processes. It is our view that language acquisition is one such learnt form of meaning-making. Such learning is driven by instinct but is not in itself an instinct.

'WANTING' AND 'LIKING'

Berridge (1996) distinguishes between the 'wanting' system just described – Panksepp's SEEKING system, the basic mammalian *appetitive* system – and the 'liking' system – which is the basic *consummation* system. (The

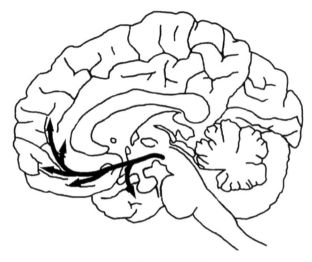

FIGURE 5.2 The SEEKING system

affective distinction between wanting and liking is fundamental; think, for example, of the difference between the excitement of sexual arousal and the release of sexual orgasm.) The term 'wanting', however, implies wanting *something in particular*; it is therefore perhaps not a good name for the primary, objectless SEEKING urge. Berridge's term 'wanting' only makes sense in connection with 'liking'; wanting in this sense is a consequence of learning. Learning, as we have already said, arises from an interaction between SEEKING and finding; it is not an instinct in itself (see also Solms and Panksepp 2012).

Chemically, the 'liking' system is primarily mu-opioid mediated. (For artificial equivalents of the feeling states it produces, try morphine, opium, or heroin.) Not surprisingly, it is connected directly with and is the primary anatomical destination of the SEEKING system; and it projects back downward to the ventral PAG (Figure 5.2). Also not surprising is the physiological fact that activation of the 'liking' system leads to deactivation of the 'wanting' (SEEKING) system. They are reciprocally interactive. This is how we learn to connect the various needs with specific objects in the world – how we learn to meet our needs in the world.

The primordial value system that liking encodes is that it is 'good' to meet one's needs, or conversely, that unrequited need is 'bad'. Combining the action of the wanting and liking systems, we learn also that pleasure for its own sake never really satisfies – that pure hedonism is less 'good' than actual satisfaction of need through appropriate action in the world. These are of course things that we all know; but that is precisely our point. The evolutionarily conserved brain mechanisms that we are describing are where such innate knowledge, such innate systems of value, comes from.

5.2.2 Lust

The second major instinctual system generates feelings of sexual lust and the copulatory behaviours associated with it. Such stereotyped feelings and behaviours in mammals, at the innate instinctual level, are the product of what Panksepp calls the LUST system. There is some doubt in the literature as to whether LUST is a true 'emotional' affect, as opposed to a 'homeostatic' affect. Panksepp and Biven (2012) argue that it deserves to be considered an emotional (instinctual) affect because it directly produces complex instinctual behaviours, from courting to orgasms, and these psychobehavioral action tendencies are the hallmark of instinctual emotions.

Not surprisingly, sexual circuitry and sexual chemistry in male and female brains are different. For example, in both genders sexual arousal produces genital engorgement, but in most females it also produces the sexually receptive position of the lordosis reflex and vaginal lubrication, whereas in most males it produces the – quite different – sexual behaviours of erection, mounting, intromission (thrusting), and ejaculation. Anatomically, in males, the anterior hypothalamus is the focus of sexuality (in rats it is the sexually dimorphic preoptic area (POA) and in humans it is the interstitial nuclei of anterior hypothalamus (INAH), which are evolutionarily homologous) and testosterone mediates the production of vasopressin, which accounts for much of male sexual behaviour. Testosterone is produced in the testicles, and acts directly on the anterior hypothalamus. In females, the ventromedial hypothalamus is the sexual locus of control and the main sexual chemicals are oestrogen and progesterone that in turn mediate the activity of oxytocin, a neuromodulator that governs much of female sexual response. Although oxytocin has been popularized as the 'love hormone', Panksepp and Biven (2012) conclude that this is an exaggeration of its role, since it does not directly produce positive affects. Instead, oxytocin may enhance the activity of endogenous opioids, which produce the positive affects. Nevertheless, it is clear that oxytocin is crucially involved in the generation of positive *social* affects, especially confidence and trust.

Mammalian sexuality is greatly complicated by the fact that the sexual body and the sexual brain develop along different trajectories in utero. The male brain is created when testosterone is converted to oestrogen and the male body is created when testosterone is converted to dihydro-testosterone (DHT). All foetal bodies are initially female, and if there is no interference, the female body will continue to develop. The female brain and mind, however, may be masculanized if the foetus is exposed to too much oestrogen at crucial times in the second trimester. Thus, the gender of the brain and of the body does not necessarily harmonize, and multiple permutations (and degrees of permutation) are possible. In short, we mammals are all bisexual to a degree.

Sexual LUST probably plays very little part in language development. However, there are important interactions between the sexually dimorphic 'maternal instinct' (the 'nurturance' or CARE system), to be described below, which seems to have evolved largely out of the female-typical LUST system. Perhaps for this reason, the pro-social behaviours associated with CARE are more prevalent in mammalian females than males. This might underpin the well-documented superiority of females over males in language development and proficiency. This is a second example of how language development might appear to have instinctual features, when in fact the instinctual element arises from the emotion systems that *motivate* language development, not from language itself.

5.2.3   Rage

The third of our primordial values dictates that it is 'bad' to be frustrated by not getting what you need or want. Irritation and anger are readily evoked in such circumstances; and these responses are directed towards the obstacle in question. The purpose of an aggressive attack is to get rid of an obstacle to satisfaction – in a word, to annihilate it. The RAGE system in the mamma-lian brain has its origins in the medial (inner) parts of the amygdala, and it terminates in the dorsal PAG (Figure 5.3). Like all the other instincts, activation of this emotional system evokes a particular set of behaviours. In this case, full-blown 'affective attack' behaviours include baring the teeth, raising the forelimbs, extending the claws (if you have them), piloerection, and lunging towards the object of your wrath. More muted anger behaviours include, for instance, pacing and growling. Such behaviours are always guided and accompanied by particular feeling states – in this case, feelings of irritability, anger, or outright rage.

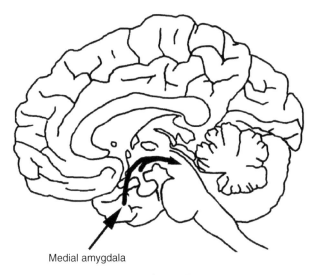

Medial amygdala

FIGURE 5.3 The RAGE system

The feelings just described do not accompany all aggressive behaviours. Neurobiologists distinguish between 'hot' and 'cold' aggression. Cold aggression is also known as 'predatory' aggression. Cold aggression is associated with activation of the SEEKING system, not RAGE. A lion chasing a springbok is not angry; it is hungry. The feeling associated with predatory aggression is more likely to be invigorated anticipation than blind hatred. This distinction has forensic implications in humans. A third type of aggressive behaviour is (perhaps inappropriately) called 'inter-male' aggression. This type of aggression is associated with territorial and dominance behaviours, and does not usually involve the destructive fights-to-the-kill that characterize RAGE. Instead, it involves threatening displays of size and sound – and warning 'nips' rather than actual attempts to destroy the intruder – that is, more bark than bite. We will return to this form of aggression later in this chapter.

The RAGE (and inter-male aggression) systems are more sensitive in males than females, and in this sense they are the mirror image of the CARE and PANIC/GRIEF systems to be described below. These anti-social male-typical instinctual systems may be *indirectly* responsible for the inferiority in language skills of males, in contrast to the pro-social systems which are more active in typical mammal females.

5.2.4   Fear

The so-called 'fight or flight' response reflects the fact that aggressive attack is not always the best way to deal with an adversary. The close link between these two responses is, however, embodied in the fact that the FEAR system, like the RAGE system, has its epicentre in the amygdala, albeit in a different part of it (Figure 5.4).

The most common behaviours activated by FEAR are freezing and fleeing responses. Again, the behaviours in question are accompanied and guided by characteristic feeling states – namely, in this case, trepidatious anxiety (accompanied, as are all basic emotions, by characteristic physiological changes, such as – in this case – rapid shallow breathing, increased heart rate, and redirection of blood from the gut to the skeletal musculature). Again, as with all instincts, the behavioural responses in question are not learned; they are innate. Mammals 'know' from day one that certain objects and situations are frightening. Newborn rodents, for example, freeze when exposed to just a single feline hair – even if they have never seen a cat before (let alone had the opportunity to discover their general attitude towards mice). It is easy to see why this is the case; if mice had to learn from experience how to respond to cats, that would be the only experiences mice ever had before they were killed! And that would be the end of mice. That is how evolution works.

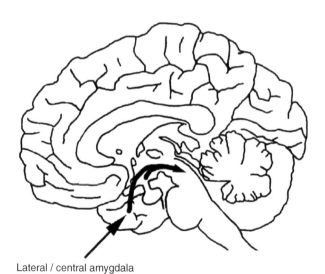

Lateral / central amygdala

FIGURE 5.4 The FEAR system

However, again, as with all instincts, we *also* learn from experience to associate certain objects with FEAR; we learn to classify (label or 'name') objects of our experience in accordance with the resemblance between their properties and those of innate instinctual stimuli – and the same applies to FEAR stimuli. Electric sockets, for example, could not possibly have been innately encoded as objects of FEAR; they did not exist in biologically ancient times. They therefore have to be *associated* with FEAR on the basis of individual experience. In this way, we classify all the objects in the world in accordance with a primordial taxonomy – something akin in the emotional realm to Kant's (1781) cognitive 'categories'. But unlike Kant's categories, it is easy to see how such emotionally driven taxonomizing behaviour bestows meaning on the world. On this basis, it is also easy to see why there might be certain universal categories of meaning, ultimately giving rise to universal features in language.

It is important to mention that once we have learnt to fear (or desire, or hate) a particular object, situation, or place, the instinctual classification of that object, situation, or place is well-nigh irreversible. Fear conditioning in particular is, as LeDoux (1998) memorably put it, 'indelible'. This fact has important implications for understanding of human mental life and behaviour.

5.2.5 Panic/Grief

The fifth basic mammalian instinct is the 'attachment' instinct. Panksepp calls it the PANIC/GRIEF instinct. This dual name reflects the fact that the experience of loss (in the context of attachment bonding, which occurs in all mammals) produces a biphasic instinctual response. The initial response of a juvenile mammal to separation from its mother is one of PANIC. Panic is of course a feeling state (but please note, it is different from FEAR). Ethologists describe the associated acute-phase behaviour as 'protest' behaviour. Protest behaviour is characterized above all by 'distress vocalizations' – that is, by crying. Each mammal species cries in its own way. While emitting these distress vocalizations it wanders around anxiously looking for mum. (The mum, too, emits distress calls, and looks for the missing pup.) But if this initial behaviour does not lead to rapid reunion, protest gives way to the second phase of the separation/loss response, namely 'despair'. Now the lost or separated mammal gives up hope. The feeling of panic is replaced by the feeling of sadness. This, some neuroscientists believe, is the normal prototype of depression (Solms and Panksepp 2012). Giving up hope (the transition from protest to despair) seems to have evolved in order to prevent isolated juveniles from announcing their vulnerability to predators and wandering too far from home base (and perhaps also to prevent metabolic exhaustion). That is, it enhances the chances of reunion and therefore increases reproductive fitness.

Distress vocalizations are another excellent example of how instinctually based 'meaning-making' might underpin the subsequent cognitive acquisition of speech and language.

Feelings of panic and sadness (the pain of social loss) appear to be the evolutionary price that we mammals pay for the biological advantages bestowed by attachment. The most basic attachment is the mother/infant bond, the evolutionary advantage of which to the infant (especially in a suckling species) is obvious. It is important to recognize that the biological advantage to the mother of this bond is the survival of her genes via her offspring; hence, the specificity of the mother/infant bond, and hence also the apparent altruism of parenthood. If distress vocalizations are a primordial form of language, it is important to note that not only mammals are equipped with the instinctual circuitry that underpins attachment behaviour but birds too have this circuitry. Hence, birds, like mammals, emit a large number of meaningful sounds relating (among other things) to sex, danger, and attachment.

The PANIC/GRIEF system, like the 'liking' system, is opioid mediated. It is interesting in this respect that it appears to have evolved out of the brain's primitive analgesic system (Figure 5.5). The mental pain of social loss in mammals seems to have (quite directly) evolved from the physical pain mechanisms of lower vertebrates. The pain associated with loss of a loved one is ameliorated by reunion (indeed, the pain motivates the seeking of reunion) in the same way that physical pain is ameliorated by morphine.

The addictive quality of love relationships is not as readily recognized as is the addictive character of dependence upon artificial opiates like heroin and morphine. Love is surely the primal addiction.

Although the PANIC/GRIEF system is paradigmatically activated through the formation of mother/infant bonds, it also underpins most other social bonds of biological significance, such as the formation of relatively permanent mating pairs and family groups.

The primal values that arise from this system are that it is 'good' to be together with loved ones and 'bad' to be separated from them, or to lose them. Nobody has to teach a mammal that it is 'bad' to separate a pup from its mum. We acquire this knowledge with our mother's milk – in fact before – for without this innate knowledge (this innate system of values)

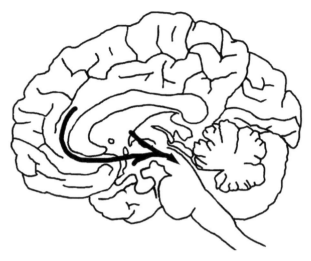

FIGURE 5.5 The PANIC/GRIEF system

the milk would not have been provided in the first place. This leads to the sixth and penultimate mammalian instinct, namely maternal CARE.

5.2.6 Care

As already noted, this instinct is more active in females than males. The same applies to the PANIC/GRIEF system, which the CARE system primes (via massive release of oxytocin, prolactin, progesterone, and the like) during pregnancy. These sex differences are (in the average case) undeniable, as indeed they are with respect to the clinical consequences in humans. Depression, for example, is almost three times more common in females than in males; and this applies especially to females of child-bearing age. RAGE, by contrast, is more prevalent in males of all ages. Likewise whereas oxytocin (a 'female' peptide) facilitates loving trust and social bonding, vasopressin (the 'male' equivalent) mediates relentless persistence.

CARE initiates unconditioned nurturant behaviours. For example, when a baby cries, we pick it up, rock it, make soothing sounds. Nobody has to teach us to do this. We just *know* what the sound of a baby crying 'means'.

The biological proto-values attached to the CARE instinct are that it is 'good' to care for little ones, and especially for one's own offspring, to love, protect, feed and groom them, and that it is 'bad' to neglect them. It is likewise 'good' to be cared for and to be cared about; it is 'good' to feel safe, secure, and loved.

5.2.7   Play

The seventh and final mammalian instinct is the PLAY instinct. People are often surprised to learn that this is an instinct, but all juvenile mammals need to play. If they are deprived of their quota of play on any particular day, they will make it up the next day – as though by homeostatic rebound. We all know what rough and tumble play is, although it varies slightly from one type of mammal to another. The play session starts with an 'invitation' posture or gesture, then the game is on: the one animal exuberantly chases the other, then jumps on the other's back; then they roll over together and wrestle or tickle each other – always accompanied by peels of laughter (or the equivalent mammal vocalization, depending on species; even rats 'laugh', see Panksepp 1998) – then they are back on their feet again, and chasing each other in the reverse direction. The associated feeling state is equally universal: it feels like *fun*. Children just love to play. On the other hand, play commonly ends in tears (or in some form of negative emotion). This provides an important clue as to what PLAY is all about, biologically speaking; it is about finding the limits of what is socially appropriate, tolerable, acceptable, permissible. When play is no longer fun for one of the participants, they don't want to play anymore. The limit has then been reached. This necessarily requires the animal to take account of the mind of the playmate. This is probably the main instinctual origin of empathy, or 'mind-reading'. A very important criterion in this respect is dominance. In any play situation, one of the participants takes the lead role and the other the submissive role. (And yes – on average – the male becomes the dominant one.) This is fun for both participants so long as the dominant one does not insist on being 'on top' all of the time. The maximum acceptable ratio seems to be roughly 60:40.

   This reveals a second, related function of PLAY, namely the establish-ment of social hierarchies – of a 'pecking order'. Accordingly, juvenile rough and tumble play increasingly gives way to competitive games, and also (in humans) to 'pretend' play, in which the participants 'try out' different social roles (Mum/Baby, Teacher/Pupil, Doctor/Patient, Cop/Robber, King of the Castle/Dirty Rascal – note the hierarchies). We do not know what goes on in the imagination of other mammals when they play, but we would confidently suggest that they too are 'trying out' different social roles, and learning what they can get away with.

All of these facts reveal some of the innate values encoded in the PLAY system: it is 'good' to have fun, but 'bad' to do so selfishly; it is 'bad' to be a bully (and to be bullied); it is 'good' to compete and win; it is 'good' to be on top, but not all the time, etc.

We don't like to recognize that humans, like all our closest animal relatives, naturally form complex hierarchies, with clear social rules (those governing primate behaviour are remarkably complex). The structures of families, clans, villages, even nations – almost any social group – are undeniably hierarchical, and have been so throughout history.

As with all of the instinctual tendencies we have described in this chapter, this is not a matter of our personal preference; it is a matter of fact. If we as a species do not face such facts, we cannot begin to contend with them. The fact that instincts exist does not mean that we can do nothing about them, that we are obliged to simply indulge them. But we ignore (or deny) them at our peril.

It is therefore not difficult to see how the instinct for PLAY gives rise to the formation of rules. Rules regulate social behaviour, and thereby protect us from the potential excesses of some of the other instincts. It is likewise not difficult to see how the need for rules partly gives rise to complex forms of communication, like (ultimately) human language. But this instinctual origin of language does not a language instinct make.

5.3   EXTENDING PANKSEPP

The above account of the instinctual mechanisms at work in the human brain is based on Panksepp's very careful comparative analysis of humans and other mammals. It may, however, be appropriate to remind readers once more that other taxonomies exist. For example, some possible extensions of Panksepp's taxonomy are discussed by Toronchuk and Ellis (2012):

5.3.1   A DISGUST System

This is proposed in Toronchuk and Ellis (2007). It may be a very old system, indeed possibly the oldest because aversive behaviour is seen in very simple animals, related to the 'second brain' (the enteric nervous system) associated with the stomach (Gershon 1999). Its function is to protect us from harm, such as ingesting rancid food, before the harm has happened: that is, it is anticipatory in nature. It is probably the basis of the 'purity' module postulated by Haidt and colleagues (Rozin et al. 2008; Haidt and Kesebir 2010), when disgust is transferred from biological to social contexts.

As stated above, Panksepp (1998) does recognize the existence of innate 'disgust' circuitry, feelings, and behaviours. However, he classifies this system as a 'sensory' (not an 'emotional') affect. Sensory affects are simpler than emotional ones. They are almost akin to reflexes (hence the retching reflex in disgust). But we must recall that disgust is far from being a simple affect in some higher animals and especially humans, where the innate action tendencies associated with revulsion and contamination and the like are quite complex.

5.3.2   A RANKING or HIERARCHY or DOMINANCE System

The existence of an instinct of this kind is suggested by Stephens and Price (2000), as being necessary to regulate conflict in affiliative groups once they have formed. An early discussion of this system was given by Robert Ardrey in his (1966) book *The Territorial Imperative*. More recently, it has been proposed by Sapolsky (2004, 2005). The point is that belonging to groups is very important for survival, and that is promoted by the PANIC/ GRIEF system, as discussed above; but once groups have come into existence, there will be competition for resources that is potentially very destructive and so must be regulated. The DOMINANCE system is the means to do so, and is apparent in all higher animal groups (as characterized by 'the alpha male', for example).

Pankespp (personal communication) believes this is not a primary instinctual system in its own right on a par with the other systems he describes, but rather is an outcome of the PLAY system, perhaps acting in conjunction with the LUST and RAGE systems. But we disagree, inter alia because it is probably a much older system than the PLAY system. It occurs, for example, in chickens (the 'pecking order'), which do not have a PLAY system. This issue is taken up by Van der Westhuizen and Solms (2014, 2015). Neuroimaging evidence for its existence is presented by Beasley et al. (2012). Psychiatric evidence also strongly points towards its existence (Stevens and Price 2000).

5.4   THEIR EVOLUTIONARY VALUE

These are all hard-wired systems: they are our evolutionary heritage, guiding the higher cognitive systems as to how to behave on a moment-by-moment basis, and also shaping neural connection strengths through the effects of

neurotransmitters spread diffusely to the neocortex form nuclei in
brainstem and limbic system (thus neural Darwinism). The fact th
hard-wired is demonstrated by the existence of the ascending systems w...
spread the relevant neuromodulators through the neocortex (Plate 2(b) (see
colour plate section)). Clearly, any biologically adequate evolutionary psychology must account for the existence of these systems, just as it must
account for the existence of the sensory systems and the neocortical structures. That justification is provided by the crucial role these systems play in
psychological functioning.

5.5   THE EMBODIED MIND

The existence and importance of these truly innate modules is part of the
theme of the embodied mind, and 'affective neuroscience', in contrast to
the trend in many earlier discussions of the brain which emphasized only
'cognitive science', that is its rational function. The concept of the embodied mind (Lakoff and Johnson 1980a; Clark 2016) is supported by
evidence of many different kinds, which are the source of continued
debate (Wilson and Golonka 2013; Matyja and Dolega 2015). Nevertheless,
the basic theme is clear: the visceral body influences the brain in many ways,
and vice versa. This is particularly clear, for example, in the mind/body
interactions arising from the fact that many immune system molecules are
also neurotransmitters or neuromodulators (Sternberg 1997, 2004), and in
even the way that placebos are causally effective even when the recipients
know that they are indeed placebos and therefore have no active ingredients
(Marchant 2016). Figure 5.6 represents a real effect!

The specific point here is twofold. Firstly, that language may well have
evolved from action grammars as an Embodied Construction Grammar
(Bergen and Chang 2003) rather than being based in the kinds of rule-
based grammars that are the focus of so much attention in linguistics. In
that case the kinds of innate language modules envisaged by Chomsky
would not have relevance to the way the brain actually embodies grammar, from a functional viewpoint. The reasonable kind of viewpoint one
may take is exemplified by Pickering and Garrod (2013), who state the
following:

> Currently, production and comprehension are regarded as quite distinct
> in accounts of language processing. In rejecting this dichotomy, we
> instead assert that producing and understanding are interwoven, and
> that this interweaving is what enables people to predict themselves and

FIGURE 5.6 The effectiveness of placebos
From www.cartoonstock.com/directory/p/placebo_effect.asp, with permission.

each other. We start by noting that production and comprehension are forms of action and action perception. We then consider the evidence for interweaving in action, action perception, and joint action, and explain such evidence in terms of prediction. Specifically, we assume that actors construct forward models of their actions before they execute those actions, and that perceivers of others' actions covertly imitate those actions, then construct forward models of those actions. We use these accounts of action, action perception, and joint action to develop accounts of production, comprehension, and interactive language. Importantly, they incorporate well-defined levels of linguistic representation (such as semantics, syntax, and phonology). We show (a) how speakers and comprehenders use covert imitation and forward modeling to make predictions at these levels of representation, (b) how they interweave production and comprehension processes, and (c) how they use these predictions to monitor the upcoming utterances. We show how these accounts explain a range of behavioral and neuroscientific data on language processing.

This all takes place in a contextual way, where neurons of even the primary sensory cortex do not encode just sensory input but integrate it with contextual information such as reward, expectation, attention, and motor action (Harris and Mrsic-Flogel 2013). Top-down inputs to the primary sensory cortical areas carry detailed information about diverse behavioural, affective, and cognitive variables.

This kind of view is developed in views of hierarchical predictive processing, which provides a potential explanatory framework for understanding a wide variety of context effects and cue integration phenomena in spoken word recognition (Farmer et al. 2013), which develops from similar proposals for how action patterns work (Clark 2013; Adams et al. 2013). Wolpert and Flanagan (2016) summarize the way action works, stating:

> Motor learning has traditionally focused on how predictive or feedforward control is updated by past errors and has generally assumed that adaptation is driven by a single process, that variability is undesirable, and that learning and control are shaped by a trade-off between speed and accuracy. Recent research [...] has begun to examine how learning shapes both predictive and reactive control mechanisms and has shown that adaptation involves multiple, interacting processes, that the motor system tunes variability to the learning task, and that accuracy is not necessarily gained at the expense of speed.

A fast process may correspond to some forms of explicit learning whereas a slow process may correspond to some forms of implicit learning. If language has evolved from action grammars, these principles will apply to speech production as well. These proposals seem broadly compatible with the ideas of neuroconstructivism (Westermann et al. 2007; Sirois et al. 2008).

This view includes an Extended Mind (EM) hypothesis, that is, 'external resources and artefacts, like written language and other forms of material culture, are central to the production of the modern human cognitive phenotype, and serve to augment and ratchet up the power of our evolved brains' (Barrett et al. 2014).

It follows from all this that evolutionary psychology theories that are adequately based in biology and the nature of the brain must take instincts and the emotional systems into account, as discussed above, as these are a key feature of the embodied mind. Many do not do so, although Fodor – of all people – included modules related to emotion systems in his proposals of modularity of mind (Fodor 1983). We can only concur with him on that score.

6

A Realistic View of Evolution, Development, and Emotions

This chapter puts together a realistic view of evolution, development, and emotions, arising out of the preceding chapters. It makes the case that emotion modules are a key link in both function and development, and hence also in evolution. Affect shapes intellect through developmental processes, responding to social experiences. The position taken here is that there are no genetically fixed cognitive modules whatever, and in particular no innate language modules that control grammatical structure. Neocortical areas are broad-purpose domains that get specialized and formed through social, physical, and ecological interactions and experiences, but are not innate in terms of cognitive content. The ascending systems associated with the limbic system modules are hard-wired because of the key role they play in activation, development, and plasticity, through channelling affective influences.

6.1 THE ISSUES

We are now in a position to pull together the issues discussed in the previous chapters, in order to attain a coherent view of innate modules (as outlined in Chapter 1). Which brain modules exist? Which are innate, and which are a result of developmental processes (insofar as one can separate these concepts: they are not in fact clearly demarcated; see Robinson 2004)? We argue that pre- and sub-cortical brain modules (in particular the sensory systems, parts of the limbic system, and the ascending systems) are clearly demarcated and uniformly replicated in physiological terms, and so demand an evolutionary explanation; whereas there is no viable developmental path for allegedly innate cortical modules with specific cognitive content coded through detailed synaptic connections. After being set up as general-purpose cognitive domains, such detailed neocortical connections arise developmentally during interaction with the environment, rather than directly from genetic information; and they then continue to change throughout life, as a result of brain plasticity.

There are other problems for the supposed innate cognitive modules. How can one square an explanation of human cognition in terms of domain-specific cognitive modules with the apparent domain general flexibility of human cognition (Carruthers et al. 2005, p. 25)? If there were such modules they would get rewritten as a result of ongoing experience and brain plasticity, which can transform the maps in the cortex (Polley et al. 2004) and eliminate synapses and neuronal branches as a result of functional activity patterns (Hua and Smith 2004). Innateness is fine for topographic maps to retinal cells (Carruthers et al. 2005, pp. 29–33), for example, which remain unchanged after formation, but not for neocortical structures, which change all the time as one learns (Carruthers et al. 2005, p. 24). The issue is stated by La Cerra and Bingham as follows:

> The model of the human neurocognitive architecture proposed by evolutionary psychologists is based on the presumption that the demands of hunter-gatherer life generated a vast array of cognitive adaptations. Here we present an alternative model. We argue that the problems inherent in the biological markets of ancestral hominids and their mammalian predecessors would have required an adaptively flexible on-line information-processing system, and would have driven the evolution of a functionally plastic neural substrate, the neocortex, rather than a confederation of evolutionarily prespecified social cognitive adaptations. In alignment with recent neuroscientific evidence, we suggest that human cognitive processes result from the activation of constructed cortical representational networks, which reflect probabilistic relationships between sensory inputs, behavioural responses, and adaptive outcomes. The developmental construction and experiential modification of these networks are mediated by subcortical circuitries that are responsive to the life history regulatory system. As a consequence, these networks are intrinsically adaptively constrained. But the task has to be relevant or 'salient' to something that impacts upon the individual's fitness or wellbeing.
>
> (La Cerra and Bingham 1998, p. 6)

Thus, the columnar organization of the neocortex (Mountcastle 1997) is indeed genetically determined, together with the statistical nature of the types of neurons and their layered synaptic connections, but not the intrinsic, detailed connection networks and weights within this general matrix that embody specific cognitive content (Le Doux 2002; Hawkins

2004; Kandel 2006, 2012). These specific connections develop through our life experiences and social interactions, which continuously alter synaptic strengths by modifying gene expression (Kandel 2005).

But how is it decided which connections to strengthen and which to weaken? Partly this is via the Hebbian 'Fire together, wire together' principle. But this does not distinguish between positive and negative experiences: those to be repeated and those to be avoided. The 'fitness' of specific connections must be linked to a biological *value* system. This is where affect comes in. All behavioural decision-making systems assess costs and benefits. A behaviour has to be worth it (La Cerra and Bingham 1998, p. 23). That assessment is largely based in the activity of the primordial emotional systems, which are indeed largely innate modules, and this solves the 'frame problem' discussed in Chapter 5: these systems give guidance as to what is important and what may be ignored. They function initially through our interaction with primary caretakers, usually the mother:

> As well as being unique to us, our representations of objects and people are constantly being modified by experience ... we aren't born with a neural representation of the world we live in. It takes time for our brains to develop the foundational neural tissue that will eventually become the scaffolding of the self ... In the primal economy, you are dependent on transactions with only one person: your mother.
>
> (La Cerra and Bingham 1998, pp. 36–37)

This works is developed in depth in Greenspan and Shanker (2004), as we discuss in the following.

6.2   THE RANGE OF INNATE MODULES

A position on which modules are innate was stated in Section 1.4. It is compatible with the view of Fodor (1983), who claimed that there were such sensory system modules but they did not occur in the cortex. This contrasts with the evolutionary psychology views of innate cortical modules discussed in Chapter 5, as proposed, for example, by Pinker (2002, pp. 90–99). To look at this in its biological context, as well as considering evolution, as emphasized strongly by Dobzhansky, one must consider also development, structure, and function, as emphasized in Chapter 1. They are all crucial to biology (Campbell and Reece 2005) and all interact with each other (Figure 6.1).

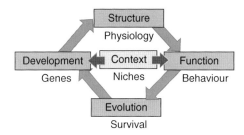

FIGURE 6.1 The interactions between evolution, development, structure, function, and environment (context). All are crucial to our survival. Context affects both development (via epigenetic effects) and function (via adaptation and learning)

One can summarize this as follows:

The contextual whole: Every biological structure that occurs in a reliable way due to developmental processes reading genes in a contextual way has a function that is key to survival, else these genes, and the developmental processes that read them, would not have been selected. Thus each biological structure and process has both evolutionary and developmental origins. It is crucial here that there are genes for developmental processes, which create structures.

This is the integrated view one should bear in mind, rather than focusing on evolution alone.

Evolution develops the genes that create the structures that enable the functions which are key to survival and reproductive success. No step in the process has meaning without the rest. In particular, both soft-wired and hard-wired CNS regions are evolutionary outcomes that are key to our reproductive fitness in different ways.

6.2.1   Structures and Development

As stated earlier, the position we take (and which all the evidence supports) is that there are no genetically fixed cognitive modules whatever, and in particular no innate language modules that control grammatical structure. Griffiths and Stotz state the issue of innate modules as follows (Griffiths and Stotz 2000):

What individuals inherit from their ancestors is not a mind, but the ability to develop a mind. The fertilised egg contains neither a 'language acquisition device' nor a knowledge of the basic tenets of folk psychology. These features come into existence as the mind grows. A serious examination of the biological processes underlying such easy terms as 'innateness', 'maturation' and 'normal development' reintroduces the very themes that are usually taken to be excluded by an evolutionary approach to the mind – the critical role of culture in psychological development and the existence of a plethora of alternative outcomes for the developing mind.

Indeed, there cannot be innate cortical modules because of the way gene expression is contextually controlled (Robinson 2004; Noble 2008; Gilbert and Epel 2009). Robinson et al. (2008) comment:

> What specific genes and regulatory sequences contribute to the organization and functioning of brain circuits that support social behavior? How does social experience interact with information in the genome to modulate these brain circuits? Here we address these questions by highlighting progress that has been made in identifying and understanding two key 'vectors of influence' that link genes, brain, and social behavior: (1) social information alters gene readout in the brain to influence behavior; and (2) genetic variation influences brain function and social behaviour. Social signals, in addition to initiating genomic state changes, can also trigger lasting epigenetic modifications of the genome, which have been defined as heritable changes in the expression of specific genes that are not due to changes in DNA sequence.

This is the same point as made by Kandel (2006): the way genes are read in the brain is influenced by our mental states and by social information. Hence, as a child develops, even if information were encoded to potentially create specific connections within the cortex, mental and social factors would intervene to produce the actual detailed patterning that encodes cognitive data and motor behaviour – and this would be different from that implied by the initial coding, if it were to exist. Our view is that such coding is not possible, for both the developmental reasons outlined above (brain plasticity affects any structures that may exist) and those explained in Chapter 3: developmental processes based in DNA codings cannot determine the detailed level of cortical wiring required to generate a cognitive module (see, for example, the discussion of how cortical circuits are built by Anderson and Coulter (2013) and Wolpert (2002)). Rather, they specify types of neurons plus the broad nature of random connections between them, that later get refined by environmentally based developmental processes stabilizing appropriate synaptic patterns, on the basis of functional activity patterns (Hua and Smith 2004). Cortical modules are *very* broad-purpose vehicles that get specialized and formed through social, physical, and ecological interactions and experiences. For example, transferring animals from standard laboratory cages to an environment that promotes expression of natural behaviours induces a large-scale functional refinement of cortical sensory maps (Polley et al. 2004). In the visual cortex, for example, patterned input drives the formation of functional subnetworks through a redistribution of recurrent synaptic connections (Ko et al. 2013).

Hard-wired modules: However, parts of the CNS are indeed hard-wired: they must provide an unchanging substrate for the plastic rest. These innate hard-wired systems are (see Chapter 1) as follows:

- **H1**: the spinal cord and 'reptilian brain', the source of reflexive and instinctive behaviour;
- **H2**: the incoming sensory connections *to* the cortex from the sensory organs (the eyes, ears, tongue, etc.), enabling us to see, hear, and so on;
- **H3**: the outgoing motor connections *from* the cortex, to muscles, enabling us to act;
- **H4**: some limbic system nuclei and connections;
- **H5**: the ascending systems linking those nuclei diffusely to neocortical regions – because of the key role they play in function, development, and plasticity.

For example, Reber et al. (2004) show how the precise wiring from retinal ganglion cells in the eye to synaptic targets in the superior colliculus of the midbrain (located below the cerebral cortex) is developmentally possible, leading to the formation of a topographic neural map.

Soft-wired domains: The soft-wired systems are (see Chapter 1) as follows:

- **S1**: the neocortex, the seat of cognition and resultant action choices;
- **S2**: the cerebellum;
- **S3**: parts of the limbic system, for instance most of the hippocampus and amygdala, and large parts of the basal ganglia.

6.2.2   Structures and Function

The hard-wired structures just listed have key functions, as follows.

- **H1**: The spinal cord and 'reptilian brain' provide background functioning that underlies all the rest, in particular homeostatic functions that keep it all going, plus reflex and instinctive functions that help survival in threatening situations.

- **H2**: The incoming sensory connections to the cortex bring to the cortex the data about the outside world, needed in order to respond appropriately. Without that data we cannot adapt to the immediate environment and know how to respond appropriately.
- **H3**: The outgoing motor connections to muscles enable the chosen responses to be effected. Without them we could not change anything in the world, or communicate with anyone else.
- **H4**: Some limbic system nuclei and connections, such as the hypothalamus because of its homeostatic role.
- **H5**: The ascending systems linking those nuclei diffusely to neocortical regions, because of the key role they play in affective activation (Panksepp 1998) and in development and plasticity (Edelman 1989, 1992), as mentioned in Chapter 6 and described in more detail in the subsequent paragraphs.

The soft-wired systems have key functions as follows:

- **S1**: The neocortex. These modules are broad purpose vehicles that get specialized and plastically shaped through social, physical, and ecological interactions and experiences. Their overall function is to generate suitable output in response to the input from the sensory systems, utilizing expectations based on internal variables ('memory', Kandel 2006, 2012), and in particular to plan ahead so that the responses have a predictive character (Hawkins 2004; Friston 2010) via suitable internal mental models. The output includes both physical actions and communication events.
- **S2**: The cerebellum, because of its role in coordinating movements and other information, and a link to language.
- **S3**: Parts of the limbic system, such as the hippocampus and amygdala, and parts of the basal ganglia, because of their role in learning and memory.

Note that the hard-wired structures are 'ready to run' at birth and relatively little modified thereafter (except that some may develop with age according to a developmental programme). The soft-wired structures are 'ready to learn' at birth, with innate abilities such as pattern recognition and prediction but no specific innate knowledge. As stated by Clark Barrett (2015), advances in evolutionary developmental biology can be applied to the brain by focusing on the design of the developmental systems that build it. Crucially, developmental systems can be plastic, designed by the process of natural selection to build adaptive phenotypes using the rich information available in our social and physical environments. The primary reason it has to be that way is developmental: there is no way it could be otherwise (Chapters 3 and 5). But this is also functionally advantageous: plasticity and the associated ability to learn are the key to adaptation to our surroundings, and to the development of the physical and abstract technology that has given humanity its survival edge. Too rigid cortical modules would be a great disadvantage.

The interaction between them: The systems **H2** and **H3** are hardwired at the extremities where they link into relatively fixed physical components (eyes, ears, muscles, and so on) but are soft-wired on the cortico-cortical side, as that is the only developmental option. This is the reason we have to learn to hear and see on the one hand, and to walk, grasp, and make desired noise patterns on the other. We have to adapt the connections in the cortex (which are initially essentially random) in response to experience; the way this happens is detailed by Ko et al. (2013). Our cortical synapses in the visual areas learn how to recognize visual patterns through activity-dependent *patterns* of plasticity: neurons first acquire feature preference by selecting feedforward inputs before the onset of sensory experience, and then patterned input drives the formation of functional subnetworks through a redistribution of recurrent synaptic connections (Ho et al. 2015). The iterative formation and elimination of synapses and neuronal branches result in the formation of a much larger number of trial connections than is maintained in the mature brain (Hua and Smith 2004). This happens in a contextual way (Frith 2007; Kandel 2012), and naturalistic experience can transform cortical sensory maps by inducing a large-scale functional refinement of these maps (Polley et al. 2004).

Additionally, cortical synapses in the motor area learn how to move chosen muscles; using feedback in the process as well as predicting and generalizing to new situations through the architecture of the system as well as neural plasticity (Poggio and Bizzi 2014). The motor abilities developed then form the foundations for tool use and development of an action grammar, and then providing a basis for language (Maynard Smith and Szathmáry 2007).

Overall this takes place in a top-down way:

Sensory perception is a learned trait. The brain strategies we use to perceive the world are constantly modified by experience. With practice, we subconsciously become better at identifying familiar objects or distinguishing fine details in our environment ... Future neural network models must incorporate the top-down alteration of cortical function by expectation or perceptual tasks. These newly found dynamic processes are challenging earlier views of static and feedforward processing of sensory information.

(Tsodyks and Gilbert 2004)

6.2.3   Structures and Evolution

Each of these structures, whether hard-wired or soft-wired, is required for human survival. The first group **H1–H5** are hard-wired in a relatively rigid way that generates fixed action patterns, and the second group **S1–S3** are soft-wired in a plastic way that generates very flexible responses in a rapidly changing physical, ecological, or social environment. But it is key that in both cases evolution provides genes and gene regulation networks that then create developmental processes (Figure 7.1): in the first case, that produce relatively fixed behavioural networks; in the second case, that produce adaptive networks with a capacity to learn and predict. We need both to survive.

In contrast to hypothetical innate cortical modules that cannot be proven to exist in a physiological sense but rather are hypothesized on the basis of behavioural patterns, our position is as follows:

Evolutionary explanation: Evolutionary theory must respect physiological facts that constrain what is possible (Noble 2013). Evolutionary biology must explain physical structures that occur in a reliable way in all humans, because this means they have a function that is crucial to our biological survival. This applies to all the hard-wired and soft-wired modules **H1–H5, S1–S3** listed above. But evolutionary explanations must respect epigenetic effects and developmental possibilities; the latter preclude any innate cortical modules embodying specific cognitive information.

The key role of the ascending systems **H5** is the focus of the following sections; they are key to emotional responses, and are genetically determined because of the importance of these responses.

Even E. O. Wilson (1975), as quoted by Ruse (1999, p. 176), put it this way:

The biologist, who is concerned with questions of physiology and evolutionary history, realizes that self-knowledge is constrained and shaped by the emotional control centres in the hypo-thalamus and limbic system of the brain. These centres flood our consciousness with all the emotions – hate, love, guilt, fear, and others – that are the parameters guiding how our cognition functions. What, we are then compelled to ask, made the hypothalamus and limbic system? They evolved by natural selection. That simple biological statement must be pursued to explain the developmental appearance of cognitive modularity in the brain.

In brief, it must be pursued to explain the way all higher-order behaviour emerges from the combination of evolution and developmental processes. That is what the proposal made here does.

6.3   EMOTION, DEVELOPMENT, AND MODULES

Tooby and Cosmides refer to the significance of emotions as follows (Barkow et al. 1992, p. 99):

> Each specific emotion appears to be an intricately structured information sensitive adaptation. In fact the emotions appear to be designed to solve a certain category of regulatory problem that inevitably emerges in a mind full of disparate, functionally specialized mechanisms – the problem of coordinating the menagerie of mechanisms with each other and with the situation being faced.

They do not, however, then emphasize the associated innate modules (the limbic system and ascending systems), and develop this to show the key role of these systems in both development and evolution, in particular dealing with the problem of frames (Barkow et al. 1992, pp. 99–108).

Rozin states this as follows (in Carruthers et al. 2006, p.41):

> In the last two decades psychology has reawakened to the importance of affect, both in understanding human life in general, and more particularly in understanding cognition. As we consider the innate mind, we should attend not only to computational mechanisms that function in the cognitive domain but also to affective processes. Including preferences and attitudes. These may facilitate or inhibit particular types of cognitive processing. Innate preferences or aversions influence the types of interactions humans have with their environment, hence their experiences, hence their mind.

Thus, affect is the key link in both function and development, hence also in evolutionary history.

Affect shaping intellect through developmental experiences: Neural Darwinism (Edelman 1989, 1992), or Neuronal Group Selection, is the adaptive process whereby strengths of synaptic connections are adaptively affected by neuromodulators diffusely spread to the cortex from nuclei in the limbic system via the ascending systems **H5**. These 'value systems' shaping brain plasticity (Edelman 1989, 1992) through neuromodulators such as serotonin and dopamine (Geary 2005, pp. 109–111) are nothing other than the means whereby the primary emotion systems identified by Panksepp (1998) and Panksepp and Biven (2012) affect brain function. They are our evolutionary inheritance giving guidance as to what is immediately important, also altering the brain's micro-connections so as to shape brain memory and behavioural repertoires. Thus, what is occurring is in fact Affective Neural Darwinism, or Affective Neuronal Group Selection (Ellis and Toronchuk 2005). This is the link between evolutionary effects, via hard-wired affective modules, and the plastic behaviour of the cortex at macro and micro levels in response to ongoing external events and internal cognitive processing. An example is disgust (Carruthers et al. 2006, p. 54; Toronchuk and Ellis 2007); others are the SEEKING and PANIC/GRIEF systems identified by Panksepp (1998). Existence of these systems is a particular case of adaptive phenotypic plasticity (Carruthers et al. 2006, pp. 98–99), where adaptation takes place to create developmental mechanisms that will produce adaptive behaviour. It is the solution to the frame problem identified by many writers (Barkow et al. 1992, pp. 9–108): these emotional systems give guidance to the cortex as to what is immediately important, and so deserving of attention.

The particular primary emotion systems (Panksepp 1998; Panksepp and Biven 2012; Toronchuk and Ellis 2007, 2012) have been discussed in Chapter 5. They come in two kinds: those based in individual survival and those based in developing group survival. The latter include the affiliation systems that drive group formation and the ranking function that then regulates group conflict, together providing the emotional drivers for the social mind, which played a key role in human evolution (Dunbar 2014).

The neural substrate: This reward-based plasticity at the macro level is based in underlying plasticity at the micro level (Pessoa and Engelmann 2010; Holey 2012). Cassenaer and Laurent (2012) state:

> In locusts, the synapses between the intrinsic mushroom body neurons and their postsynaptic targets obey a Hebbian spike-timing-dependent plasticity (STDP) rule. Although this property homeostatically regulates the timing of mushroom body output, its potential role in associative learning is unknown. Here we show in vivo that pre–post pairing causing STDP can, when followed by the local delivery of a reinforcement-

mediating neuromodulator, specify the synapses that will undergo an associative change. At these synapses, and there only, the change is a transformation of the STDP rule itself. These results illustrate the multiple actions of STDP, including a role in associative learning, despite potential temporal dissociation between the pairings that specify synaptic modification and the delivery of reinforcement-mediating neuromodulator signals.

This is the kind of effect discussed by Edelman (1998).

The brain is predicting all the time on the basis of its past experience (Hawkins 2004) and then correcting its expectations via a Bayesian process (Friston 2010; Brown and Kuperberg 2015). At the micro level this is done by adjusting neural connection weights, which in turn occurs by control of gene regulation networks (Kandel 2005, 2006). This process can create the effective folk understanding that many evolutionary psychologists talk about, not through innate knowledge, but by ordinary learning processes whose attention is directed by affective systems. The innate features are the guiding affective systems, together with the structured cortical columns, ready to learn. (We are considering only the cortical systems here; of course not all learning is cortical.) The feedback process of prediction and correction provides the cognitive content of these cortical areas

6.4   EMOTION, EVOLUTION, AND MODULES

This is the position taken here. How does it relate to cortical modules? What we suggest is that we do not have the situation proposed by Geary (2008):

Evolution → folk modules (3)

Folk modules → learning effects (4)

Rather through the mechanism just identified, the genetically fixed affective systems and the associated ascending systems shape the way the cognitive system learns as it interacts with its environment (Ellis 2008):

Evolution → emotional systems (5)

Emotional systems + experience → effective folk psychology behaviour (6)

Effective folk psychology behavior → learning effects. (7)

Indeed,

> because the multiple environments that genes interact with have endless degrees of variation, the developmental outcomes of traits or behaviours can be influenced in a near infinite number of ways [hence] evolutionary

change involves changes in the developmental systems ... the critical learning steps leading to symbolic thinking were embedded in our cultural learning processes and not in the structure of our genes.

(Greenspan and Shanker 2004, pp. 3, 5)

This will be discussed further in Chapter 7.

6.5   LANGUAGE, DEVELOPMENT, AND MODULES

As mentioned in the aforementioned discussion, language has been the key domain where innate cortical modules have been proposed. This section will look at that issue in depth.

6.5.1   Arguments for and against Language Modules

These have been discussed in Chapter 5. Here we examine how it looks when we take the emotional underpinnings of language into account, rather than regarding it as a purely cognitive affair. We do not claim to be experts in linguistics and will not attempt a full theory of how grammar develops and is effected in neural terms. Rather, we will refer to sufficient literature in the embodied language tradition to show that it is indeed possible to have a plausible viewpoint based on this foundation, with lexical priming as the basis of grammar rather than rule-based cognitive processes.

Tomasello summarizes the arguments against innate language modules (Tomasello 2003, pp. 284–290), and that is in essence just a special case of the arguments against innate cognitive modules made here, which we need not repeat. Rather, we will look at plausible alternatives.

6.5.2   The Realistic Alternative

How then is spoken language learned? Through ongoing experience of the use of language in meaningful contexts (Tomasello 2003), developing an Embodied Construction Grammar (Feldman 2008), particularly via mother/child bonding and the child's search for meaning in this developing relationship (Greenspan and Shanker 2004). This then continues to the understanding of written language in a meaningful context as well, as is beautifully described in *Chloe's Story* by Carole Bloch (Bloch 1997). In linguistic terms, language emerges through collocations, colligations, and lexical priming, based in functional webs as

The Nervous System

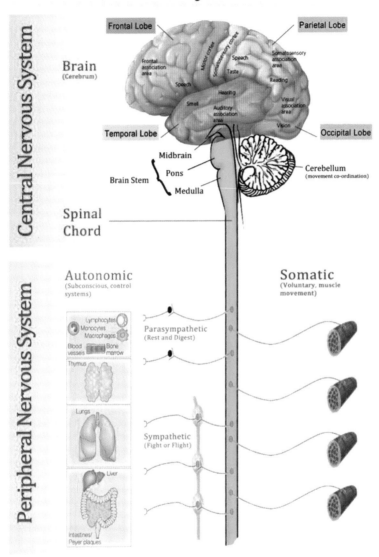

PLATE 1 The nervous system.
Source: James Follett

(a)   (b)

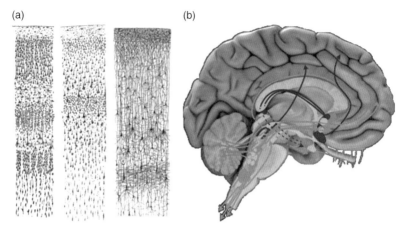

PLATE 2 (a) Cortex structure (left), (b) ascending systems (right). The finer cortical connections on the left are soft-wired; the connections from the limbic system to the cortex indicated on the right are hard-wired.

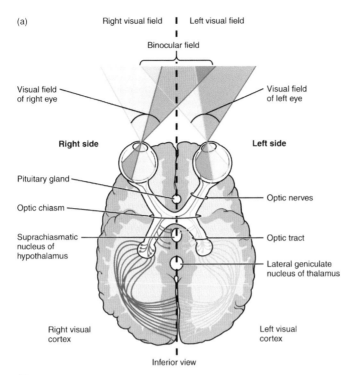

(a)

Right visual field | Left visual field

Binocular field

Visual field of right eye

Visual field of left eye

Right side

Left side

Pituitary gland

Optic chiasm

Suprachiasmatic nucleus of hypothalamus

Optic nerves

Optic tract

Lateral geniculate nucleus of thalamus

Right visual cortex

Left visual cortex

Inferior view

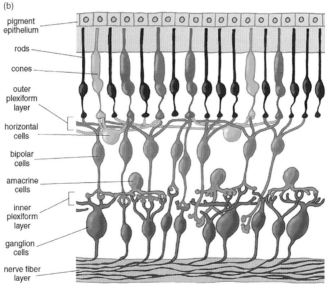

(b)

pigment epithelium

rods

cones

outer plexiform layer

horizontal cells

bipolar cells

amacrine cells

inner plexiform layer

ganglion cells

nerve fiber layer

PLATE 3 (a) The optic tract, (b) the retinal synaptic connections. These are hard-wired: a very specific pattern of connection is laid down by developmental processes, except for the link to the cortex (bottom of (a)), which is soft-wired (connections are not made to specific predetermined cortical *neurons*). Plate 3(a) From Martini, F. H.; Tallitsch, R. B., *Human Anatomy*, 8th Ed., ©2015. Reprinted by permission of Pearson Education, Inc., New York, New York. Plate 3(b) from 'How the Retina Works' by Helga Kolb, American Scientist 2004, Volume 91. Reprinted by permission of Sigma Xi.

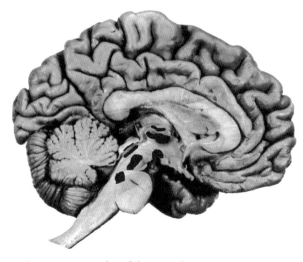

PLATE 4 Some major nuclei of the reticular activating system and PAG.

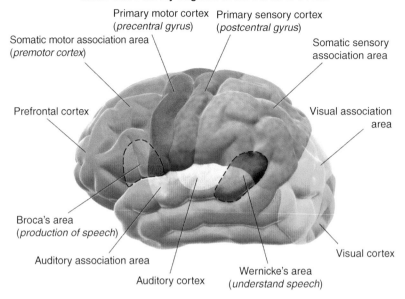

Motor and Sensory Regions of the Cerebral Cortex

Primary motor cortex (*precentral gyrus*)

Primary sensory cortex (*postcentral gyrus*)

Somatic motor association area (*premotor cortex*)

Somatic sensory association area

Prefrontal cortex

Visual association area

Broca's area (*production of speech*)

Visual cortex

Auditory association area

Auditory cortex

Wernicke's area (*understand speech*)

PLATE 5 Association areas. From Blausen.com staff. "Blausen gallery 2014". Wikiversity Journal of Medicine. DOI:10.15347/wjm/2014.010. ISSN 20018762.

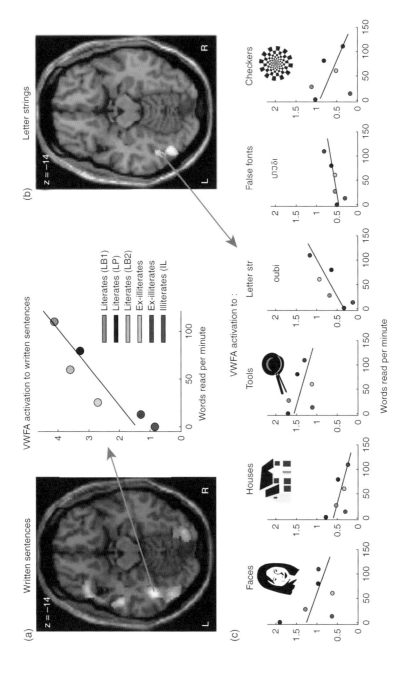

PLATE 6 The visual word form area. From Dehaene and Cohen (2011), see also DeHaene (2009). Reprinted with permission from Elsevier.

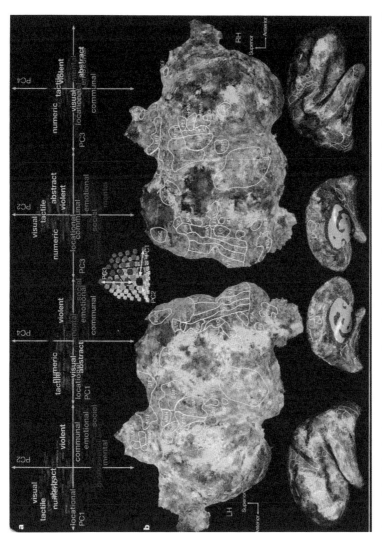

PLATE 7 Semantic models: Principal components of voxel-wise semantic models, revealing four important semantic dimensions in the brain. From Huth et al (2016). Reprinted with permission from *Nature*.

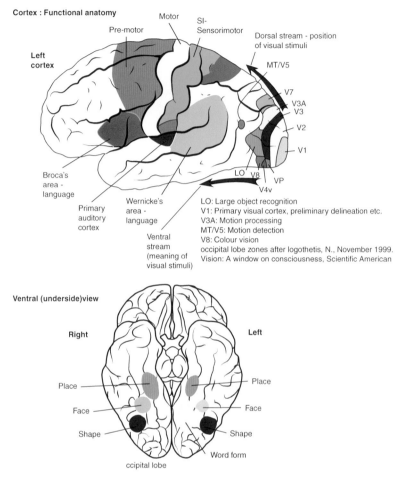

Cortex : Functional anatomy

Motor
Pre-motor
SI-Sensorimotor
Dorsal stream - position
of visual stimuli

Left cortex

MT/V5

V7
V3A
V3
V2
V1

Broca's
area -
language

LO
V8
VP
V4v

Wernicke's
area -
language

Primary
auditory
cortex

Ventral
stream
(meaning of
visual stimuli)

LO: Large object recognition
V1: Primary visual cortex, preliminary delineation etc.
V3A: Motion processing
MT/V5: Motion detection
V8: Colour vision
occipital lobe zones after logothetis, N., November 1999.
Vision: A window on consciousness, Scientific American

Ventral (underside)view

Right
Left

Place
Place

Face
Face

Shape
Shape

Word form

ccipital lobe

PLATE 8 Physical domains in the cortex. Some physical domains in the cortex (visual cortex, auditory cortex, motor cortex, and so on) correspond to operational modules in the brain. But rewiring of external connections to these domains can result in a change of their function.

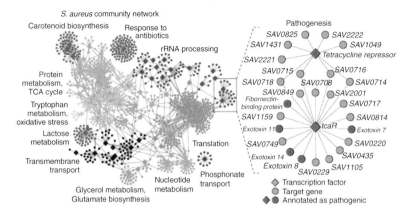

PLATE 9 Hierarchical structure of a gene regulatory network (Marbach et al 2012). Reprinted with permission from Nature.

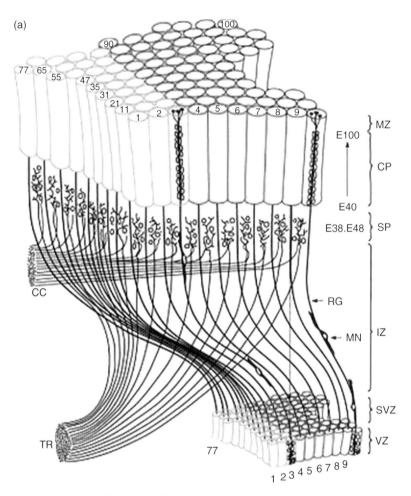

PLATE 10 (a) Sketch of cortical columns made up of interconnected neurons. The detailed neural connections in these columns determine brain function and individuality (also Plate 2(a)).

(b)

PLATE 10 (cont.) (b) Detailed microsketch of cortical columns. Image provided by Marcel Oberlaender, Max Planck Group "In Silico Brain Sciences", Center of Advanced European Studies and Research, Bonn, Germany.

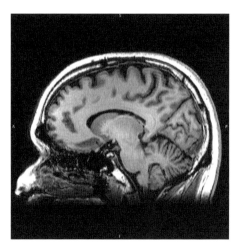

PLATE 11 The nucleus accumbens.

characterized by Pulvermüller (2002, pp. 82–87), with grammar an outcome of lexical structure (Hoey 2005), as a word – object association matrix based in a neural network can provide syntax almost for free (Solé 2005). This is largely compatible with a Functional Linguistic Grammar approach (Halliday 1977, 2003).

In more detail, the view we propose is essentially encompassed by four books. Tomasello (2003) puts forward a usage-based theory of language acquisition, based in sense-making and symbolizing experience. Feldman (2008) discusses how such processes lead to an Embodied Construction Grammar (ECG), based at the macro level in metaphors and frames and at the micro level in weight of connections in neural networks. Halliday and Matthiessen (2014) discuss the nature of the resulting functional grammar and its social imbedding. Greenspan and Shanker (2004) in effect support the views developed in the other four books, but add in the crucial ingredient of affect – the emotional binding between mother and child being a key driving factor in the acquisition of language, and showing that poverty of stimulus arguments have simply not adequately taken into account the intense interaction between real mothers and their children. It is this book that particularly reflects the view we put forward here, because of its emphasis on the importance of affect.

6.5.3 Cognitive Prerequisites and the Social Context

Spoken language requires an ability to speak and hear, based in the structures of the buccofacial apparatus on the one hand and the ears on the other (Deacon 1997; Christiansen and Kirby 2005). The ability to make sense of what we hear and to speak, then, depends on how these organs are linked to the cortex, which must learn how to use them. However, signing is a type of language that does not have these requirements: rather, it requires the ability to see on the one hand and manipulate the hands and fingers on the other. Additionally, the brain must be cognitively prepared for language: there must be an ability to classify, remember, and predict patterns (Tomasello 2003); there must be contextual drivers for using these functions in a communicative way; and there must be a representational ability: the cortical columns must have the ability to assign labels to patterns of excitations of neurons, and to do so recursively (assigning labels to patterns of labels), hence allowing development of recursive syntax.

There are three key cognitive prerequisites for language development.

1. **Intention-reading, Theory of Mind:** Children's learning is not isolated association-making and induction, but is integrated with other
   cognitive and social cognitive skills related to understanding the intentions of others (Tomasello 2003, pp. 3–4, 20–31). Of particular importance for language acquisition is intention-reading, broadly conceived,
   which is also called Theory of Mind (sharing attention, following the
   attention of others, directing the intention of others, and imitatively
   learning the intentional activities of others). Together, these define the
   functional dimension of linguistic communication, which in all cases
   involves the attempt of one person to manipulate the intentional or
   mental states of other persons. These are domain-general skills in that
   they enable a variety of other cultural skills and practices such as tool-
   making, pretend play, recognizing frames and roles, and taking part in
   rituals.

2. **Categorization ability** (Tomasello 2003, pp. 428–431): This involves
   pattern recognition and remembering patterns, allowing prediction
   of future events. It includes the ability to form perceptual and conceptual categories of similar objects and events, the ability to form
   sensory motor schemata from recurrent patterns of perception and
   action, the ability to perform statistically based analyses of perceptual
   and behavioural sequences using an intuitive Bayesian type of analysis, and so an ability to assign probabilities to types of likely future
   events. This is all based in properties of neural networks (Elman et al.
   1998; Hawkins 2004; Feldman 2008; Friston 2010; Churchman 2013).

3. **Symbolic ability**: Assigning names (labels) to objects and actions,
   allowing off-line thought about actions, events, and objects. At the
   neural level, assigning names to patterns of activations (Elman et al.
   1998, p. 126), and then to patterns of patterns (another layer of
   naming), allowing recursion, which is then the key to complex
   linguistic forms. Thus, there must be the ability to form complex
   schemas and to categorize these and their internal constituents into
   abstract categories, as well as the ability to make sophisticated pragmatic inferences, functional re-analyses, and analogies based in these
   basic capacities (Tomasello 2003, p. 16).

The first two prerequisites are the basic general-purpose abilities underlying thought, and so providing the general functional foundation for
language. The third introduces the foundation for symbolic behaviour

and so for language, and is what specifically separates us from the great apes (apart from issues of greater prefrontal volume). Neither its genetic nor its structural foundation is yet clear, but the difference must exist, as our language abilities are so clearly quite different from those of the great apes.

Given this language preparedness, the rest can follow by experience, guided by emotion systems, leading to *cognitive functional linguistics*, also called *usage-based linguistics* (Tomasello 2003, p. 5), based in the idea that the essence of language is its symbolic dimension, with grammar being derivative.

6.5.4   Embodied Language

In broad consonance with this viewpoint, Feldman bases his embodied theory of language on information processing through neural computation. On this view, language and thought are not best studied as formal logic but as adaptations that enable creatures like us to thrive in a wide variety of situations (Feldman 2008, p.7). Concrete words and concepts directly label our embodied experiences; words related to spatial relations derive form specialized circuitry in the visual system; the way we conceptualize the structure of events appears to derive from the neural structure of our system of motor control; and abstract thought grows out of concrete embodied experiences, typically sensory-motor experiences. Grammar arises from neural circuitry pairing embodied concepts with sounds or signs, and children first learn grammar by pairing sound combinations with familiar experiences (Feldman 2008, pp. 7–8). This is all realized through adapting the detailed synaptic weights in the cortical neural networks to give the desired abstract representation (Feldman 2008, pp. 115–122).

The embodied theory of meaning suggests the child needs to have conceptual structures for understanding experiences before the words labelling them can make any sense; these structures that shape expectations of what will happen are called *frames*, for example a restaurant frame or a school frame. Coordinated motor activities such as grasping are called motor schemas, and conceptual thought builds on conceptual schemas such as support, contain, source/path/goal, and so on. Their origins are via actions experienced and learned. Essentially, all our cultural, abstract, and theoretical concepts derive their meanings by mappings through metaphor to embodied experiential concepts (Lakoff and Johnson 1980; Feldman 2008, p. 199).

Because the principles of these mappings are constant, we know how to use them in novel cases (Feldman 2008, p. 210). Feldman explores how the lexicon is built up through experience and generalization, and Feldman (2008, pp. 283–294) and Bergen and Chang (2003) show how this can be built up to give an embodied construction grammar.

In the end, Feldman's point is that *grammar is not based in a set of abstract rules that our mind uses to determine what to say: it is embodied in the strengths of synaptic connections in the prefrontal and speech areas of the cortex.* That is what makes it an embodied grammar. *These strengths are developed through our experiences as we interact with the world around.* This is what makes it a construction grammar. They reflect the nature of that interaction, particularly ours.

Action grammar and language: Similar views are expressed by Knott (2012), who proposes that the syntax of a concrete sentence – a sentence that reports a direct sensorimotor experience – closely reflects the sensorimotor processes involved in the experience. In fact, he argues, the syntax of the sentence can be interpreted as a description of these sensorimotor processes. He presents detailed models of the sensorimotor processes involved in a man grabbing a coffee cup (drawing on research in psychology and neuroscience) and of the syntactic structure of the transitive sentence reporting the episode (drawing on Chomskyan Minimalist syntactic theory). He proposes that these two independently motivated models are closely linked – that the logical form of the sentence can be given a detailed sensorimotor characterization and that, more generally, many of the syntactic principles understood in Minimalism as encoding innate linguistic knowledge are actually sensorimotor in origin. This accords with the evolutionary proposals of Maynard Smith and Szathmáry (2007).

6.5.5   Acquiring Language: The Emotion Link

Coles (1998, 1999), Shanahan (2007, 2008), and Painter (2004) make the link between learning language and emotion. Greenspan and Shanker (2004) do so in a way closely related to the claims made here. Their view is that our ability to reason is founded not simply on genetics but specifically on emotional responses by infants to those they interact with, with these emotional interactions forming the key link in the development of symbols and language. Indeed, they claim that emotions actually give birth to our ability to create symbols and think.

They develop this proposal in depth, and here we can only touch on some of the points they make.

The basic argument is that in order to develop symbols, we must transform our basic emotions into a series of successively more complex emotional *signals*. This human capacity to exchange emotional signals with each other begins in early life during a long practice period and leads to symbols, language, abstract thinking, and a variety of complex emotional and social skills that enable social groups to function (Greenspan and Shanker 2004, p. 17). There are two conditions that need to be met for humans to progress from the fixed action level to a level where they can create meaningful symbols and thoughts. The first is that relevant emotional experiences must invest symbols as they form. We don't have meaningful symbols unless affect invests the images: without this you can have imagery but not symbols (p. 25). The second is that a symbol emerges when a perception is separated from its action. This is the developmental process that provides the link in understanding how symbol formation and thinking emerges from action-based perception (pp. 25–27). The foundation is that the baby needs to have a warm pleasurable relationship with a caregiver so that there is another human being towards whom she experiences deep emotions and therefore with whom she wants to communicate (pp. 28–29). Chains of emotional signalling develop that are reciprocal, co-regulated emotional interactions (pp. 31–32). 'The answer to the question of how human beings form symbols is that symbols come about by separating a perception, which is the ability to form an image, from its action. This is achieved by co-regulated emotional interactions with other human beings' (p. 37).

They state that emotions provide the mechanisms through which social groups form and society functions (p. 46). A child progressively masters a number of functional emotional (f/e) capacities, where the significance of an infant's smile cannot be divorced from the context in which it occurs. 'A baby first learns "causality" not through pulling a string to ring a bell or other similar behaviour, as Piaget (1951) thought, but through the exchange of emotional signals (I smile and you smile back). Therefore this lesson is emotional and cognitive at the same time' (p. 51). Each sensation as it is registered by the child also gives rise to an affect or emotion. This dual coding of experience is the key to understanding how emotions organize intellectual abilities and indeed create the sense of the self (p. 56). After developing intimacy and engagement, emotions become transformed into signals for communication (p. 59). The child learns how to predict patterns of adult behaviour and react accordingly (p. 61). Pattern recognition that is learnt through social interactions can then be applied to solve problems in the physical world as well. The ability to plan and sequence actions is learnt through interactive play where emotional goals are used to guide actions (p. 66).

The emergence of formal symbols is discussed in pp. 70–72, starting with emotional interactions through which images acquire meaning. They can be symbolized by words or pretend play, which then can be used to share meanings, including a sense of justice and other concepts that can unite groups socially; this will include inclusion and exclusion, as well as hierarchy and rank (p. 77). General reasoning emerges from understanding emotional interactions, and is then applied to the more impersonal world (p. 73). New social skills emerge from the ability to connect ideas. These skills form the basis for participating in larger groups, communities, and societies, where individuals both need to follow and help define the rules that will enable a large number of people to live safely and securely and solve challenges together (p. 74). This is the origin of what Dunbar (2014) has called the social brain (pp. 115–116). It has emerged – and can only emerge – in the context of the close nurturing relationships that a child experiences with her caregivers (p. 102). The way this happens in grammatical terms is discussed by Halliday (1993).

In summary: *Having developed symbolism on an emotional basis, it is then possible to divest some symbols of felt emotions and develop purely logical systems like formal logic, mathematics, and formal linguistics. These are all very useful tools, and valid in their own right. The problem comes when it is claimed that they were the direct product of biological evolution alone. They were not: they are the product of cultural evolution, enabled by the adaptive learning systems that are indeed the product of biological evolution. These issues replay in the developmental life of each individual.*

6.5.6   Poverty of Stimulus

Is there a poverty of stimulus, as claimed by Chomsky and others? The poverty of stimulus argument is stated by Simpson et al. in Carruthers et al. (2005, pp. 6–8):

> If we truly suppose that children are empiricist learners, then it is not at all obvious how they would come to even some of the most basic assumptions about language: that it is a system of communication, that meanings are associated with words as opposed to individual sounds, that strings of sounds can be assigned more than one meaning and more than one syntactic structure, and so on. The sorts of errors children make are highly circumscribed.

This is, however, not the case if we take the ongoing intense mother/child interaction into account (Bloch 1997; Greenspan and Shanker 2004). Empirical evidence comes from neural network models, which can indeed preform the required learning task; for example, Amodei et al. (2016) state that 'Our English speech system is trained 11,940 hours of labelled speech data containing 8 million utterances' (which is 4 years at 8 hours a day, 6.5 years at 5 hours a day, or 8 years at 4 hours a day). 'We train our RNN Models over millions of unique utterances, which enables the network to learn a powerful implicit language model. Our best models are quite adept at spelling, without any external language constraints. Further, in our development datasets we find many cases where our models can implicitly disambiguate homophones.' The learning effect is much enhanced if invested with emotional meaning, as explained by Greenspan and Shanker.

6.5.7   Innateness and Grammar

The recent wave of development of Deep Learning Neural Networks has shown how suitable structured multi-layer neural networks, starting with random initial connections in the inner layers and suitable back-propagation algorithms applied to the outer layers, can learn very complex tasks in an efficient way, including language grammar and syntax. They demonstrate that there simply is no need for innate information to be encoded in cortical modules in order that a language capacity can develop (Amodei et al. 2016).

We show that an end-to-end deep learning approach can be used to recognize either English or Mandarin Chinese speech – two vastly different languages. Because it replaces entire pipelines of hand-engineered components with neural networks, end-to-end learning allows us to handle a diverse variety of speech including noisy environments, accents and different languages ... Decades worth of hand-engineered domain knowledge has gone into current state-of-the-art automatic speech recognition (ASR) pipelines. A simple but powerful alternative solution is to train such ASR models end-to-end, using deep learning to replace most modules with a single model (Hannun 2014). We present the second generation of our speech system that exemplifies the major advantages of end to-end learning. The Deep Speech 2 ASR pipeline approaches or exceeds the accuracy of Amazon Mechanical Turk human workers on several benchmarks, works in multiple languages with little modification, and is deployable in a production setting. It thus represents a significant step towards a single ASR system that addresses the entire range of speech recognition contexts handled by humans. Since our system is built on end-to-end deep learning, we can employ a spectrum of deep learning techniques: capturing large training sets, training larger models with high performance computing, and methodically exploring the space of neural network architectures.

The grammar will be developed socially in a cultural evolutionary context of developing effective communication methods, initially based in action grammar; and will then necessarily embody language universals, as pointed out by Deacon (2003). Deep learning neural networks will then be able to structure detailed cortical connections realizing the ability to understand and speak according to the local lexicon and grammar, through ongoing social interaction from the day the child is born.

6.5.8   Origin of language universals

Where then do the language regularities come from that Chomsky recognized and categorized as being due to a deep grammar module? On this view they are due to essential syntactic limitations on any language whatever in order that it be an adequate symbolic system for describing the world around. They are due to fundamental semiotic constraints on any symbolic representation of our experiences and environment, as explained in detail by Deacon:

> Many of these core language universals reflect semiotic constraints, inherent in the requirements for producing symbolic reference itself . . . these constraints shape the self-organisation and evolution of communication in a social context . . . combinations of words inherit constraints from the lower order mediating relationships that give words their freedom of mapping. These classes of constraints limit the classes of referentially consistent higher order symbol constructions.
>
> (Deacon 2003, pp. 112, 118)

He emphasizes that symbolic reference is a system of relationships, not a mere collection of mappings, so there are universal systemic constraints on what can and cannot constitute higher-order forms of symbolic reference. Tomasello states it this way (Tomasello 2003, p. 18):

> Of course there are language universals. It is just that they are not universals of form – that is not particular kinds of linguistic symbols or grammatical categories or linguistic constructions – but rather they are universals of communication and cognition and human physiology. Because all languages are used by human beings with similar kinds of social lives, all peoples have the need to solve in their languages certain kind of communication tasks, such as referring to specific entities or

predicating things about those entities. All human beings have the same basic tools for accomplishing those tasks – linguistic symbols, markers on those symbols, ordering of symbols, and prosodic patterns ... This leads to some language universals for example something like nouns and verbs as expressions of reference, and predication using linguistic symbols of certain kinds. Such universals are therefore emergent phenomena, based ultimately on universals of human cognition, human communicative needs, and human vocal-auditory processing.

This is intriguingly demonstrated by Rosenfelder (2010), who discusses in a practical way the requirements to create a coherent artificial language, and thereby illustrates the nature of the language universals mentioned by Deacon and Tomasello. In any case the Universal Grammar hypothesis has substantial problems (Dąbrowska 2016; Everett 2016; Goldberg 2016). An emergent grammar hypothesis can be argued to be more plausible (Archangeli and Pulleyblank 2015). 'Evidence from genetics, comparative work on non-human primates, and cognitive neuroscience suggests that humans have evolved complex sequence learning skills, which were subsequently pressed into service to accommodate language; in particular our ability to process recursive structured does not rely on recursion as a property of the grammar, but instead emerges gradually by piggybacking on domain-general sequence learning abilities' (Christiansen and Chater 2015).

6.5.9   The Nature of Linguistics

Linguistics has many dimensions, and various approaches to its study emphasize these different dimensions. We do not claim to have a grand theory of how these all fit together, but rather propose that a full theory must take into account all these viewpoints, each of which captures part of the complex whole.

1. **Abstract structure:** This view emphasizes formal structure (Chomsky 1965), and regards grammar as equivalent to formal rules for syntax. This approach allows one to analyse language once developed, but is not a realistic theory of development, use, or evolution of language. It is based in a rule-based system, which is enabled by neural network computations. What is particularly important is that they can implement an 'IF X(x) THEN Y ELSE Z' logical structure, which is the core of logical argumentation, classification, and exploration of alternative action plans. This is enabled by the

underlying neural network because synapses have a threshold nature: they fire if the total incoming signal is above a threshold, but not otherwise. They can also provide all the basic logical operations (OR, AND, NOT, and XOR) needed to enable complex logical computations $X(x)$ in the decision criteria (Pulvermüller 2002, pp. 96–106).

2. **Embodied approaches:** Grammar is based in an underlying biological structure: namely the neural network structure (Elman et al. 1998; Hawkins 2004), allowing naming and recursion. The specific details of that structure that enable naming and recursion in the prefrontal and speech areas of the cortex have not been identified but presumably involve downward connections from higher to lower levels in order to implement recursion. From this viewpoint, grammar is embodied in neural connection weights rather than in formal rules (Feldman 2003).

3. **Function:** Language is based in communication and its semiotic functions (Deacon 1997, 2003) in a social context (Tomasello 2003) leading to functional theories of grammar, as developed from the work of Halliday (1977, 1993; Halliday and Matthiessen 2014). These are approaches to language considered as a tool for social communication, and so considered as the key to understanding linguistic processes and structures to be the functions of language and the linguistic elements that carry them out. Functional theories therefore instead of focusing on formal relations between linguistic elements focus on the way language is actually used in communicative contexts, with phrases as the focus rather than words or phonemes, and evidence provided by statistical studies of how language is actually used in ordinary social circumstances (individual or societal).

4. **Development and learning:** These approaches emphasize the basis of language in the mother/child interaction (Greenspan and Shanker 2004), leading to an embodied construction grammar (Feldman 2003), starting with pointing and with holistic 'holophrases' that then get resolved into their parts (Tomasello 2003, pp. 36–40). In these processes the child is acting as a scientist exploring hypotheses and then testing them out (Gopnik et al. 2000; Gopnik 2009). The neural circuits underlying this engagement in exploratory and playful activities for their own sake, rather than as steps towards other extrinsic goals, are discussed in Oudeyer et al. (2007).

5. **Evolutionary origin, action grammar** (Maynard Smith and Szathmáry 2007): The evolutionary origin of communicative language is subject to much debate; various views are expressed in the

book edited by Christiansen and Kirby (2005). We will not attempt a detailed proposal here, but rather just support the view, consonant with the rest of what is proposed here, that the deep evolutionary roots of language lie in the attempts of primate individuals to influence the behaviour of conspecifics (Tomasello 2003, p. 11), and this is a crucial part of the development of the social brain (Dunbar 2014), whereby language evolved as a device for bonding large social groups, whose existence made a key difference to survival. This bonding was an outcome of the affiliation/bonding primary emotional system in humans identified by Stevens and Price (2000), developing from Pankskepp's PANIC/SEPARATION system that occurs in all mammals.

The suggestion is that given this context, language grammar develops from action grammar, leading to the use of many action-based metaphors (Lakoff and Johnson 1980a). On the usage-based view, processes of grammaticalization and syntactization can create grammatical structures out of concrete utterances (Tomasello 2003, p. 13). But (contrary to what is stated by Tomasello), there is a need for a specific genotype outcome that differs between us and the great apes: namely whatever is required to underlie the possibility of attaching labels (names) to patterns of activations of synapses (Elman 1991, 1993), and to do so in a recursive way. A key feature here is identifying when different names have been attached to the same entity (Li and Clifton 1994).

In biological terms, a reasonable organizing principle for the evolution of higher reflective abilities of humans is to think in terms of greater functional/emotional capacity, defined as *the ability of the organism to engage in co-regulated affective communication, where this communication becomes more and more differentiated over time* (Greenspan and Shanker 2004, pp. 183, 190–191). And this is based in the evolution of the primary emotional systems that underlie bonding and hierarchy, for these are the ones that underlie the development of the social brain.

6. **The Language Pattern View, with evidence based in corpus studies:** This approach considers how language is actually used, based in studying statistical data from corpora (large collected bodies of texts). Hoey (2005) develops corpus linguistics as a basis of language, with collocations (co-occurrence of specific words near each other in the text more often than would be the case in a random text) setting the basic patterns of usage, and grammar emerging from this. The question of why specific language seems natural is answered through

the creation of texts via combinations of collocations. Lexical priming is the driving force behind language use, structure, and change: every word is primed for collocational use, with colligations (priming for grammatical functions) shaping grammar. As a word is acquired through encounters with it in speech and writing, it becomes cumulatively loaded with the contexts and co-texts in which it is encountered (Hoey 2005, p. 8). This happens in a nested way: the product of priming becomes itself primed in ways that do not apply to the individual words making up the combinations.

The result of these processes is development of grammar patterns. The pattern of a word is all the words and structures which are regularly associated with the word and which contribute to its meaning (Hunston and Francis 2000, p. 37). Patterns can be established for nouns, verbs, adjectives, and adverbs by setting up concordance lines for multiple uses of the word and its variants (e.g. explain, explains, explained). This has been done in depth for verbs (Francis et al. 1998) and for nouns and adjectives (Francis et al. 1998), giving a corpus-driven approach to establishing actual grammatical patterns, as a contrast to rule-based approaches to grammar.

7. **The integrative view: The distributed functional view:** The key point in all this is that one must take the whole context of language use into account in order to adequately describe what is happening. Thibault (2011) articulates aspects of an emerging perspective shift on language: the distributed view. According to this view, languaging behaviour and its organization are irreducible to the formal regularities that have characterized mainstream linguistics over the past century. Language, in the distributed view, is a radically heterogeneous phenomenon that is spread across diverse spatiotemporal scales, ranging from the neural to the cultural. It is not localizable on any one of them, but it involves complex interactions between phenomena on many different scales. A crucial distinction is thus presented and explained, viz. first-order language and second-order language. The former is grounded in the intrinsic expressivity and interactivity of human bodies-in-interaction. Second-order patterns emanate from the cultural dynamics of an entire population of interacting agents on longer, slower cultural-historical time-scales.

This is broadly consonant with the functional linguistic view. As noted by Nichols (1984),

[Functional grammar] analyzes grammatical structure, as do formal and structural grammar; but it also analyzes the entire communicative situation: the purpose of the speech event, its participants, its discourse context. Functionalists maintain that the communicative situation motivates, constrains, explains, or otherwise determines grammatical structure, and that structural or formal approaches are not merely limited to an artificially restricted data base, but are inadequate even as structural accounts. Functional grammar, then, differs from formal and structural grammar in that it purports not to model but to explain; and the explanation is grounded in the communicative situation.

This leads to **Systemic Functional Linguistics** (**SFG**) as developed by Halliday, which is viewed as a network of interrelated sets of options for making meaning, based in the social-semiotic nature of language. Language has this form because that is what it is has evolved to do in a social context. The practical outcome is correlations between words demonstrated by corpus linguistics and related lexical primings associated with expectations.

Halliday (1993) expresses his approach as follows: Despite the fact that educational knowledge is massively dependent on verbal learning, theories of learning have not been specifically derived from observations of children's language development. But language development is learning how to mean; and because human beings are quintessentially creatures who mean (i.e. who engage in semiotic processes, with natural language as prototypical), all human learning is essentially semiotic in nature. We might, therefore, seek to model learning processes in general in terms of the way children construe their resources for meaning – how they simultaneously engage in 'learning language' and 'learning through language'.

Halliday and Matthiessen describe the nature of written and spoken language as follows:

> Writing is not the representation of speech sound. While every writing system is related to the sound system of its language in systematic and non-random ways (exactly how the two are related varies from one language to another), the relationship is not a direct one. There is another level of organization in language to which both the sound system and the writing system are related, namely the level of **wording**, or 'lexicogrammar'. (We shall usually refer to this simply as 'grammar', as in the title of the book; but it is important to clarify from the start that grammar and vocabulary are not two separate components of a language – they are just the two ends of a single continuum) The sound system and the writing system are the two modes of **expression** by which the lexicogrammar of a language is represented, or **realized**.
>
> (Halliday and Matthiessen 2014, p. 7)

The central role of clauses in this view is described as follows:

> The clause is the central processing unit in the lexicogrammar – in the specific sense that it is in the clause that meanings of different kinds are mapped into an integrated grammatical structure. For this reason the first half of this book is organized around the principal systems of the clause: theme, mood and transitivity. In Part II we move outward from the clause, to take account of what happens above and below it – systems of the clause complex, of groups and phrases, and of group and phrase complexes; and also beyond the clause, along other dimensions so to speak. The perspective moves away from structure to consideration of grammar as system, enabling us to show the grammar as a meaning-making resource and to describe grammatical categories by reference to what they mean. This perspective is essential if the analysis of grammar is to be an insightful mode of entry to the study of discourse. (Halliday and Matthiessen 2014, p. 10)

This is all compatible in broad terms with Hoey's proposal of representing language at the usage level through lexical priming. We are grateful to Peter Fries (Michigan) for the following notes on this (private communication):

> Systemic Functional Linguistics (SFL) and corpus linguistics have shared since their beginning similar positions concerning the appropriate data to use for linguistic description. Specifically advocates of both approaches use data gathered from language actually being used for some social purpose rather than made-up examples constructed by the analyst. Both approaches also are interested in counting relative frequencies of the entities they investigate, although, perhaps the reasons for counting and the conclusions reached as a result of the counting may differ in detail.

As one can see from Hoey (2005), corpus linguists focus very heavily on how words pattern – with other words and/or with grammatical structures. Systemicists, on the other hand, view a language as a complex set of interrelated choices, each place one encounters a choice (in our terms, each system) being connected with some difference in meaning and also with some difference in form to realize that meaning – *form* here referring to some word or some aspect of grammatical structure, such as order of elements, say subject and predicator. Systemicists believe that within any system (in the SFL technical sense), the relative frequency with which the various options within that system are taken is part of the meaning of taking one or another option. Of course if that is true, then every time we use language we alter the frequencies of the choices in all systems. In this way, language change is inherent in language use.

Thus, advocates of SFL tend to describe language at a 'deeper', more abstract level than do corpus linguists. Hoey's work is typical of that of many corpus linguists in that he tends to use relatively simple grammatical concepts such as noun phrase, verb phrase, beginning or end of sentence or paragraph, etc. In other words, he follows in the tradition of John Sinclair of trying to use categories that don't commit him to one or another specific theoretical tradition. Descriptions within the systemic tradition factor out various aspects of each grammatical structure encountered into a number of separate functions, and each function results from a constellation of choices 'made' by the speaker. (The word *made* here must be interpreted as a theoretical concept not actually a description of what the speaker actually does. Perhaps it's best interpreted as a description of the *result* of what the speaker has done.)

SFL and corpus linguistics work together quite well because they complement one another both in their weaknesses and in their strengths. Corpus linguistics is really good at discovering large-scale covert patterns in the language we use, patterns that relate strongly to the meanings we express and the ways we express them. But typically the wordings/meanings corpus linguists address are meanings of relatively small (word-length or phrase-length) elements. Good information for supplementing a detailed analysis of a single text, but not very good for a complete analysis of a single text in context.

It is difficult to take what we learn about individual expressions (or even an extended set of individual expressions) and use that information to interpret a whole text because such an approach misses the operation of the internal dynamics of text itself. By contrast, one important interest of systemicists has been to use SFL as a tool to address what texts mean. That requires locating and describing the patterns of meanings (and deviations from these patterns of meanings) expressed in a text and noticing how the patterns interact. They are interested in the very internal textual dynamics that corpus approaches typically miss.

SFL scholars who focus on language development in children would agree about the key role of affect in behaviour and development (Painter 2004). Furthermore, SFL scholars, and usage-based grammar advocates in general, do not buy the 'poverty of stimulus' argument used by formalists. Rather they take an approach that learning language is primarily a matter of learning to mean – first learning that communication with some other is possible, and then taking part in gradually more and more sophisticated communicative events. The tools used start as simple form meaning associations and gradually develop more and more complicated aspects as children become aware of the benefits of altering the systems they have in certain ways in order to participate more fully in interactions with important others.

In the SFL view language is *not* invented by the child alone. Rather the communicating community has a great deal to do with the developments. Specifically, the interest of the adults in their children leads them to (a) understand the intents of the child even with minimal tools for communication, and (b) track how the efforts of the child to communicate relate to those inferred intents. Thus, the meaningful responses of the adults to what the children are doing and 'saying' contribute a great deal to the development of the children. A quick summary of language development from pre-language to the development of grammatical metaphor is given in Painter et al. (2007).

Fries concludes:

> I like to use the notion of resonance (and damping) as a metaphor to describe the internal dynamics of texts. The image is that the meanings (e.g. of a word /phrase/text portion) may be potentially present in many (all?) contexts in which it may appear, but the different specific textual contexts each resonate certain meanings and dampen others with the result that the reader 'hears' different meanings in the different contexts. I like the notion of resonance since it also allows for the possibility that the context may even supply a new meaning that is not normally conveyed by the word when thought of in isolation, but which the context brings out. I'm thinking of those special cases where several individual singers each sing notes that are in special harmonic relation to one another and the result is that the audience hears a note that no one is actually singing. I have identified a couple cases of that sort of thing in texts.

This is a notion of emergence, showing clearly why one must interpret the text at the higher level; the deep meanings are simply not present in the component parts on their own (Ellis 2016). It resonates with the holistic views of how sensory perception, including vision, takes place (Frith 2007; Kandel 2012). Visual sensory data are sent from the retina to the thalamus and tectum; excitatory connections pass sensory information on from relay neurons in the thalamus to the cortex, but additionally descending input to the thalamus comes from cell bodies located in level 6 of the cerebral cortex (Alitto and Usrey 2003), exerting both an excitatory and inhibitory influence on relay neurons. These connections transmit selected feedback signals to the thalamus, shaping its contextual response to what is seen, including writing, which can be demonstrated by studies of how reading takes place to always be controlled in a contextual way based on what is expected to be seen (Goodman et al. 2016). Predictive top-down integration of prior knowledge takes place (Sohuglu et al. 2012), based in canonical microcircuits (Bastos et al. 2012), and internal models of the motor and social situation (Wolpert and Flanagan 2016), continually shaping how we perceive and what we pay attention to.

The key contextual feature in early childhood, shaping this all, is the relation to the caregiver. This is all compatible with the view of how language works as proposed by Tomasello:

> The glue that holds this all of these factors together is always the child's attempts to understand the communicative intentions of other persons as she interacts with them socially and linguistically ... children learn words most readily in situations in which it is easiest to read the adult's communicative intentions. Usage based linguistics holds that the essence of language is its symbolic dimension, that is, the ways in which human beings use conventional linguistic symbols for purposes of interpersonal communication. (Tomasello 2003, pp. 44, 49, 283)

How this happens is detailed in depth by Tomasello; and this is all driven by the PANIC/GRIEF (attachment) system, as is in effect noted by Greenspan and Shanker.

In conclusion, there are many approaches to grammar, each of which captures some of its aspects. They broadly fit together to give a viable view that is not based in innate cortical modules but is based in semiotic and social usage and experience. We have not attempted a rigorous view of how they fit together, but rather have put forward the view that they are aspects of a whole that can be striven for, and is to quite a degree already captured in the SFL approach.

6.6   GENDER

It is very well established that girls, on average, perform better than boys in language tasks throughout development (with the superiority being approximately one standard deviation (15%) on most tasks). Likewise, language disorders are more common in boys than girls. This is associated with sex differences in regional activation of cortex in both visual and auditory language tasks (Burman, Bitanc and Booth, 2008).

On the Chomsky–Pinker view, these findings would imply that the output of the innate 'universal grammar module' is superior in girls, for some inexplicable – and genetically unproven – reason. This is not possible; no sex differences have been demonstrated in the single gene variant (ARHGAP11B) that controls specifically human cortical expansion.

More plausible is the developmental mechanism of language acquisition we have outlined in the aforementioned discussion, in which infant/ mother interaction plays such a prominent role. There are substantial sex differences (in favour of females – in all mammals) in the hormones and peptides that mediate the relevant prosocial brain systems (CARE, PANIC/ GRIEF) governing the basic emotions for attachment and nurturance, such as oestrogen, oxytocin, prolactin, and progesterone (Panksepp 1998; Panksepp and Biven 2012). On our view, it is within the context of such behaviours that language skill develops. It seems obvious that degrees of language development would co-vary with degrees of social connectedness. There are also large sex differences in PLAY, another prosocial basic emotion, a major precursor of empathy, but it is less clear how exactly this might relate to language development. Perhaps, the need for social negotiation and mutuality in successful PLAY episodes is the key here.

Incidentally, males show superiority over females in spatial cognition. This would be readily explicable, on the same basis, by the fact that males in all mammal species are more physically active (and more aggressive) than females. Increased physical exploration of the spatial environment seems bound to result in superior spatial skills. Here too, the proponents of innate cortical modularity would have to postulate a male-specific genetic variant for spatial cognition – a claim for which there is, once again, absolutely no empirical evidence.

6.7   PRIMARY EMOTION SYSTEMS AS THE LYNCHPIN FOR EVOLUTION AND DEVELOPMENT

We have focused in depth on language because that has been the most dominant source of claims on innate cognitive modules, but the same principles apply in all the other cases claimed, such as folk physics and folk psychology modules. Gopnik (2009) expresses this as follows:

> The basic idea is that children develop their everyday knowledge of the world by using the same cognitive devices that adults use in science. In particular, children develop abstract, coherent, systems of entities and rules, particularly causal entities and rules. That is, they develop theories. These theories enable children to make predictions about new evidence, to interpret evidence, and to explain evidence. Children actively experiment with and explore the world, testing the predictions of the theory and gathering relevant evidence. Some counter-evidence to the theory is

simply reinterpreted in terms of the theory. Eventually however when many predictions of the theory are falsified, the child begins to seek alternative theories. If the alternative does a better job of predicting and explaining the evidence, it replaces the existing theory.

This is the origin of 'folk physics', 'folk biology', and 'folk psychology'. No innate modules are needed to account for them. The need to understand is driven by the SEEKING system, which provides the pleasurable motivation for the hard work involved, and which is closely related to the process of 'prediction error coding' described earlier (Friston 2010; Schultz 2016).

Summary: We have

- Sensory systems that are hard-wired at the sensory end, but soft-wired at the cortical end, hence we have to *learn* to see
- Motor systems that are hard-wired at the muscle end, but soft-wired at the cortical end, hence we have to learn to grasp and manipulate objects and walk
- Cortical columns have no domain-specific knowledge: this is not possible because of developmental and genetic constraints. They are soft-wired, and have a highly plastic nature, and their development and connectivity in response to social and other experience is shaped to a considerable degree by hard-wired components of the limbic and ascending systems – that is, by the primary emotion systems.

Theories of evolutionary psychology must take this seriously: in particular, they must reflect the crucial role of affect in cognitive development and hence in evolution, or they will be missing the key element in what is going on. And all this takes place in the context of the broad way the mind works: all the time seeking to make sense, predicting what will happen (Hawkins 2004), and paying attention to deviations from those predictions, which shape what we see and experience (Frith 2007; Goodman et al. 2016) through reciprocal connections that link processing at each level within the cortex (Pulvermüller 2002, p. 110) and between the cortex and the thalamus (Pulvermüller 2002, pp. 80–81; Alitto and Usrey 2003; Sherman 2016).

7

Conclusion

This chapter gives a summary of our argument in relation to recent developments in evolutionary theory, and outlines further possible developments. It considers possible implications for educational policy, as advocated, for example, by David Geary, and lists some of the outstanding issues to be sorted out to consolidate the view presented here at the heart of a progressive research programme. (We thank Carole Bloch for assistance with the section on learning to read and write.)

7.1   A CONSISTENT VIEW

The view we have put above, with detailed explanation of the reasons for believing it to be true, is that *there are no innate neocortical modules with specific cognitive content.* Such modules are impossible because of the details of how gene expression leads to cortical columns and layers being laid down by developmental processes (see Bakken et al. 2016 for a more detailed discussion). Rather, what is genetically determined in the neocortex is the broad structure of columns and layers of specific neuron types, with some pre-specified structure in the overall patterns of synaptic connectivity but with all detailed synaptic connections and weights being fixed through developmental processes (Wolpert 2002; Gilbert 2006) as the mind interacts with the physical, ecological, and social environment, the latter being of particular importance (Dunbar 2014; Sterelny 2014). Where the pattern of the connections is indeed innately determined is in the connections (via subcortical relays) of the sensory systems to the sense organs, the motor system to muscles, and the ascending 'arousal' systems. The latter contain evolutionarily specified information (coded in affective terms) that, together with limbic nuclei and circuits, guides developmental systems in shaping detailed neocortical connections *as a consequence of*

136

interactions with the external and internal environments. This information is embodied in a set of primary emotion systems (Panksepp 1998) that originated through evolutionary processes because they are so successful in shaping responses to the situations we encounter, in a highly flexible and adaptive way (Panksepp and Biven 2012). This is all set out in the previous chapters, and is broadly consonant even with Fodor (1983, 2000).

It is useful here to have at hand a recent series of articles, coordinated by Ansaldo and Enfield (2016), looking at the issue of the claimed existence of an innate language faculty from psychological and linguistic perspectives. In this series of papers,

- Dąbrowska (2016) reviews the fundamental arguments in support of the Universal Grammar hypothesis and maintains that all three can be proven wrong.
- Christiansen and Kirby (2005) argue that an innate Language Faculty is evolutionarily unlikely.
- Culbertson and Kirby (2016) propose that our linguistic knowledge is best seen as a unique interaction of domain-general capacities with what becomes language.
- Adger and Svenonius (2015) maintain that aspects of our best theories of syntactic phenomena are simply special cases of more general principles, but those more general principles are not established at the moment.
- Goldberg (2016) looks at the 'subtle and intricate' implicit knowledge of language that speakers seem to possess. These cases do not warrant the positing of innate syntactic structures, as they can be explained by the functions of the constructions involved which are learned and conventionalized, and they only require domain-general constraints on perception, attention, and memory.
- Archangeli and Pulleyblank (2015) propose that humans make sense of linguistic data primarily through three non-linguistic abilities: categorical thinking, sensitivity to frequency, and symbolic generalization.
- Evans (2016) argues that language must have both a conceptual and a linguistic system operating in a symbiotic relation, each of which is semantic in nature and contributes to meaning construction, but the former is evolutionarily older and is the one to which the latter is adapted.
- Everett (2016) argues against phonological nativism, which suffers from at least two shortcomings, namely: properties invoked in phonological nativism are not successfully explained in evolutionary

terms; it confuses design features of any given system with innate, rather than acquired, constraints.

These arguments buttress our conclusions. However, we emphasize that the primary and solid reason we are confident in them is that they are based in considering possible developmental mechanisms whereby innate cognitive modules could come into being in the neocortex. There are none. Hence, there can be no such modules.

7.2   THE BROADER CONTEXT: RELATION TO EVOLUTION

The argument of this book is related to major developments taking place in evolutionary theory, and it sits easily in the Evo-Devo tradition aimed at uniting evolutionary theory and developmental studies (Carroll 2006; Sansom and Brandon 2007). Through taking into account current developmental biology and physiology, this extended synthesis provides a view of evolutionary origins with a much more solid biological base than the Modern Synthesis does (Pigliucci and Müller 2010; Noble 2013), because the latter is largely based in looking at correlation rather than causation via biological mechanisms (Sansom and Brandon 2007). Although Evo-Devo is not at this time a unified theory (Laubichler and Maienschein 2007), the various approaches have broad strands of argument that are common and that broadly agree with the view put here. We are concerned both with viewing developmental mechanisms as causal mechanisms for the processes of evolution, and with evolution as the basis for existence of specific developmental programmes. As well as being solidly rooted in developmental biology, our view takes epigenetics, niche construction, and multi-level selection seriously, the latter being a necessary outcome of developmental programmes because they are based in interactions between different levels. In the case of human beings, the view put forward here is consistent with some form of the Social Intelligence Hypothesis (Sterelny 2014) or Social Brain Hypothesis (Dunbar 2014), which are broadly similar to proposals for the key mechanisms making the difference between humans and other hominids, although the former is somewhat wider in scope.

7.2.1   Evolutionary Psychology Issues

Evolutionary psychology is highly contested. It is strongly supported by its proponents, as summarized in Buss (2005), while Panksepp and

Panksepp (2000) draw attention to 'The seven deadly sins of evolutionary psychology' (with a summary of their views and a variety of responses given in Panksepp and Panksepp (2001)). A special issue of *This View of Life* (TVOL 2016) entitled 'What's Wrong (and Right) about Evolutionary Psychology?' has a range of views, from 'What Is Wrong with Evolutionary Psychology? Nothing' by Terry Burnham Darwin, through 'In Your Brain. Four Reasons Why Evolutionary Psychology Is Controversial' by Bernard Crespi, to 'Evolutionary Psychology Is Neither' by Jonathan Marks. A book by Robert Richardson (2007) is entitled *Evolutionary Psychology as Maladjusted Psychology*, and queries its status as an explanatory theory.

Despite these questionings, evolutionary psychology has great popular traction due partly to evangelistic efforts on its behalf, and it has indeed produced some interesting studies. Nevertheless, its main thesis of massive modularity, in the sense of hard-wired cognitive modules, seems to be fatally flawed, as discussed earlier, primarily because it implicitly supposes developmental mechanisms that cannot in fact exist. It is not soundly based in developmental biology or physiology. The underlying assumption is that these are epiphenomena with all the real informational work being carried out by genes. But this is an inversion of the demonstrable flow of causation. Developmental processes turn genes on and off so as to achieve the desired phenotypic results. The flow of control is top-down (Kandel 2005; Noble 2012; Ellis 2016; and see figure 12.2 on page 317 in Pigliucci and Müller 2010).

7.2.2   Evolution and Development

The Evo-Devo viewpoint (Carroll 2006; Sansom and Brandon 2007) aims at integrating evolutionary and developmental theories. Central is the fact that environmental context at all scales determines which genes get read at what time (Gilbert and Epel 2009), and so determines developmental outcomes, and hence the outcome of our evolutionary history. Pigliucci and Müller (2010, p. 14) express this as follows:

> The views of several contributors to this volume converge on the view of genes as followers in the evolutionary process, ensuring the routinization of developmental interactions, the faithfulness of their inheritance, and the progressive fixation of phenotypic traits that were initially mobilized through plastic responses of adaptive developmental systems to changing environmental conditions. In this way, evolution progresses through the

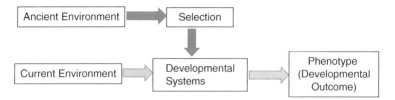

FIGURE 7.1 The ancient environment selects developmental systems that provided desirable outcomes in that context. These developmental systems then function in the context of the current environment to produce specific outcomes adapted to that different environment. The developmental system includes genes, gene regulatory networks, proteins, metabolic regulatory networks, and signal transduction networks at the micro scale. At the macro scale they include the primary affective systems and associated neuromodulators and ascending neuronal systems from the limbic system to the cortex. The evolutionary path (diachronic emergence) is shown in the lighter-shaded arrows; the developmental path (synchronic emergence) in the darker arrows

capture of emergent interactions into genetic-epigenetic circuits which are passed to and elaborated on in subsequent generations.

Because selection acts on phenotypes, not directly on genotypes or genes, novel traits can originate by environmental induction as well as mutation, then undergo selection and genetic accommodation; genes are probably more often followers than leaders in evolutionary change (West-Eberhard 2003, 2005).

This is the proper evolutionary background for our viewpoint: an emphasis on developmental systems and phenotypic plasticity as key players in the evolutionary process, broadly in accord with the Developmental Systems Theory (Oyama et al. 2001), taking the relation between physiology and evolution seriously (Noble 2008, 2013), and leading to some kind of extended synthesis; see Pigliucci and Müller (2010).

Given this broad understanding, what is selected? Selection takes place at both the micro and macro levels. At the micro level, there is selection for the following (Wagner 2011):

1. **The genotype**, which is the traditionally proposed target of selection. But this is not just specific segments of DNA; indeed, there are two distinct concepts of a gene in the literature: whatever factors cause phenotype change, and coding segments of DNA (Noble 2011). These are not the same. Here we will mean the latter, because this is a well-defined concept as used by molecular biologists. The former includes in

addition all the items listed below, the imprecise usage of which enables tautologous (and so unhelpful) claims that genes cause everything.

2. **Gene regulatory networks**, which decide which genes will get read where and when. This is where epigenetics comes in and results in the contextual dependence of developmental biology.

3. **Metabolic regulatory networks**, which control how energy is made available for cell activities, and includes in particular the citric acid cycle.

4. **Signal transduction networks**, related to the interactions of cells with each other, regulating the development of a wide range of physiological structures.

5. **Proteins**, which provide structural material as well as binding, catalysis (through enzymes), and switching (Petsko and Ringe 2009). They create extraordinary molecular machines (Roux 2011) that cannot possibly have self-assembled.

   At higher levels, there is a cascade from selection of properties that make group and individual survival more likely down to properties of physiological systems and the microbiology systems (just listed) that makes their existence possible. Thus, there is in particular selection for the following:

6. **Group properties** associated with social intelligence and the social brain, which made the rise of Homo sapiens possible, for example by making intergenerational cultural transmission possible.

7. **Individual properties** that either underlie social intelligences, and so make the success of social groups possible, or are propitious for individual survival independent of the existence of the group, such as greater individual strength, speed, or intelligence.

There is a cascade down from these higher-level properties to the lower-level ones: there is selection for the groups which are likely to survive better because of their social cooperation and consequent development of technology. This is possible because of a combination of intellectual (cognitive and emotional) properties of individuals; and this is made possible by the underlying physiological systems based in interacting cells and microbiology systems that enable them to function.

In addition, **Niche construction** takes place: the group alters the environment in such a way as to make its own survival more likely (Odling Smee in Pigliucci and Muller 2010). Overall, it is *developmental* systems that are selected for. It is those systems – at both the micro level, as listed above, and at the macro level, as described in previous chapters – that shape the connectivity of the brain.

7.2.3   Evolution: Multilevel Selection

There is a heated debate on the one hand about whether selection takes place only in regard to individuals or also in relation to groups, leading to a large literature on cheaters, cooperation, and defection, and on the other hand whether selection can be regarded as acting only on genes with all the other levels going along for the ride as epiphenomena, or it is an essentially multilevel affair. The former relates to proposals for group selection and kin selection ('inclusive fitness theory'); the latter leads to arguments about what are the true replicators, and regards developmental biology as epiphenomena carried along by the underlying genetic mechanisms.

The previous section has argued that selection must certainly be multilevel as regards the physiological mechanisms of the body, and this is made explicit by Noble (2008, 2012). As regards human individuals and groups, we believe selection must also be multilevel, because as well as there being individual features that enhance the likelihood of survival (such as strength, speed of running, or intelligence), there are also group features that enhance survival prospects such as the ability to cooperate and communicate in such a way as to develop superior technology (Bronowski 2013). Sterelny (2014, pp. xii–xiv) expresses this fundamental effect as follows:

> Human cognitive competence is a collective achievement and a collective legacy . . . It remains likely that selection on groups (especially on culturally defined groups) has been important in human evolution . . . The expansion of cross-generational cultural learning in the human lineage is a core cause of the increasing phenotypic difference between humans (ancient and modern) and the great apes.

Selection for this group advantage then chains down to individuals who have propensities to function well in groups (because of their emotional and intellectual attributes) and then down to genotypes that will provide developmental programmes leading to the emergence of such individuals. This will not be a selection process for specific genes, but for genotypes in an equivalence class that will lead to such beneficial results (Ellis 2016). We emphasize that we are not here basing our conclusion on mathematical models, but on the nature of the causal mechanisms at play. Any mathematical or statistical models used to test such a viewpoint must adequately represent the multilevel mechanisms just discussed.

7.2.4 Development: Epigenetics and Contextual Effects

Implicit in the usual evolutionary psychology discussions is the reductionist bottom-up paradigm: all the real work takes place at the lower (physical) level, specifically at the level of genes, and all the higher (biological and psychological) levels are epiphenomena. However, this ignores all the top-down effects that occur in the real world, from physics to molecular biology to neurophysiology to psychology and society (Ellis 2016). It also takes a naïve view as regards the complexity of the real relation between genes and behaviour (Moore 2015; Tabery 2015; Schaffner 2016).

In fact, developmental processes (Wolpert 2002; Gilbert 2006) are crucially based in contextual effects such as positional information, and rely on epigenetic effects (Gilbert and Epel 2009; Moore 2015), for example based in DNA methylation, for their effectiveness. This is a form of top-down causation (Noble 2008). In the developing mind, such effects shape synaptic strengths (Wolpert 2002; Kandel 2005, 2006), in contrast to the purely bottom-up gene-based processes envisaged in evolutionary psychology texts.

7.2.5 Humankind

There is still much debate about what were the key physiological and social differences that led to the rise of Homo sapiens through development of intelligence and technology, in contrast to the other hominids. We agree broadly with those proposing that the crucial difference is captured in some form of Social Brain Hypothesis (Dunbar 2014) or Social Intelligence Hypothesis (Sterelny 2014). As stated by Sterelny (2014, pp. xi, xii):

> In explaining most human cognitive competence, I emphasize the power of learning mechanisms rather than preinstalled, specific information ... coevolutionary positive feedback loops are responsible for the large and rapid phenotypic divergence between us and our closest living relatives.

Niche construction takes place in this context because society creates social and physical structures which are extensions of the mind – indeed, the mind does not only organize the brain; it uses external material objects to extend its cognitive powers, and they become part of its daily functioning (Clark and Chalmers 1998; Clark 2008). Thus, our minds create contexts which then shape the development, and in the longer term the evolution, of our brains. Sterelny (2014, p. xii) puts it this way: 'Human cognitive competence often depends on organizing the physical environment in ways that enhance our information processing capacities.'

7.2.6   The Overall View

Griffiths and Stotz (2000) summarize it all this way:

> The developmental systems perspective in biology is intended to replace the idea of a genetic program. This new perspective is strongly convergent with recent work in psychology on situated/embodied cognition and on the role of external scaffolding in cognitive development. Cognitive processes, including those which can be explained in evolutionary terms, are not inherited or produced in accordance with an inherited program. Instead, they are constructed in each generation through the interaction of a range of developmental resources. The attractors which emerge during development and explain robust and/ or widespread outcomes are themselves constructed during the process. At no stage is there an explanatory stopping point where some resources control or program the rest of the developmental cascade. Human nature is a description of how things generally turn out, not an explanation of why they turn out that way. Finally, we suggest that what is distinctive about human development is its degree of reliance on external scaffolding.

This is consistent with what we have presented in the aforementioned discussion.

7.3   THE KEY ROLE OF EMOTIONS

What is missing in virtually all of these analyses (on both sides of the Evolutionary Psychology debate) is the crucial role that is played by *emotions*. The competing and converging analyses almost all tend to focus on *cognitive* abilities, meaning the ability to rationally understand alternatives and calculate 'best' options according to some payoff criterion, as envisaged in standard economic theory and game theory, instead of acknowledging the crucial role played by emotions in our action choices. Even the growing literature on cognitive biases and failures of rational choice (Kahneman 2011) still focuses on the issue as if the process is indeed at bottom one of rational choice, calculated in terms of various trade-offs, when in reality it is usually some kind of emotional satisfaction that drives choice in the first place, modified to some degree by rational cognition. This is 'the law of affect' (Panksepp et al. In press). In many cases 'rational choices' are in fact rationalizations of choices made on non-rational grounds.

The exception to this general tendency to ignore the role of emotions in evolutionary psychology is, firstly, the work of Panksepp and Panksepp (2000, 2001) and Panksepp and Biven (2012), who develop a viewpoint very similar to what we present here. Strangely, they have not had much impact in the Evolutionary Psychology literature. Secondly, is the book by Lee et al. (2009), which adopts a view very similar to that in this book as regards the importance of emotions and the associated neural systems in terms of their relation to evolution and the acquisition of language.

7.3.1 Developmental History

Emotional systems firstly shape our immediate reactions through the effects of neurotransmitters and neuromodulators, but secondly shape neural network connectivity and strengths through processes of Neuronal Group Selection (Edelman 1989, 1992; Ellis and Toronchuk 2005). Thus, emotions crucially shape both behaviour and development of cognition (Damasio 1994, 1999).

7.3.2 Evolutionary History

Because of this mechanism, emotions are the lynchpin between experience and cognitive development. The implication is that any discussion of the evolutionary history of humanity that omits the role of the emotion systems is missing the key factor that underlies how development takes place, and hence shapes our mental evolutionary trajectory. Because survival is based in developmental outcomes, evolutionary history was driven successively by instinctual, social-emotional, and then intellectual development, as these different capacities became available.

This is reflected in the classical but oversimplified triune brain structure (Figure 2.1), where, as pointed out by McLean (1989), we in effect have three interacting brains stacked on top of each other, reflecting the order of their evolutionary development. The 'reptilian' systems evolved to give stereotyped survival behaviours, which are valuable, but sometimes also non-adaptive. They don't adjust to the current environment. The limbic primary emotion systems developed in order to give survival more nuanced guidance in an adaptive way, based on life experiences. Through altering network weights in the cortex, these shape patterns of responses in the current context as we experience local conditions. These are flexible adaptive developmental systems, operating in parallel to the fixed-response patterns embodied in the so-called reptilian brain. The neocortex evolved to provide the additional advantages of rational thought and planning, adapting the stereotyped action tendencies of the basal ganglia and other automatized subcortical systems.

Phylogeny indeed does roughly recapitulate ontogeny in terms of the relation between these particular physical structures and our evolutionary history. The reason is that ontogeny *creates* phylogeny: 'Ontogeny is the mechanical cause of phylogeny. And it must be so, for ontogeny is a mechanical process, while phylogeny is a historical phenomenon' (quote from Lovtrup 1984 in Sanson and Brandon 2007, p. 25).

7.3.3   Emotions and Brain Modules

As a consequence, the limbic system and associated affective systems are innate modules, selected for and coded for in the genotype because of their crucial role in brain function, development, and evolution. Any theory of brain modules must account for them – as our analysis above does. This agrees with Fodor's account of brain modules (Fodor 1983, 2000). It should be a primary objective of evolutionary psychology to account for the natural selection of *these* structures – but they are ignored by almost all in the literature, except by Panksepp and his colleagues.

7.4   LEARNING IMPLICATIONS

Any theory of brain function necessarily has educational implications (Goswami 2004; Ansari and Coch 2006). We will pick up just two specific areas where the idea of innate cognitive modules has been suggested to have educational implications: namely as regards supposed folk psychology, folk biology, and folk physics modules (Geary 2008), and as regards teaching reading and writing (Shaywitz 2003). If such innate modules do not exist, as we claim here, obviously the educational implications will be different. We look first at Geary's claims in this section, and then at Shaywitz's claims in the next. Finally, we comment more broadly on the educational implications of the fact that emotions underlie brain plasticity, as explained above.

7.4.1   Education and Evolutionary Theory

Possible implications for educational policy are proposed in particular in 'An evolutionarily informed education science' by David Geary (2008), hereafter referred to as EIES. Much else has been written on the topic, but this paper has the virtue of being a more-or-less self-contained, rather complete description of the programme and its basic ideas. A response has previously been given by one of us (Ellis 2008); here we elaborate on that response in a different way.

While we agree with a lot of what Geary says, we also disagree with essential points in his proposal. He says:

> The integration of evolutionary theory into the social sciences has been slow and contentious, but nevertheless has been successfully used to frame empirical findings and generate testable hypotheses in areas ranging from mate choice to morality (see Buss, 2005). Cultural influences, such as a parental socialization, mores, and so forth, are a common counter argument to the influence of evolved biases in human behaviour, but this is unnecessary.
>
> (EIES, p. 179)

It seems quite apparent that the huge amount of evidence for brain plasticity contradicts the last phrase, and much of the evolutionary psychology literature recognizes this tension. Indeed, Geary seems to backtrack on his position on the following page. He states there: 'The gist is that the evolution of the human mind and brain resulted from the advantages that gradually emerged as a result of our ancestors' ability to modify (e.g., building shelters, dams) and control ecologies and to cope with rapidly changing social dynamics' (EIES, p. 180). This is in line with our discussions in previous chapters of this book, and depends crucially on brain plasticity rather than inborn behavioural patterns or understandings, petrified as responses to some specific supposed environment of evolutionary adaptedness (EEA).

As regards innate cognitive systems, Geary says (EIES, p. 180):

> Human brain and cognitive systems that have evolved to attend to, process, and guide behavioral response to evolutionarily significant information compose biologically primary or core domains of human cognition, and coalesce around folk psychology, folk biology, and folk physics ... These are predicted to be modular to the extent that they are biased to process specific forms of information, and they are predicted to be plastic to the extent that sensitivity to variation in the corresponding information patterns provides an advantage.

He then splits these three domains up into many subdomains. The folk biological modules orient attention towards important features of the biological world, with submodules specialized on flora and on fauna. The folk physical systems support navigation, the formation of mental representations of physical features of the ecology, and the construction of tools. They are not experienced as explicit data; rather, the corresponding information is processed implicitly and the behavioural component is more-or-less automatically executed. However, the evidence he brings to support the modularity claimed is behavioural, not anatomical. There is no evidence whatever of brain regions specialized for folk physics as opposed to folk biology as opposed to folk psychology. Such innate modules simply do not exist as physical entities.

7.4.2   Innate Modules versus Intuition

The key question here is why behavioural patterns (which certainly exist) are supposed to arise from innate brain modules. Is there another explanation? There is no evidence that such *innate* cognitive modules exist as psychological entities: they are just hypothesized to fit a particular evolutionary story. It is worth quoting what Geary says about development of evolved cognitive mechanisms (EIES, p. 182):

> Folk systems evolved to cope with information and conditions that are consistent across generations and within lifetimes. As shown by the left side of Figure 2,[1] these mechanisms guide attention to and enable the quick processing of corresponding information and more or less automatic behavioral rule of thumb responses. The result is that most of the forms of information that were encountered in day-to-day living during our evolutionary history are processed automatically and with little cognitive effort. There are, however, situations in which evolved responses are not sufficient; heuristics often lead to attributional errors (Tversky & Kahneman, 1974), and behavioral strategies do not always lead to the desired outcome. These are represented by the right side of Figure 2: If the evolution of the human brain and mind was driven in part by the need to deal with rapid change in ecological or social conditions, then brain and cognitive systems that function to mentally represent and manipulate dynamic change in information patterns are predicted to evolve.

This gets it just right, except for the key point that the 'folk systems' are not evolved systems; they are developed functions. He is here describing *intuition*, based in our life experiences, not pre-wired cognitive modules. Intuition is our automatized distillation of our previous experience,

---

[1] Reproduced as Figure 7.2 below.

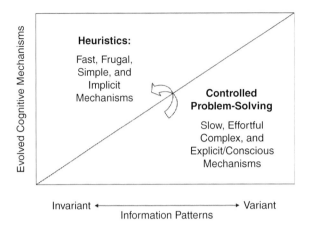

FIGURE 7.2 The way conscious problem-solving routines get embodied in intuitive problem-solving patterns. This is the source of effective folk understandings and behaviour. Whether the term 'modules' is appropriate is a moot question
From *The Origin of Mind: Evolution of Brain, Cognition, and General Intelligence*, by D. C. Geary (p. 168), 2005, Washington, DC: American Psychological Association. Copyright 2005 by the American Psychological Association. Reprinted with permission.

packaged for fast analysis and response (Myers 2003). It is not inherited, for how could the intuition of a fighter pilot, a brain surgeon, or a basketball player be genetically determined?

Evolved mechanisms enable humans to cope with and learn from evolutionarily novel situations, and then repetitive successful patterns of problem-solving behaviour get automatized so they can be rapidly deployed without conscious thought. Geary characterizes well how this happens (EIES, p. 183): 'The result is represented by the arrow at the center of Figure 2,[2] that is, the transfer of information, procedures, and heuristics learned from effortful, controlled problem solving to long-term memory, including semantic and procedural memory.' The result is to *create* effective folk modules of the kind described by Geary, as a result of our experiences; no innate modules are needed for this to happen. These modules have universal characteristics because all humans face the same set of basic problems (where to get food, how to find a mate, how to contend with other people, and so on). They have many differences, too, because different cultures solve these problems in different ways, within the limits of what is possible.

[2] Figure 7.2 here.

Geary proclaims the existence of such modules but (i) does not give any proof that they are in fact physical modules, rather than temporary coalitions of different brain domains as the need arises, (ii) does not give any proof that they are innate rather than learned, (iii) does not clearly distinguish supposed cortical (cognitive) modules from pre- and sub-cortical (sensory-motor and affective) modules. On our view, such capacities exist because of the inbuilt developmental systems that inevitably lead to their coming in to being, and determine their specific nature in the context of ongoing experiences of the unique physical, ecological, and social environments in which we live. All such environments have universal features that lead to universal aspects of these capacities. They also differ in many ways, leading to the many differences recognized by anthropologists and sociologists.

A main claim made by Geary is that

> The ability to inhibit folk systems and engage in controlled problem solving are defining features of the human brain and mind and are the key to understanding our extraordinary ability to create and to learn evolutionarily novel information. [T]he core of these mechanisms is conscious psychological simulations, and working memory and controlled problem solving.
>
> (EIES, p. 183, also 188)

The second part is fine. But if there are no innate neocortical modules, as we argue, then there is a problem with the first part of this statement.

7.4.3   Primary and Secondary Abilities

Central to this argument is the distinction between what Geary labels as primary and secondary abilities and learning (EIES, pp. 188–189), the former being natural because they are inbuilt through evolutionary processes that adapt to conditions in the supposed EEA, and the latter being unnatural because they are based in cultural practices and arise at later times. There are a number of problems here. Firstly, there was no single EAA: our ancestors adapted to a whole variety of different contexts including the African savannah but also sea shores and semi deserts, where many survival needs were quite different. Furthermore, if there is a module for language, why is there not one for fire-building, for example, or cooking, or fishing, or farming, or flint tool-making? These have all been important in evolutionary development, at about the same era, and indeed many of them have been claimed to be important for language development.

Flint tool-making appeared throughout the world over a considerable period of human history, and then disappeared again, having outlived its 'secondary' adaptive usefulness. Language, by contrast, is presumed to be 'primary' (natural; not based in cultural practices). But the most important issue is that this is the wrong distinction. There is indeed a distinction such as Geary proposes between subjects that are easy to learn and those that are more difficult. That distinction, however, is between *pattern-based* understandings, which neural networks are beautifully adapted to, and *rule-based* understandings, which can indeed be handled by neural networks, but which are not the natural way they operate. The rise of cognitive understanding is to a large extent the discovery of rules, firstly qualitative and then quantitative, that capture or order the experiences we encounter. We need intergenerational education for two reasons: (1) to pass on knowledge of data and patterns that has been accumulated through the experience of previous generations; (2) to pass on the understanding of how to encapsulate such experiences in rule-based systems. Neither is related to innate cognitive modules. It is in order to pass on these topics in a modern society, with its wealth of technological knowledge, that we need a formal educational system.

Many of the understandings we arrive at by scientific exploration are counter-intuitive, and indeed at first sight contradicted by daily experience, which experience is well incorporated in the understandings and internal models of the physical and biological world which we develop through our own life experiences. These understandings are what Geary labels as 'folk physics' and 'folk biology'. We do indeed have to learn to modify those understandings in the light of scientific knowledge,[3] so in that sense Geary's claim above is correct. But that is not because they have been passed down to us genetically from our ancestors; it is because they are indeed the way we experience the world as we interact with it, and we have learnt that that is the case through those experiences. They are effective theories that successfully encapsulate our interactions with our environment. Goswami and Bryant (2007, pp. 4–7) show how this happens in the three areas of naïve physics, biology, and psychology, corresponding to Geary's claimed folk systems.

Thus, when Geary claims (EIES, p. 194) that self-initiated behavioural experiences 'provide the social and ecological feedback needed to adjust

---

[3] For example, Aristotle's form of physics is the 'obviously' correct form, because it is supported by so much data from daily life. It took 1,000 years to arrive at Newton's counter-intuitive laws of motion.

modular architecture to variation in information patterns in these domains', that is correct, but they are not adjusting ancestrally determined folk theories, as he envisages: they are rather the basis for adjusting our own developing theories in response to our experiences. That is nothing other than the usual basic process of learning which, when formalized, becomes the scientific method (Gopnik et al. 2000).

7.4.4 Evolutionary Educational Psychology

According to Geary (EIES, p. 185), Evolutionary Educational Psychology is the study of the relation between folk knowledge and abilities and accompanying inferential and attributional biases as these influence academic learning in evolutionarily novel cultural contexts, especially schools. The fundamental premises are that

(a) these primary abilities are modifiable, but only within inherent constraints;

(b) children are inherently motivated to learn in folk domains, with the associated attentional and behavioural biases resulting in experiences that automatically and implicitly flesh out and adapt these systems to local conditions; and

(c) there are evolved aspects of mind and brain – the function of which is to enable people to cope with within-lifetime variation in social and ecological conditions. These mechanisms operate by enabling people to generate mental representations (predictions) of potential future conditions and then rehearse behaviours to cope with potential variation in these conditions. These include the core components of fluid intelligence and are the key to understanding secondary learning.

Our view, rather, is that

(a) aspects of mind and brain have evolved to provide developmental processes that facilitate the development of folk psychology, folk biology, and folk physics because of the profound nature of brain plasticity;

(b) children are inherently motivated to learn because of the properties of some of the primary emotion systems resulting in experiences that automatically and implicitly develop and adapt these systems to local conditions;

(c) brain plasticity at both micro and macro levels are evolved aspects of the brain – the function of which is to enable people to cope with local social and ecological conditions, as it is the basis of all learning;

(d) cognitive consciousness and the core components of fluid intelligence enable generation of mental representations of potential future conditions and rehearsal of behaviours to cope with these conditions.

Geary continues:

> The gist is that knowledge and expertise that prove to be useful in the social milieu or ecology in which the group is situated are retained and transferred across generations. The transfer occurs in the form of cultural artifacts, such as books, or learning traditions, such as apprenticeships. Across generations, the store of cultural knowledge accumulates. The result is a gap between accumulating cultural innovations and knowledge and the forms of folk knowledge and abilities that epigenetically emerge with children's self-initiated activities. There must, of course, be an evolved potential to learn evolutionarily novel information and an associated bias to seek novelty (EIES, p. 18).

This is correct, except for the phrase 'the forms of folk knowledge and abilities that epigenetically emerge'. There are none; 'that epigenetically emerge' should rather be 'that emerge developmentally'. Any study of such processes must take seriously the multiple levels of organization involved in the mind–brain–education nexus, and take seriously both traditional education research and traditional cognitive and affective neuroscience research (Ansari and Coch 2006; Willis 2008).

7.4.5 Learning and Motivation

As regards motivation to learn, Geary states (EIES, p. 186):

> If the complexities of social dynamics are the key to understanding the evolution of the human mind and brain, then a core motivational bias during development will be to engage in activities that flesh out knowledge related to the self, social relationships, and group dynamics – the core folk psychological domains.

Indeed. But he does not point out that motivation is mainly an emotional issue, not an intellectual one. From our viewpoint, the primary educational drivers are basic emotion systems (see Chapter 6), such as

- the SEEKING system, driving the desire to explore (and understand),
- the PLAY system, driving the desire to experiment and test limits,
- the RANKING or DOMINANCE system, driven by competition to be top.

Now some of the motivation to learn will rather be through cognitive willpower, a decision to do the hard work necessary to learn and master difficult subjects; but that willpower has to be sustained by some emotional energy. PLAY supports a key aspect of learning (which is why it has resulted in existence of a genetically determined primary emotional system); but you don't often play because you *think* you should play, you play because you *want* to play. Similarly, if you work hard at sport or an academic subject in order to be top, it is not because you *think* you want to come first; it is because you do indeed *want* to come first; and that is where the emotional energy to do the hard work comes from. Apart from the general cognitive capacities of the cortex, it is these primary emotion systems that are the real evolutionary heritage facilitating learning. They should therefore be of major concern to any evolutionary educational theory. This link needs to be developed further. Geary states (EIES, p. 191):

> Children's evolved behavioral biases, such as social play, and their observation of and learning from culturally successful adults results in the automatic and effortless modification of folk systems and the learning of the forms of culturally important activities, such as hunting, that have a long evolutionary history. For these domains and activities, there are corresponding motivational biases that ensure that children engage in the necessary activities. If we assume that children are inherently motivated to learn in secondary domains and learn them as effortlessly as they learn in primary domains, then we risk undervaluing the importance of focus and effort for secondary learning. The necessity of focus and effort follows directly from the attentional and inhibitory working memory mechanisms that I proposed evolved for secondary learning (Geary, 2005). Without an explicit assumption that learning will require effort, we risk having children assume that school learning will occur effortlessly. When effort is required for learning and children begin to experience failure, they are at risk for making attributions that may undermine their later engagement with school.

The problem with such theories is that there is no evidence whatever for either a cognitive or motivational module associated with actions such as hunting. Indeed, juvenile bushmen are *taught* hunting, based in the skill of tracking (Liebenberg 1990), by their elders; and this is a well-developed social process; it is not innate. It is this kind of unsupported claim that leads to the negative perception of evolutionary psychology as being based in 'just-so' stories. Geary's point about 'secondary learning' is valid if we replace the concept of secondary learning with that of rule- or logic-based learning, as discussed earlier, and look for the motivational biases in the primary and secondary emotions, and particularly the primary emotion systems, for whose existence there is excellent evidence, as a starting point. The important further task is to relate the positive secondary emotions (such as pride) with educational practice in order to persuade children to pay the necessary attention and devote the effort required for the task.

7.5 LEARNING WRITTEN AND SPOKEN LANGUAGE

A crucially important issue in education is how children learn to read and write. A strong claim has been made (on the basis of evolutionary psychology ideas) that spoken language is easy to learn because innate language modules make such learning natural for human beings, whereas learning written language is difficult to learn because it is 'unnatural' in an evolutionary sense; therefore, different teaching methods should be used in that case. It is suggested that this supports an essentially bottom-up, phonics-based teaching method (Shaywitz 2003; Shaywitz and Shaywitz 2005, 2008). But if there are no innate language modules, this argument does not hold. The alternate view is that the processes of learning spoken and written language are essentially the same, both being ongoing explorations of symbolic systems capable of representing the world around us, albeit realized in different modalities. If the learning conditions are right, both are motivated by the desire to understand interesting and important communication events in the growing child's life, and learning can take place on the basis of informal feedback just as well as with formal learning procedures (Bloch 1997). In particular, the implication that the teaching of reading and writing must be undertaken basically in a bottom-up, phonics-based way does not hold (Goodman et al. 2016). This is discussed in depth in Ellis (2016), Section 8.6, which was written with Carole Bloch, who helped shape what follows.

It is crucial to recognize here the larger picture in such studies. Hruby and Goswami (2011) point out,

> As literacy scholars have long appreciated, reading is more than just the mental processes inside the head of a reader. Social, linguistic, and cultural factors all play a role both during a reading event and in reading development over time. Current developmental science has

suggested that these contextual factors do not just happen to a reader, but are aspects of a developing child's social and cultural environment, a symbolic landscape that the child learns to appropriate, represent, and negotiate in a generally functional and eventually strategic fashion.

This is in line with the view of the reading process of Kenneth Goodman and colleagues (Goodman et al. 2016), emphasizing that decoding text is one aspect of a complex meaning-making process: it is a psycho-linguistic guessing game, based on context and partial information. But this is true of the spoken word as well; the same contextual processes are at work in both cases. Evolution has prepared us to be social animals, and given us developmental abilities that can adjust to whatever communication channel is available. It has not favoured one channel (speaking, writing, or signing) over another; the fact that most people normally learn to speak first is the result of the context in which we are raised (a carer who continually speaks to us in meaningful ways) together with our possessing normal hearing and speaking abilities (enabling us to hear and respond).

7.5.1   Evolutionary Bases?

The view of reading as presented from an evolutionary psychology viewpoint is summarized by Shaywitz as follows (Shaywitz 2003, p. 50):

> Reading is not built into our genes, there is no reading module wired into the human brain. In order to read, man has to take advantage of what nature has provided: a biological module for language. For the object of the readers attention (print) to gain entry to the language module, a truly extraordinary transformation must occur. The reader must somehow convert the print on the page into a linguistic code – the phonetic code, the only code recognized and accepted by the language system. However, unlike the particles of spoken language, the letters of the alphabet have no inherent linguistic connotation.

This is simply wrong. Although the brain is language-ready when we are born, there is no inbuilt biological module for language in the cortex (Chapter 7). The few relevant examples from the literature demonstrate how children who are not exposed to speech early on normally have serious difficulties learning to speak (Hudson 2000). Rather, there is a basic ability to identify patterns in our environment and name them, plus an emotional predisposition that motivates us to learn language in order to communicate our needs and desires, particularly with our caregivers (Greenspan and

Shanker 2004). It is not true that the human brain is hard-wired to process spoken language but not written language. Both are learnt by the same kinds of pattern recognition and association abilities of the brain that underlie all learning (Frith 2007), both proceeding by the same method of searching for meaning and experimentation. It is just that reading and writing are less immediately social.

The language system recognizes phonetic and printed codes equally, once it has been trained in comprehending these. The quote above arbitrarily assigns 'linguistic connotation' to the one and not the other. But they are just different representations of the same concepts; they are equally valid as linguistic representations. Both are arbitrary codes for ideas. The mapping between them (phonics to written words) is a map between two arbitrary representations. Neither is more fundamental than the other, even though we normally learn one before the other. That is a result of developmental situations; specifically, that the mother's speech is already heard by the developing foetus when in the womb, whereas a child has to learn to see before it can learn to read. Also, a child usually experiences a large amount of spoken interaction with its primary caregiver at a very early age but much less interaction with written or printed language. That stimulation usually comes much later, after oral language understanding is well underway; and reading/writing is more solitary than listening/speaking.

The implication of all this is that the underlying language learning propensity is a universal one which involves the learner in a holistic search for personal meaning and a drive to make meaning from the moment s/he encounters it and begins engaging in social communication and self expression. ('This is associated with that; this predicts that; this leads to that', etc.) While written and oral language are not identical, they are learned in the same fundamental way, and the brain then automatically translates words between them, recognizing that they are just different physical instantiations of the same idea.

7.5.2 Language Modalities

Our genetic heritage is a plastic brain that, through developmental mechanisms, has language acquisition abilities but not inborn ready-to-use linguistic rules. Normally spoken language is developed first, because that is the form of communication that envelops the infant. It can then be expressed in various modalities, specifically spoken words, sign language, or written words. As stated by Pinker in Christiansen and Kirby (2005, p. 17): 'a word is an arbitrary sign: a connection between a signal and a concept shared by members of the

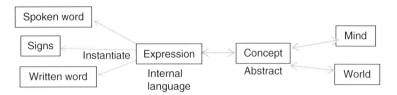

FIGURE 7.3 Spoken and written languages are different instantiations of the same expressions representing abstract concepts. Any associated brain modules arise developmentally, as they cannot have been genetically determined. Once the link is learnt, one does not have to go via written words to understand the spoken words

community'. But that signal can be instantiated in different ways: in spoken words, sign language, or written words. The link is illustrated in Figure 7.3.

The relation is described as follows by Huybregts et al. (2016):

> Language as an internal cognitive system must be distinguished from its externalisation as speech or sign. Internal language involves a wide array of hierarchically structured expressions that describe complex concepts and intentions. To convert concepts into speech, the syntactic hierarchical structure must be 'flattened' into a linear sequence of wordlike elements. The externalisation process, whether the words take the form of speech or sign, is a secondary process that evolved more recently than internal cognition.

This applies equally to writing. In this sense, speech, signing and writing are equally secondary processes. The brain is language-ready, but not hard-wired to use any particular language modality. Sign language (Stokoe 1960) is just as natural (or unnatural) as spoken or written language. Deaf children can learn sign language without hearing any spoken language, and this happens just as easily as normal language acquisition; according to Peperkamp and Mehle (1999), 'there is evidence suggesting that the acquisition of signed languages is equally fast and follows the same developmental path as that of spoken languages'.[4] Swisher (1987) comments that sign languages are different in some ways from spoken languages because of the constraints and possibilities afforded by the visual-gestural modality, yet they remain fundamentally similar to spoken languages in many ways. Sign languages (like spoken ones) have syntactic, semantic, morphological, and phonological levels of

---

[4] 'A deaf child born to parents who are deaf and who already use American Sign Language (ASL) will begin to acquire ASL as naturally as a hearing child picks up spoken language from hearing parents.' www.nidcd.nih.gov/health/american-sign-language. Butler (1980) gives the story of an individual child facing such a journey.

analysis, and they are used to accomplish the same communicative functions. As to spoken language, for deaf people it is conveyed by mouth shape ('lip reading'), i.e. by a different instantiation than sound. This is, therefore, still another symbolization of the same underlying language system (Figure 7.3).

What is the difference between brain domains involved in spoken and written language? Perfetti and Frishkoff (2009) state the following:

> Comprehension involves not one mental model, but two . . . A text base amounts to a representation of meaning that is close to the language of the text, essentially amodal and propositional. In contrast, a situation model comprises nonpropositional and nonverbal information, and may include modality specific (e.g., visual–spatial), as well as semantic representations . . . There should be no surprise to learn that the components of text processing are distributed rather than localized. They depend fundamentally on processes of information encoding, memory, and retrieval, along with basic left hemisphere language processes . . . the ironic conclusion is that the only special structures for text processing are those that are special for language processing. Beyond these, text processing requires broadly distributed brain resources for the various cognitive, social, and affective processes that are integral to language and communication, including domain general processes for memory updating that involve the (anterior and posterior) cingulate cortex.

Price and Friston (2007) describe the issue of brain domains as follows:

> Structure – function relationships can be described at multiple levels. Each level may be appropriate in a different context. Nevertheless, we argue that it is more useful to label a region with a function that explains all patterns of activation. As an example, we have described the range of tasks that the posterior lateral fusiform is engaged by, and proposed that the common denominator is a role in sensorimotor integration. Understandably, a sensorimotor integration label may not be particularly attractive to cognitive psychologists as it does not correspond to any of the components hypothesised to be involved in reading or object processing. Nevertheless, it does provide a prediction about the conditions under which the left posterior lateral fusiform area responds. In this sense the sensorimotor label is more useful than task-specific labels.

Again, lipreading is the same kind of holistic enterprise as reading or listening. According to lipreading.org:[5]

---

[5] www.lipreading.org/beginners-guide-to-lipreading, and see http://video.nationalgeo graphic.com/video/short-film-showcase/watch-what-its-like-to-read-lips.

- Lip reading allows you to 'listen' to a speaker by watching the speaker's face to figure out their speech patterns, movements, gestures and expressions. Often called 'a third ear', lip reading goes beyond simply reading the lips of a speaker to decipher individual words.
- Learning to lip read involves developing and practicing certain skills that can make the process much easier and more effective. These include:
    - Learning to use the cues provided by the movements of the speaker's mouth, teeth and tongue
    - Reading and evaluating the information provided by facial expressions, body language and gestures in conjunction with the words being said
    - Using vision to assist with listening
    - Using prior knowledge to fill in the gaps that can occur in understanding since it is impossible to read every word said.

Interestingly, it is easier to read longer words and whole sentences than shorter words.

These holistic principles apply also to listening and, indeed, apart from those aspects involving vision, to all modes of comprehending language. They are just different instantiations of the same basic process. One is, once again, reminded of Sur's (2000) experimental finding in ferrets.

Cohen and Dehaene (2004) write:

> Is there specialization for visual word recognition within the visual ventral stream of literate human adults? We review the evidence for a specialized visual word form area and critically examine some of the arguments recently placed against this hypothesis . . . We conclude that learning to read results in the progressive development of an inferotemporal region increasingly responsive to visual words, which is aptly named the visual word form area (VWFA).

But that is how learning to speak works as well: learning to understand speech results in the progressive development of a lateral temporal region increasingly responsive to spoken words. This takes place not by invoking an innate language module, but (Chang, Dell, and Bock 2006) by learning through language processing involving incremental prediction, which is carried out by the production system. Prediction necessarily leads to prediction error, which drives all ongoing learning, including both adaptive adjustment to the mature language processing system and language acquisition.

This is part of the broad understanding of the brain as using a hier-archical generative model that aims to minimize prediction error within a bidirectional cascade of cortical processing (Clark 2013). This is in line also with the idea of *neuroconstructivism,* the guiding principle of which is context dependence, within and between levels of organization, resulting in partial representations distributed across distinct functional circuits (Westerman et al. 2007; Sirois et al. 2008).

7.5.3 Educational Implications

Shaywitz proposes that the implications of her views regarding the needs of children with reading difficulties are that an essentially phonics-based approach is necessary for all children, in terms of teaching reading and writing. The claim is that normal as well as dyslexic students learn to read faster through methods that break down words into small segments (phonics). Abadzi expresses this view as follows:

> to attain high-level skills, learners must first master component tasks in small bits. To increase performance speed and accuracy, practice and feedback for error correction are necessary. Only with manageable tasks and feedback can learners progress to more complex skills.
>
> (Abadzi 2006, p. 21)

That view, however, does not take into account how reading actually takes place, as demonstrated by a variety of observations of readers engaged with real text (Goodman et al. 2016). Note that while experiments based on single words or nonsense phonemes are able to throw light on some of the underlying mechanisms, they are simply unable to elucidate how reading of meaningful texts takes place, because that is a highly contextual activity where prediction of what should come next is a key factor and the reading 'particles' are phrases rather than phonemes.

Geary (EIES, pp. 190–191) states his view on the topic thus:

> Children's natural interest in novelty and their motivation to learn their culture will get them started but is not predicted to maintain long-term academic learning, contra Rousseau and other 'romantic' approaches to education. These approaches have rested on an assumption of a smooth continuity between primary domains, such as language, and secondary domains, such as reading, and thereby assume children are inherently motivated to engage with secondary materials, such as books, and will learn to read automatically and effortlessly during this engagement. I am proposing that this is an

educationally fatal error, except perhaps during the transition from primary to secondary learning.

If there is no essential difference between what he labels as primary and secondary domains, as we maintain, this argument falls away. He further states (EIES, p. 191):

> From an evolutionary perspective the transition from pictures to print is not the same as the transition from naming real objects to naming pictures of objects. This is because print is an arbitrary set of abstract symbols that do not resemble objects in the real world much less resemble the specific objects they – specific words – represent. Of course, the word sounds for objects differ from one language to the next and are arbitrary, but the language system has evolved to easily develop associations between pronounced words of any human language and objects, people, places, and so forth, to which they refer.

We do not see the difference. Word sounds are just as arbitrary as print symbols. The process of association is essentially the same in both cases. Finally he says (EIES, p. 192):

> Given its cultural origin and recent emergence, the reading of written symbols is by definition a complex evolutionarily novel skill. On the basis of my model, learning how to read these symbols and especially to decode and blend their phonetic features is predicted to require engagement of the systems that have evolved to acquire secondary competencies ... If this proposal is correct, explicit instruction in phonetic decoding, blending, and other aspects of formal reading are predicted to be necessary for most children ... With a theoretically anchored approach to education, we can avoid these types of debilitating debates for other evolutionarily novel, secondary domains.

This omits all the conditions necessary to *motivate* children to read. Consideration of the kind of environment that is conducive to reading exploration (Bloch 2014, 2015) is crucial, as are interactive adult role models to demonstrate to children the power and point of reading and writing. One must also realize the fact that in practice reading is not a bottom-up process of assembling phonemes to create words, words to create phrases, and so on, but rather is a top-down process of prediction and psycholinguistic guessing where phoneme and even word identification is only a small part of what is going on (Smith 2004; Goodman et al. 2016). In particular, a core condition for easy access to literacy is the human use of and desire for story (Gottschalk 2012). As stated by Bloch (2015):

Motivation and know-how to do the tough and complex work of learning to read (and write) comes most easily when a child becomes riveted
over time to meaningful stories contained in writing and in what books
hold for them. It's also tough and complex work for a baby to learn to
speak. But their immature oral babbling becomes conventional talk over
a relatively short space of time because they are absolutely intent on
communicating – using their emerging language capabilities and knowledge as they learn how to share ideas with others. Learning to read and to
write can be very similar (Goodman & Goodman 2014). Children
entranced by stories find the energy and commitment to learn how
print works and how to shape it for themselves because they want to
use it – they sense its social power for them.

Above all, EIES omits reference to the experimental evidence on how
reading in fact happens, summarized by Goodman et al. (2016), which
does not fit his paradigm. It also omits data such as that of Glezer et al.
(2009), who state:

> Theories of reading have posited the existence of a neural representation
> coding for whole real words (i.e., an orthographic lexicon), but experi-
> mental support for such a representation has proved elusive. Using fMRI
> rapid adaptation techniques, we provide evidence that the human left
> ventral occipitotemporal cortex (specifically the 'visual word form area',
> VWFA) contains a representation based on neurons highly selective for
> individual real words, in contrast to current theories that posit a sub-
> lexical representation in the VWFA.

We don't read phoneme by phoneme and assemble the results into words;
just as in the case of other sensory systems (Kandel 2012), we read in a
gestalt-holistic way, which is why we can read mis-formed or ungrammatical sentences just as well as well-formed ones (Grill-Spector and Witthoft
2009). The thalamus probably plays an essential role in such sensory
processing (Alitto and Usrey 2003; Sherman 2016) through thalamo-cor-
tical loops which support a temporal context representation in the service
of predictive coding (O'Reilly et al. 2014).

7.5.4 Language and Gestalt Holism

This aspect of language and holism is also developed by Anderson et al.
(1985) in their report *Becoming a Nation of Readers: The Report of the
Commission on Reading*. The first chapter of the report stresses reading as
the process of constructing meaning from written texts. The second

chapter, on emergent literacy, argues that reading must be seen as part of a child's general language development and not as a discrete skill isolated from listening, speaking, and writing. The third chapter, on extending literacy, stresses that as proficiency develops, reading should not be thought of as a separate subject, but as integral to learning in all content areas. They go on to comment on the need for motivation to read, along the lines of what we state above.

A similar view is put by the National Council of Teachers of English (NCTE 2008), who state:

> Reading is a complex and purposeful sociocultural, cognitive, and linguistic process in which readers simultaneously use their knowledge of spoken and written language, their knowledge of the topic of the text, and their knowledge of their culture to construct meaning with text. Each of these types of knowledge impacts the sense that readers construct through print. Readers easily comprehend text with familiar language but are less successful at comprehending text with unfamiliar language. Readers easily comprehend text on familiar topics but are less successful at comprehending texts on unfamiliar topics. At the same time, the interpretations readers construct with texts as well as the types of texts they read are influenced by their life experiences.

From this basis, the foundations of learning to read follow:

> Learning to read is a life-long process. People begin developing knowledge that they will use to read during their earliest interactions with families and communities. In their pre-school years, children learn to understand and use spoken language and learn about their world through meaningful interactions with others. Children also learn about written language as more experienced readers provide meaningful demonstrations of reading and writing. Some of the earliest demonstrations they receive include reading environmental print (such as the word stop on a stop sign), making and using grocery lists, writing and reading notes, and reading and discussing childrens stories and letters from friends . . . Through these demonstrations by others, children learn the pleasures and purposes of print. They also learn to read and write their names and the names of family members. In addition, they learn vocabulary typical of written language, such as how different types of texts such as grocery lists, personal letters, and fairy tales are structured. They also learn basic concepts of print such as the message of print in books continues across pages. The more children interact with spoken and written language, the better readers they become.

This is a view of reading that is much deeper than that supposed by or derived from evolutionary psychology. It is part of the much larger picture of how all sensory modes function, as explained by Kandel (2012).

7.5.5   Mathematics

Similar issues arise with regard to learning mathematics: like writing, it is claimed to be unnatural and hence to need different learning methods than learning to speak.

One should distinguish here between number sense and abstract mathematics proper. It may well be that some kind of number sense for small numbers (e.g. one, a couple, few, many) is built into pre-cortical structures, and specifically the visual-motor tectum or thalamus. Algebraic problem solving is a completely different matter. It involves the kind of formalized reasoning that is indeed unnatural because it is not the way innate neural networks operate.

There are indeed specific neocortical areas that are usually involved in mathematical thinking, for example the horizontal segment of the intra-parietal sulcus (Dehaene et al. 2003). However, principal functions of this sulcus are visuomotor tasks comprising target selections for arm and eye movements, object manipulation, and visuospatial attention (Grefkes and Fink 2005), so it is not a specifically innate *mathematical* domain. It is, however, focused on the kind of data about the world that will naturally lead to an understanding of numbers. Dehaene et al. (1999) give evidence that the human capacity for exact arithmetic depends on both linguistic competence and on visuo-spatial representations. Fair enough. This is however a far cry from developing Pythagoras' theorem, proving that the square root of two is irrational, or proving the fundamental theorem of calculus. These are indeed what might be termed secondary competences that have to be learned, as discussed above. They are part of our cultural heritage, passed on by intergenerational teaching.

7.6   EDUCATIONAL METHODS AND FEAR OF LEARNING

As there are no innate folk physics or biology modules, there is no need to 'unlearn' what misleading understandings they may be imposing on us, as claimed by Geary. Rather educational policy and implementation must adapt on the one hand to the exploratory developmental way the brain works, making mistakes on the way to getting a correct understanding, and on the other hand must take into account the crucial role of affect in the classroom and its effects on learning motivation (Willis 2008).

7.6.1   The Basic Learning Process

The basic learning process is by trial and error, by experiment and observation of the results followed by inference and adaptation. Through brain plasticity we adapt the brain to our experience as we learn for ourselves. Teachers can help in that process. But if they prioritize rote learning over creative and critical thinking and action, then this is not true learning as it is not adaptive – it is a fixed action pattern.

The challenge is to teach independent adaptive thinking that takes past experience and current knowledge into account. The paradox is that concepts, knowledge and skills have to be discovered and understood by the learner, or else the result is inadequate, partial, and leads to largely low-level thinking and learning. In addition to motivating, enticing and nurturing, an effective teaching role is thus more one of demonstrating, explaining, and creating opportunities that facilitate learning for the learner.

We are of course verging on long-standing debates about educational methods here, and will not say more about it except that claiming to solve them on the basis of artificial evolutionary psychology ideas is highly problematic.[6]

7.6.2   Teaching and the Emotional Environment

What does follow from a proper understanding of evolutionary psychology – that is, one that takes its emotional underpinnings into account as discussed above – is that the emotional context of the class is at least as important as teaching technical competence in subject material. This context can be predicted to be a major determinant of educational outcomes. Methods that discourage the basic learning process through *exploration* are regressive. We give just two examples.

7.6.2.1   *Maths Education and Fear of Learning*

It is likely that a major contributing factor of the high rate of drop-out of students in general, and girl students in particular, from mathematics

---

[6] This point is made in the responses to Geary in the special issue of *Educational Psychologist*, where his article (Geary 2008) is published.

classes is fear of mathematics. This is partly due to the reputation of the subject as being difficult, apparently propagated in particular among girls. It is also partly due to teaching methods, where mistaken attempts to get the answer result in a negative response or even some form of punishment, rather than encouragement rewarding exploration of possible options. Yes of course the right answer has to be obtained in the end, but there are often multiple ways to get there, and the student will only understand them if they have been allowed to discover the correct way by making mistakes which lead to adjustments that arise from an understanding of how they went wrong.

An encouraging milieu will make all the difference, and particularly one that encourages exploration. If mathematics raises a negative emotional response in the student, good responses are highly unlikely.

7.6.2.2 *Teaching Writing: Spelling, Composing and Fear of Learning*

A similar issue arises with regard to learning to write: are immature or unconventional efforts discouraged or punished, or are initial attempts and exploration encouraged? This is particularly true regarding spelling: if teachers give children negative messages when they make spelling mistakes, especially in the early stages of learning, this will raise negative emotions in regard to written language learning that will be detrimental for both pupils and teachers. The kind of context which nurtures literacy learning through exploration is set out by Bloch (1997, 2014, 2015), which indicates what can succeed well: motivate children through stories and personally meaningful attempts, and foster a climate where you expect them to use their growing understanding of and skill with written language. The details are taught and learned as part of this holistic process.

7.6.3 The Educational Divide

We agree with Geary that academic subjects are in general more difficult to learn than 'folk' subjects, but we disagree as to the cause of the problem. At heart it is because academic subjects are (abstract) rule based rather than (concrete) pattern based. This means that more motivation is needed to persist with these studies than in the other case, and this is also true in purely data-based subjects (memorizing facts and places, for example). Here is where emotion comes in. And that means learning policy must be based on a serious study of motivational systems, such as those described by Panksepp (1998).

7.7   REPRISE, AND WORK TO BE DONE

Finally, we return to the language issue because it has been the key point for so much other work, and then we look at what remains to be done, to develop the view outlined here.

7.7.1   Return to Chomsky and Linguistics

The view put forward in this book is mainly based in developmental biology, but it can be argued for also on other grounds. Our overall thesis as regards language modules is in accord with the views of Hilary Putnam, who engaged extensively with Chomsky in order to understand Chomsky's viewpoint (Putnam 1967). He says:

> The innateness hypothesis (henceforth, the I.H.) is a daring – or apparently daring; it may be meaningless, in which case it is not daring – hypothesis proposed by Noam Chomsky ... the I.H. is the hypothesis that the human brain is programmed at birth in some quite specific and structured aspects of human natural language.

After a technical discussion of this hypothesis, he says:

> The I.H. is supposed to justify the claim that what the linguist provides is a hypothesis about the innate intellectual equipment that a child brings to bear in language learning ... Clearly, it is the idea that these abilities and these intuitions are close to the human essence, so to speak, that gives linguistics its sex appeal, for Chomsky at least.

He summarizes the arguments advanced by Chomsky to support the I.H. as being:

(a) The ease of the child's original language learning
(b) The fact that reinforcement, 'in any interesting sense', seems to be unnecessary for language learning.
(c) The ability to 'develop the competence of the native speaker' has been said not to depend on the intelligence level
(d) 'Linguistic universals' are allegedly accounted for by the I.H.
(e) 'What else could account for language learning?' The task is so incredibly complex (analogous to learning, at least implicitly, a complicated physical theory, it is said), that it would be miraculous if even one tenth of the human race accomplished it without 'innate' assistance.

He then responds persuasively to each. We will just give two of his arguments here. As regards linguistic universals, he comments:

> A single origin for human language is certainly required by the I.H., but much weaker than the I.H. But just this consequence of the I.H. is, in fact, enough to account for 'linguistic universals'! For, if all human languages are descended from a common parent, then just such highly useful features of the common parent as the presence of some kind of quantifiers, proper names, nouns, and verbs, etc., would be expected to survive. Random variation may, indeed, alter many things; but that it should fail to strip language of proper names, or common nouns, or quantifiers, is not so surprising as to require the I.H.

This view is backed up by Deacon's argument as regards the constraints imposed by the iconic nature of language (Deacon 2003), and is also backed up by Goldberg (2016) who says:

> Much has been written about the unlikelihood of innate, syntax specific, universal knowledge of language (Universal Grammar) on the grounds that it is biologically implausible, unresponsive to cross-linguistic facts, theoretically inelegant, and implausible and unnecessary from the perspective of language acquisition. While relevant, much of this discussion fails to address the sorts of facts that generative linguists often take as evidence in favour of the Universal Grammar Hypothesis: subtle, intricate, knowledge about language that speakers implicitly know without being taught. This paper revisits a few often-cited such cases and argues that, although the facts are sometimes even more complex and subtle than is generally appreciated, appeals to Universal Grammar fail to explain the phenomena. Instead, such facts are strongly motivated by the functions of the constructions involved.

As regards the poverty of stimulus claim, Putnam responds:

> Let us consider somewhat closely the ease with which children do learn their native language. A typical mature college student seriously studying a foreign language spends three hours a week in lectures. In fourteen weeks of term he is thus exposed to forty-two hours of the language. In four years he may pick up over 300 hours of the language, very little of which is actual listening to native informants. By contrast, direct method teachers estimate that 300 hours of direct-method teaching will enable one to converse fluently in a foreign language. Certainly 600 hours – say, 300 hours of direct-method teaching and 300 hours of reading – will enable any adult to speak and read a foreign language with ease, and to use an incomparably larger vocabulary than a young child.

This is broadly in line with the claims of Greenspan and Shanker (2004). The overall conclusion is that

> the theorems of mathematics, the solutions to puzzles, etc., cannot on any theory be individually innate; what must be innate are heuristics, i.e., learning strategies ... Invoking Innateness only postpones the problem of learning; it does not solve it. Until we understand the strategies which make general learning possible – and vague talk of classes of hypotheses – and weighting functions is utterly useless here – no discussion of the limits of learning can even begin.

There are many competing theories here. It is adventurous to suggest that evolutionary psychology can give the answers, particularly when it is such a controversial approach.

What about the use of formal learning theory and Gold's theorem to show innate language modules must exist? The relation between that theory and real-world education is distant, as discussed by Johnson (2004):

> In general, the relation of Gold's Theorem to normal child language acquisition is analogous to the relation between Gödel's first incompleteness theorem and the production of calculators. Gödel's theorem show that no accurate calculator can compute every arithmetic truth. But actual calculators don't experience difficulties from this fact, since the unprovable statements are far enough away from normal operations that they don't appear in real life situations. Similarly, child language acquisition may be restricted by Gold's Theorem, but this restriction only applies to cases that don't occur in any normal environment, and thus have no practical significance ... In sum, Gold's Theorem appears interesting to cognitive science when identifiability and acquirability are confused. When we distinguish these notions, we undermine the argument that Gold's Theorem is supposed to support.

These kinds of theoretical arguments don't take seriously the real-world situation of children learning language, or other aspects of the world that they understand through the effective models they develop, that Geary calls Folk Psychology, Folk Physics, and Folk Biology. Macro brain plasticity and resultant learning does the job nicely, based in the underlying micro-plasticity, which facilitates emergent brain functioning, language acquisition, and learning to read as set out by Goodman et al. (2016). The learning process is the same in all cases.

It is, however, more taxing for subjects that involve data that cannot be acquired through informal learning in everyday social-emotional life, or abstract arguments that are rule-based rather than pattern-based. A different kind of more formally structured learning is required in these cases. Nevertheless in all cases the motivation is based in our emotion systems. Which of the kinds of educational strategies shown in Figure 8.5 will be best for specific contexts cannot be determined by evolutionary considerations; that is an issue to be settled by trial and error in real educational contexts.

Finally, what about the alleged existence of specific pre-determined brain areas for language functions? The biological evidence shows this is not the case. According to Goswami (2004):

> Neurons themselves are interchangeable in the immature system, and so dramatic differences in environment can lead to different developmental outcomes. For example, the area underpinning spoken language in hearing people (used for auditory analysis) is recruited for sign language in deaf people (visual/spatial analysis). Visual brain areas are recruited for Braille reading (tactile analysis) in blind people.

Developmental processes use brain plasticity to develop brain areas to suit the particular emerging context best. The effective modules that arise are determined in this way, not through genetic determinism. Although they of course use genes to obtain the desired results, by controlling suitable epigenetic processes that determine which gene will get read when in what location, via gene regulatory networks. As to macro-level processes:

> Simple learning mechanisms, operating in and across the human systems for perception, motor-action and cognition as they are exposed to language data as part of a social environment, suffice to drive the emergence of complex language representations ... Many of the criticisms [of the UG assumption] address generative linguistics' taking the uniquely human faculty of language and then studying it in isolation, divorced from semantics, the functions of language, and the other social, biological, experiential and cognitive aspects of humankind. This autism has two consequences. First, it concentrates the study of language on grammar, ignoring such areas as lexis, fluency, idiomaticity, pragmatics and discourse. Second, it dramatically restricts the potential findings of the study of grammar: If the investigation never looks outside of language, it can never identify any external influences on language.
>
> (Ellis 1998)

Hawkins states the issue nicely thus (Hawkins 2004, p. 181):

> Language fits nicely into the memory-prediction framework [of how the cortex functions] without any special language sauce or dedicated language machinery. Spoken and written words are just patterns in the

world, as are melodies, cars, and houses. The syntax and semantics of language are not different from the hierarchical structure of other every-day objects. And in the same way that we associate the sound of a train with the visual image of a train, we associate spoken words with our memory of their physical and semantic counterparts.

7.7.2   Taking it Forwards

The theoretical proposals made here need further development, and in particular possible avenues of further validation of the theory should be investigated by making specific experimental predictions and explorations. This might be along the lines proposed by La Cerra and Bingham (1998) and by Barrett et al. (2014). The latter suggest that the various forms of e-cognition (i.e. embodied, embedded, enactive) represent a true alterna-tive to standard computational approaches, with an emphasis on 'cognitive integration' or the 'extended mind hypothesis' in particular. This offers good promise for human psychology because it incorporates the social and historical processes that are crucial to human 'mind-making' within an evolutionarily informed framework, provided one takes emotion into account as well as cognition. The major properties of language under-standing can be naturally explained within a multi-representational hier-archical actively generative architecture whose goal is to infer the message intended by the producer, and in which predictions play a crucial role in explaining the bottom-up input (Kuperberg and Jaeger 2015).

Key issues are as follows:

1. The difference in developmental programmes underlying the hard-wired and soft-wired brain domains, as discussed above. There is a vast amount of data here; what is required is firstly pulling it together in a way that makes very clear the technical issues at stake and plausible specific developmental programme differences, and then designing experiments to test them. This is at the heart of the claims made in this book.

2. The key further missing element is what change in neural network structure made the rise of symbolic understanding and language possible: what makes the human brain language-ready, in contrast to the brains of other hominids? Specifically, what aspects of the structure and connectivity of cortex underlie firstly the labelling of a pattern of excitations, and secondly the labelling of a pattern of labels (i.e. recursion: applying the first procedure to a pattern of excitations

representing a pattern of labels). This probably has something to do with prefrontal connectivity (re-representation) and with what Edelman (1989) calls 're-entry'.

3. Further development of the ongoing debate on what aspects of the evolutionary environment and responses to it led to the development of symbolism and language. In particular, was enlarged prefrontal connectivity the cause or the outcome of this development? The key role of language, leading to its adaptive value, is probably facilitating the social acquisition, use, and transmission of ecological and technological expertise (Sterelny 2014, p. 15). Was this sufficient as a driving evolutionary force? Or was it primarily because language facilitated individual goal-directed thought? Or can they not be separated? In this connection we should also recall that language is probably based in a mode of cognition (nested abstraction) which only secondarily became a mode of communication.

4. Providing detailed observational evidence as regards the response given here to the 'Poverty of Stimulus' argument, both in qualitative terms (such as is given in Bloch 1997 and Greenspan and Shanker 2004), and in quantitative terms, detailing hours of interaction between mothers and children and the nature of those interactions.

5. Carefully structured further studies of brain plasticity, designed to test or confirm the degree of flexibility in what have been designated as areas with specific higher cognitive functions. In the case of humans this will presumably be largely through lesion studies.

6. More work on the nature of the innate primary emotion systems and associated nuclei, circuits, and neuromodulators. If these are the lynchpin of how cortical plasticity functions, as claimed here, the specific nature of these systems is a key issue for both developmental theory and evolution. In particular do the other ones piggy-back on a few basic ones? If so, how does that work? Is the variation of Panksepp's proposals by Toronchuk and Ellis (2012) correct? If not, what is? How do primary emotions relate to secondary emotions, which become key players in brain plasticity as social consciousness develops?

We believe that the biologically based viewpoint put forward in this book will provide a solid foundation for further investigations of these aspects of the nature/nurture issue, and the question as to why and how innate mental modules develop in the brain.

Appendix: Language Infinities

George Ellis and William Stoeger, SJ[1]

The ability to use spoken and written language is one of the most significant attributes that separates humans from the rest of the animal kingdom (Deacon 1997; Bickerton 2001); consequently, it is inevitably the subject of major academic disputes. In particular, there is a disjunction between those who propose a biologically based embodied-language approach (see, for example, Feldman's book *From Molecule to Metaphor* (Feldman 2008)) and those utilizing a much more abstract formal language theory (see, for example, a recent survey by Komarova and Nowak (2005), hereafter KN).

While the latter approach throws interesting light on some aspects of language (reflected, for example, in various papers published in *Nature* (Nowak, Plotkin and Jansen 2000; Nowak, Kamarova and Niyogi 2002)), one may query whether its formal nature, centring on a proposed algorithmic implementation of a Universal Grammar, adequately reflects the biological underpinnings of the workings of the human mind.

We here illustrate this unease by focusing on a strong claim made by KN: namely that there are an infinite number of languages containing an infinite number of sentences (KN, p. 320).[2] This is not just proposed as a statement about formally defined languages; it is explicitly claimed that natural languages are infinite (KN, p.323). This is based on the idea that sentences can have an unbounded length: you can just keep adding subsidiary clauses ad infinitum to obtain arbitrarily long sentences. But such a 'sentence' is not really a complete thought – until it is complete. However, it never will be, because that is what infinity means – something that is never completed! Thus, from some common points of view, it is not really a

---

[1] Deceased. Published with consent of his estate.
[2] There is in fact a whole literature on this topic, which one can access by searching for 'language is infinite' on Google; however, it is convenient to peg the present discussion on the statements in KN.

sentence to begin with. In any case this viewpoint has nothing to do with real-world biologically usable languages, for the simple reason that the human brain has finite storage capacity and only survives for a finite length of time, and so can only carry out a finite number of operations in its lifetime.[3] Hence, there is a finite limit to the length of a possible sentence in a biologically realistic language context, while sentences actually usable for communication purposes, the raison d'être of language, are very much shorter.

One can calculate an absolute limit on what a human being can possibly read in their lifetime by estimating how many words can be read by a machine doing so continuously for 24 hours a day every day for say 120 years at a rate of say 10 words a second (giving 37,843,200,000 words). This is obviously not infinite. No real person can exceed this limit in their lifetime (inter alia because they have to sleep). But in a realistic approach, one recognizes that if a sentence has meaning, the reader must remember the beginning by the time they reach the end.[4] Given the famous features of short-term memory that we can only hold 7 items in mind simultaneously on a short-term basis (Miller 1956), one can estimate that a maximum-length readily understandable sentence has 7 subclauses, each with a maximum of 7 words, so 49 words. As sentences become longer than this, they become increasingly un-understandable as a function of the sentence length, and hence unusable for communication purposes; one is probably safe in saying that a sentence more than an order of magnitude larger than this (10 × 49 = 490 words) is of no use for communication purposes and will not occur in any real language except as a possible flowery demonstration of verbal dexterity rather than being intended for genuine communication.[5]

Thus, the number of practically usable sentences in any real language is finite and they can in principle all be listed, contrary to what is envisaged by KN ('Natural languages are infinite: it is not possible to imagine a finite list that contains all English sentences', KN, p. 323). This alleged infinity is

---

[3] The same kind of restriction applies to any real digital computer; the hypothetical infinite tape of a Turing machine is equally unrealistic. In a sense this embodies a form of the halting problem.

[4] Typical advice to aspiring writers is given in www.technical-writing-course.com/essay-writing-length.html: 'Make sure you do not allow long sentences – over 40 words – to creep into your writing style . . . Faced with long sentences, readers often give up halfway through or forget the start of the sentence by the time they reach the end. The more words in a sentence, the harder it becomes to understand.'

[5] For examples of such excesses, see http://en.wikipedia.org/wiki/Longest_English_sentence. In contrast, the present (somewhat lengthy) sentence has 76 words (just compatible with the more optimistic assessment of 9 phrases of 9 words giving 81 words), and the current paragraph has 429 words. The sentence should have been split in two between 'purposes' and 'one is'.

simply not a realistic description of genuine languages as used for communication by the human species. It is true that sentences will appear in contexts where long-range dependencies occur, so meaning is not confined to single sentences. But then the maximum number of sentences that can be contained in a conversation or a book is also finite; for a single author perhaps the equivalent of 30 volumes of 1,500 pages each might be a upper limit for their coherent presentation of theories and thoughts over their entire life, so that the maximum number of combinatorial sentences in such presentations is also finite. The possible set of human thoughts expressible in written or spoken language is large but finite. As many have remarked, infinity is not just a very large number: it is a magnitude that is never attained, is always beyond reach. To be real, something has to be completed or have definite boundaries – but the essence of mathematical infinity is that it's never completed; consequently, what is complete in the real world is always finite.

This is of course a rather abstract argument, but in our view this strongly stated use of the concept of infinity in formal language theories definitively demonstrates their lack of realism as compared with embodied-language theories. It indicates that the underlying theory does not take seriously the fundamental purpose and context of language use (communication between living people).[6] Indeed, the great mathematician David Hilbert remarked that '*the infinite is nowhere to be found in reality, no matter what experiences, observations, and knowledge are appealed to*' (Hilbert 1964). We believe this stricture should be taken seriously, and used to separate fanciful from realistic theories, be they theories of language or of physics.[7]

The fundamental underlying point is that it is all very well having some mathematical theory of how the world works, such as a mathematical theory of learning, but the job of an applied mathematician is then to see if this abstract theory (in this case, Gold's Theorem, see Gold 1967) actually corresponds to what happens in the real world. The answer is no. Johnson (2000) makes this clear. He says:

> Most of this work is of interest only from the standpoint of mathematical logic or theoretical computer science ... A language can be thought of as merely the set of sentences that are grammatical in that language ... [For

---

[6] The fundamental definition of a sentence KN employs really does not represent any sentence in any language – it has neither syntax nor meaning, nor does it need to be complete.

[7] One could perhaps propose that the theories referred to here don't *really* mean infinity; they really just refer to a very large number. But that would contradict the very purpose of introducing such abstract theories: they are supposed to introduce a precision of thought that was previously lacking.

Gold's Theorem] we also need mathematically precise representations of (i) the learner's environment, (ii) the nature of the learners, including the set of hypotheses that the learner selects from, and (iii) a criterion of successful learning. (Particular representations of (i), (ii), and (iii) can be thought of as a model of learning.)

It is fantasy to suggest that such a mathematical model can adequately represent real-world learners or learning. Mathematical models are only useful if they can be shown to adequately represent aspects of the real world. That is not the situation in this particular case.

APPENDIX REFERENCES

Bickerton, D. (2001) *Language and Human Behaviour* (Seattle: University of Washington Press).

Deacon, T. (1997) *The Symbolic Species: The Co-evolution of Language and the Human Brain* (London: Penguin Books).

Feldman, J. A. (2008) *From Molecule to Metaphor: A Neural Theory of Language* (Cambridge, MA: MIT Press); www.icsi.berkeley.edu/NTL/.

Gold, E. M. (1967) 'Language identification in the limit' *Information and Control* 10:447–474.

Hilbert, D. (1964) 'On the infinite'. In P. Benacerraf and H. Putnam (Eds.), *Philosophy of Mathematics* (Englewood Cliff, NJ: Prentice Hall): 134.

Kamorova, N. L. and M. A. Nowak (2005) 'Language, learning, and evolution'. In M. H. Christensen and S. Kirby (Eds.), (Oxford: Oxford University Press): 317–337.

Johnson, K. (2000) 'Gold's theorem and cognitive science' *Philosophy of Science* 71:571–592. Available at www.lps.uci.edu/~johnsonk/Publications/Johnson.GoldsTheorem.pdf.

Miller, G. A. (1956) 'The magical number seven, plus or minus two: Some limits on our capacity for processing information' *Psychological Review* 63:81–97.

Nowak, M. A., Kamarova, N.L. and Niyogi, P. (2002) 'Computational and evolutionary aspects of language' *Nature* 417:611–617.

Nowak, M. A., Plotkin, J.B. and Jansen, V.A.A. (2000) 'The evolution of syntactic communication' *Nature* 404:495–498.

REFERENCES

Abadzi, H. (2006) *Efficient Learning for the Poor: Insights from the Frontier of Cognitive Neuroscience* (Washington, DC: World Bank).

Adams, R.A., Shipp, S. and Friston, K.J. (2013) 'Predictions not commands: Active inference in the motor system' *Brain Structure and Function* **218**:611–643.

Adger, P. and Svenonius, D. (2015) 'Linguistic explanation and domain specialization: A case study in bound variable anaphora' *Frontiers in Psychology*, 24 September 2015 | http://dx.doi.org/10.3389/fpsyg.2015.01421.

Alitto, H.J. and Martin Usrey, W. (2003) 'Corticothalamic feedback and sensory processing' *Current Opinion in Neurobiology* **13**:440–445.

Amodei, D., Anubhai, R., Battenberg, E., Case, C., Casper, J., Catanzaro, B., Chen, J., Chrzanowski, M., Coates, A., Diamos, G., Elsen, E., Engel, J., Fan, L., Fougner, C., Han, T., Hannun, A., Jun, B., LeGresley, P., Lin, L., Narang, S., Ng, A., Ozair, S., Prenger, R., Raiman, J., Satheesh, S., Seetapun, D., Sengupta, S., Wang, Y., Wang, Z., Wang, C., Xiao, B., Yogatama, D., Zhan, J., and Zhu, Z. (2015) 'Deep speech 2: End-to-End speech recognition in English and mandarin. arXiv preprint arXiv:1512.02595.

Anderson, S. and Coulter, D. (2013) 'Neuroscience. Neuronal birth to cortical circuitry' *Science* 340:1058–1059.

Anderson, R.C. and Others (1985) *Becoming a Nation of Readers: The Report of the Commission on Reading* (Urbana: Illinois University, Center for the Study of Reading).

Ansaldo, U. and Enfield, N.J.(2016) 'Editorial: Is the language faculty nonlinguistic?' *Frontiers in Psychology*, 10 June 2016 | http://dx.doi.org/10.3389/fpsyg.2016.00861.

Ansari, D. and Coch, D. (2006) 'Bridges over troubled waters: Education and cognitive neuroscience' *Trends in Cognitive Sciences* **10**:146–151.

Archangeli, D. and Pulleyblank, D. (2015) 'Phonology without universal grammar' *Frontiers in Psychology*, 04 September 2015 | http://dx.doi.org/10.3389/fpsyg.2015.01229.

Ardrey, R. (1966) *The Territorial Imperative: A Personal Inquiry Into the Animal Origins of Property and Nations* (USA: Kodansha).

Ayala, F. (2012) *The Big Questions: Evolution* (London: Quercus).

Baker, M. (2001) *The Atoms of Language* (New York: Basic Books).

Bakken, T.E. et al. (2016) 'A comprehensive transcriptional map of primate brain development' *Nature* 535:367–375.

Barkow, J.H., Cosmides, L. and Tooby, J. (1992) *The Adapted Mind: Evolutionary Psychology and the Generation of Culture* (Oxford: Oxford University Press).

Barrett, H. Clark (2015) *The Shape of Thought How Mental Adaptations Evolve* (Oxford University Press).

Barrett, J., Dunbar, R. and Lycett, J. (2002) *Human Evolutionary Psychology* (Princeton: Princeton University Press).

Barrett, L., Pollet, T.V. and Stulp G. (2014) 'From computers to cultivation: Reconceptualising evolutionary psychology' *Frontiers in Psychology* 5:867.

Bastos, A.M., Usrey, W.M., Adams, R.A., Mangun, G.R., Fries, P. and Friston, K.J. (2012) 'Canonical microcircuits for predictive coding' *Neuron* 76:695–711.

Beasley, M. Sabatinelli, D. and Obasi, E. (2012) 'Neuroimaging evidence for social rank theory' *Frontiers in Human Neuroscience*, 08 May 2012 [doi:10.3389/fnhum. 2012.00123].

Beer, S. (1972) *Brain of the Firm* (Chichester: Wiley).

Bennett, M.R. and Hacker, P.M.S. (2006) 'Language and cortical function: Conceptual developments' *Progress in Neurobiology* 80:20–52.

Bergen, B.K. and Chang, N. (2003) 'Embodied Construction Grammar in Simulation Based Language Understanding'. In J.O. Ostman and M. Fried (Eds.), *Construction Grammars(s): Cognitive and Cross-Language Dimensions* (Amsterdam: John Benjamins): 147–190.

Berridge, K.C. (1996) 'Food reward: Brain substrates of wanting and liking' *Neuroscience and Biobehavioral Reviews* 20:1–25.

Berry, M.W., Dumais, S.T. and O'Brien, G.W. (1995) 'Using linear algebra for intelligent information retrieval' *SIAM Review* 37:573–595.

Biber, D. Conrad, S. and Reppen, R. (2006) *Corpus Linguistics: Investigating Language Structure and Use* (Cambridge: Cambridge University Press).

Bickerton, D. (2001) *Language and Human Behaviour* (Seattle: University of Washington Press).

Binder, P-M. and Ellis, G.F.R. (2016) 'Nature, computation and complexity' *Physica Scripta* 9:064004 (1–9).

Bishop, C.M. (1999) *Neural Networks for Pattern Recognition* (Oxford: Oxford UniversityPress).

Bloch, C. (1997) *Chloe's Story: First Steps to Literacy* (Cape Town: Juta).

Bloch, C. (2014) 'Growing young readers and writers: Underpinnings of the Nal'ibali National Reading-for-Enjoyment Campaign'. In H McIlwraith (Ed.), *The Cape Town Language and Development Conference: Looking beyond 2015* (London: British Council): 50–56.

Bloch, C. (2015) 'Nal'ibali and libraries: Activating the gift of reading together' Conference: IFLA 2015 [**library**.ifla.org/1282/1/076-bloch-en.pdf].

Boeckx, C. and Benítez-Burraco, A. (2014) 'The shape of the human language-ready brain' *Frontiers in Psychology* 5:282.

Booch, G. (2007) *Object-Oriented Analysis and Design with Applications* (Menlo Park: Addison-Wesley).

Brakel, L.A.W. (2013) *The Ontology of Psychology: Questioning Foundations in the Philosophy of Mind* (New York: Routledge).

Bronowski, J. (2013) *The Ascent of Man* (London: BBC Books).

Brown, M. and Kuperberg, G.R. (2015) 'A hierarchical generative framework of language processing: Linking language perception, interpretation, and production abnormalities in schizophrenia' *Frontiers in Human Neuroscience* **9**:643.

Bruner, J.S. (1975) 'The ontogenesis of speech acts' *Journal of Child Language* **2**:1–19.

Bruner, J.S. (1983) *Child's Talk: Learning to Use Language* (Oxford: Oxford University Press).

Buller, D.J. (2005) *Adapting Minds: Evolutionary Psychology and the Persistent Quest for Human Nature* (Cambridge, Mass: MIT Press).

Burman, D., Bitanc, T. and Booth, J. (2008) 'Sex differences in neural processing of language among children' *Neuropsychologia* **46**:1349–1362. doi:10.1016/j.neuropsychologia.2007.12.021.

Buss, D.M. (1994) *Evolutionary Psychology* (Boston: Allyn and Bacon).

Buss, D. (2005) *The Handbook of Evolutionary Psychology* (Hoboken, NJ: John Wiley).

Butler, D. (1980) *Cushla and Her Books* (Boston: The Horn Book, Inc).

Butterworth, B. (1999) *What Counts: How Every Brain is Hardwired for Math* (New York: The Free Press).

Calvin, W.H. and Bickerton, D. (2001) *Lingua ex Machina: Reconciling Darwin and Chomsky with the Human Brain* (Cambridge, Mass: MIT Press).

Campbell, D.T. (1974) 'Downward causation'. In F J Ayala and T Dobzhansky (Eds.), *Studies in the Philosophy of Biology: Reduction and Related Problems* (Berkeley: University of California Press).

Campbell, N.A. and Reece, J.B. (2005) *Biology* (San Francisco: Benjamin Cummings).

Cardoso, S.D., Teles, M.C. and Oliveira, R.F. (2015) 'Neurogenomic mechanisms of social plasticity' *The Journal of Experimental Biology* **218**:140–149.

Carpenter, G.A. and Grossberg, S. (1988) 'The ART of adaptive pattern recognition by a self-organising neural network' *Computer* **21**:77–88.

Carroll, S.B. (2006) *Endless Forms Most Beautiful: The New Science of Evo Devo* (New York: W W Norton).

Carruthers, P., Laurence, S. and Stich, S. (2005) *The Innate Mind: Structure and Contents* (Oxford: Oxford University Press).

Carruthers, P., Laurence, S. and Stich, S. (2006) *The Innate Mind: Volume 2: Culture and Cognition* (Oxford: Oxford University Press).

Carruthers, P., Laurence, S. and Stich, S. (2007) *The Innate Mind Volume 3: Foundations and the Future* (Oxford: Oxford University Press).

Carruthers, P., Woodward, J. and Cowie, F. (2004) 'Is the mind a system of modules shaped by Natural selection?' Chapters 15 and 16 in it Ed. C Hitchcock (Oxford: Blackwell): 291–334.

Cartwright, J. (2000) *Evolution and Human Behaviour* (Hampshire: Palgrave).

Cassenaer, S. and Laurent, G. (2012) 'Conditional modulation of spike-timing-dependent plasticity for olfactory learning' *Nature* **482**:47–52.

Chang, Franklin, Dell, Gary S. and Bock, Kathryn (2006) 'Becoming syntactic' *Psychological Review* **113**:234–272.

Changeaux, J-P., Courrege, P. and Danchin, A. (1973) 'A Theory of the epigenesis of neuronal networks by selective stabilization of synapses' *Proceedings of the National Academy of Sciences of the United States of America* **70**:2974–2978.

Chanraud, S., Pitel, A.L., Müller-Oehring, E.M., Pfefferbaum, A. and Sullivan, E.V. (2013) 'Remapping the brain to compensate for impairment in recovering alcoholics' *Cerebral Cortex* **23**:97–104.

Chechik, G., Meilijison, I. and Ruppin, E. (1999) 'Neuronal Regulation: A mechanism for synaptic pruning during brain maturation' *Neural Computation* **11**:2061–2080.

Chomsky, N. (1965) *Aspects of the Theory of Syntax* (Cambridge, Mass: MIT Press).

Chomsky, N. (1995) 'Language and nature' *Mind* **104**:1–61.

Christiansen, M.H. and Chater, N. (2015) 'The language faculty that wasn't: A usage-based account of natural language recursion' *Frontiers in Psychology* **6**: |Article1182.

Christiansen, M.H. and Kirby S. (2005) *Language Evolution* (Oxford: Oxford University Press).

Churchland, P.M. (2013) *Plato's Camera: How the Physical Brain Captures a Landscape of Abstract Universals* (Cambridge, Mass: MIT Press).

Churchland, P.S. and Sejnowski, T.J. (1988) 'Perspectives in cognitive neuroscience' *Science* **242**:741–745.

Clark, A. (2008) *Supersizing the Mind: Embodiment, Action, and Cognitive Extension* (Oxford: Oxford University Press).

Clark, A. (2013) 'Whatever next? Predictive brains, situated agents, and the future of cognitive science' *Behavioral and Brain Sciences* **36**:181–204.

Clark, A. (2016) *Surfing Uncertainty: Prediction, Action, and the Embodied Mind* (Oxford: Oxford University Press).

Clark, A. and Chalmers, D. (1998) 'The extended mind' *Analysis* **58**:7–19.

Clark, D.L., Boutros, N.S. and Mendez, F.E. (2012) *The Brain and Behaviour: An Introduction to Neuroanatomy* (Cambridge: Cambridge University Press).

Cohen, L. and Dehaene, S. (2004) 'Specialization within the ventral stream: The case for the visual word form area' *NeuroImage* **22**:466–476.

Cohen, L., Lehéricy, S., Chochon, F., Lemer, C., Rivaud, S. and Dehaene, S. (2002) 'Language specific tuning of visual cortex? Functional properties of the Visual Word Form Area' *Brain* **125**:1054–1069.

Coles, G. (1998) *Reading Lessons: The Debate over Literacy* (New York: Hill and Wang).

Coles, G. (1999) 'Literacy emotion and the brain' Reading online.

Corning, P.A. (2005) *Holistic Darwinism* (Oxford: Oxford University Press).

Cosmides, L. (1989) 'The logic of social exchange: Has natural selection shaped how humans reason? Studies with the Wason selection task' *Cognition* **31**:187–276.

Craik, F. and Bialystok, E. (2006) 'Cognition through the lifespan: Mechanisms of change' *Trends in Cognitive Sciences* **10**:131–138.

Craver, C.F. (2007) *Explaining the Brain* (Oxford: Clarendon Press).

Crick, F. (1994) *The Astonishing Hypothesis* (New York: Scribner).

Cudeiro, J. and Sillito, A.M. (2006) 'Looking back: Corticothalamic feedback and early visual processing' *Trends in Neuroscience* **29**:298–306.

Culbertson, J. and Kirby, S. (2016) 'Simplicity and specificity in language: Domain-general biases have domain-specific effects'. *Frontiers in Psychology*, 12 January 2016 | http://dx.doi.org/10.3389/fpsyg.2015.01964.

Dąbrowska, E. (2016) 'What exactly is universal grammar, and has anyone seen it?' *Frontiers in Psychology*, 23 June 2015 | http://dx.doi.org/10.3389/fpsyg.2015.00852.

Damasio, A. (1994) *Descarte's Error: Emotion, Reason and the Human Brain* (New York: Harper Collins).

Damasio, A. (1999) *The Feeling of What Happens: Body, Emotion and the Making of Consciousness* (London: Vintage).

Damasio, A. (2010) *Self Comes to Mind: Constructing the Conscious Brain* (Penguin: Random House)

Darwin, C. (1872) *The Expression of the Emotions in Man and Animals* (London: Murray).

Deacon, T. (1997) *The Symbolic Species: The Co-evolution of Language and the Human Brain* (London: Penguin Books).

Deacon, T. (2003) 'Universal grammar and semiotic constraints'. In M Christiansen and S Kirby (Eds.), *Language Evolution* (Oxford: Oxford University Press): 111–139.

Dehaene, S. (2009) *Reading in the Brain* (New York: Penguin Viking).

Dehaene, S. and Cohen, L. (2011) 'The unique role of the visual word form area in reading'. *Trends in Cognitive Sciences* 15:254–262.

Dehaene, S., Cohen, L., Sigman, M. and Vinckier, F. (2005) 'The neural code for written words: A proposal'. *Trends in Cognitive Sciences* 9:335–341.

Dehaene, S. and Dehaene-Lambertz, G. (2016) 'Is the brain prewired for letters?' *Nature Neuroscience* 19:1192–1193.

Dehaene, S., Piazza, M., Pinel, P. and Cohen, L. (2003) 'Three parietal circuits for number processing'. *Cognitive Neuropsychology* 20:487–506.

Dehaene, S., Spelke, E., Pinel, P., Stanescu, R. and Tsivkin, S. (1999) 'Sources of mathematical thinking: Behavioral and brain-imaging evidence'. *Science* 284:970–974.

Dejean, C., Courtin, J., Karalis, N., Chaudun, F., Wurtz, H., Bienvenu, T.C.M. and Herry, C. (2016) 'Prefrontal neuronal assemblies temporally control fear behaviour'. *Nature* 535:420–424.

Dell, G.S. and Chang, F. (2014) 'The P-chain: Relating sentence production and its disorders to comprehension and acquisition'. *Philosophical Transactions of the Royal Society B* 369:20120394.

Devlin, J.T., Jamison, H.L., Gonnerman, L.M. and Matthews, P.M. (2006) 'The role of the posterior fusiform gyrus in reading'. *Journal of Cognitive Neuroscience* 18:911–922.

Devlin, K. (2000) *The Math Gene: How Mathematical Thinking Evolved and Why Numbers are Like Gossip* (New York: Basic Books).

de Waal, F. (1996) *Good Natured: The Origins of Right and Wrong in Humans and Other Animals* (London: Harvard University Press).

Dobzhansky, T. (1971) 'Nothing in biology makes sense except in the light of evolution'. *American Biology Teacher* 35:125–129.

Donald, M. (2000) 'The central role of culture in cognitive evolution: A reflection on the myth of the "isolated mind".' In L. Nucci (Ed.), *Culture, Thought and Development* (Mahwah, NJ: Lawrence Erlbaum Associates): 19–38.

Donald, M. (2001) *A Mind so Rare: The Evolution of Human Consciousness* (New York: W. W. Norton).

Dunbar, R.I.M. (2003) 'The social brain: Mind language and society in evolutionary perspective' *Annual Review of Anthropology* 32:163–181.

Dunbar, R. (2014) *Human Evolution* (London: Pelican Books).

Dunbar, R., Barrett, L. and Lycett, J. (2005) *Evolutionary Psychology* (Oxford: Oneworld).

Edelman, G.M. (1989) *Neural Darwinism: The Theory of Group Neuronal Selection* (Oxford: Oxford University Press).

Edelman, G.M. (1992) *Brilliant Air, Brilliant Fire: On the Matter of Mind* (New York: Basic Books).

Edelman, G.(2001) 'Consciousness: The remembered present' *Annals of the New York Academy of Sciences* 929:111–122.

Ekman, P. (1992) 'An Argument for Basic Emotions' *Cognition and Emotion* 6: Issue 3–4.

Ekman, P. and Friesen, W.V. (1971) 'Constants across cultures in the face and emotion' *Journal of Personality and Social Psychology* 17:124–129.

Ellis, G.F.R. (2008) 'Commentary on "An evolutionarily infirmed education science" by David C Geary' *Educational Psychologist* 44:206–217.

Ellis, G.F.R. (2016) *The Emergence of Complexity and the Mind: The Role of Top-down Causation* (Heidelberg: Springer).

Ellis, G.F.R, Noble, D. and O'Connor, T. (Eds.) (2012) 'Top-down causation: An integrating theme within and across the sciences?' *Royal Society Interface Focus Special Issue* 2:1–140.

Ellis, G.F.R. and Toronchuk, J.A.(2005) 'Neural development: Affective and immune system influences'. In R. D. Ellis and N. Newton (Ed.), *Consciousness and Emotion* (Amsterdam: John Benjamins): 81–119.

Ellis, N.C. (1998) 'Emergentism, connectionism and language learning' *Language Learning* 48:631–664.

Elman, J.L. (1991) 'Distributed representations, simple recurrent networks, and grammatical structure' *Machine learning* 7:195–225.

Elman, J.L. (1993) 'Learning and development in neural networks: The importance of starting small' *Cognition* 48:71–99.

Elman, J.L., Bates, E.A., Johnson, M.H., Karmiloff-Smith, A., Parisi, D. and Plunkett, K. (1998) *Rethinking Innateness: A Connectionist Perspective on Development* (Cambridge, Mass: MIT Press).

Evans, V. (2016) 'Design features for linguistically-mediated meaning construction: The relative roles of the linguistic and conceptual systems in subserving the ideational function of language' *Frontiers in Psychology*, 19 February 2016 | http://dx.doi.org/10.3389/fpsyg.2016.00156.

Everett, D.L. (2016) 'An evaluation of universal grammar and the phonological mind' *Frontiers in Psychology*, 08 February 2016 | http://dx.doi.org/10.3389/fpsyg.2016.00015.

Farmer, T.A., Brown, M. and Tanenhaus, M.K. (2013) 'Prediction, explanation, and the role of generative models in language processing' *Behavioral and Brain Sciences* 36:211–212.

Fauconnier, G. (1997) *Mappings in Thought and Language* (Cambridge: Cambridge University Press).

Feferman, S. (2006) 'The nature and significance of Gödel's incompleteness theorems' *Institute for Advanced Study, Princeton: Gödel Centenary Program.* Available at https://math.stanford.edu/~feferman/papers/Godel-IAS.pdf.

Feldman, J.A. (2008) *From Molecule to Metaphor: A Neural Theory of Language* (Cambridge, Mass: MIT Press); http://www.icsi.berkeley.edu/NTL/.

Fernando, C. and Szathmary, E. (2010) 'Natural selection in the brain'. In *Towards a Theory of Thinking On Thinking* (Heidelberg: Springer): 291–322.

Flood, R.L. and Carson, E.R. (1990) *Dealing with Complexity* (New York: Plenum Press).

Florio, M., Albert, M., Taverna, E., Namba, T., Brandl, H., Lewitus, E., Haffner, C., Sykes, A., Wong, F., Peters, J., Guhr, E., Klemroth, S., Prüfer, K., Kelso, J., Naumann, R., Nüsslein, I., Dahl, A., Lachmann, R., Pääbo, S. and Huttner, W. (2015) 'Human-specific gene ARHGAP11B promotes basal progenitor amplification and neocortex expansion' *Science* **347**:1465–1470. doi:10.1126/science.aaa1975.

Flurkey, A.D., Paulson, E.J. and Goodman, K.S. (2008) *Scientific Realism in Studies of Reading* (Mahwah, NJ: Lawrence Erlbaum).

Fodor, J.A. (1983) *The Modularity of Mind: An Essay on Faculty Psychology* (Cambridge, Mass: MIT Press).

Fodor, J.A. (1985) 'Précis of the modularity of mind' *Behavioral and Brain Sciences* **8**:1–42.

Fodor, J. (2000) 'The mind doesn't work that way: The scope and limits of computational psychology'. In J E. Adler and L J. Rips (Ed.), *REASONING: Studies of Human Inference and Its Foundations* (Cambridge: Cambridge University Press): 878–914.

Francis, G., Hunston, S. and Manning, E (1998) *Collins COBUILD Grammar Patterns: Nouns and adjectives* (London: Harper Collins).

Francis, G., Hunston, S. and Manning, E. (1998) *Cobuild grammar patterns 2: Nouns* (London: Harper Collins).

Freud, S. (1911) 'Formulations on the two principles of mental functioning' *Standard Edition* **12**:215–226.

Friederici, A.D. (2011) 'The brain basis of language processing: From structure to function.' *Physiological Reviews* **91**:1357–1392.

Friston, K. (2008) 'Hierarchical models in the brain' *PLoS Computational Biology* **4**: e1000211.

Friston, K. (2010) 'The free-energy principle: A unified brain theory?' *Nature Reviews Neuroscience* **11**:127–138.

Friston, K.J., Tononi, G., Reeke, G.N., Sporns, O. and Edelman, G.M. (1994) 'Value-dependent selection in the brain: Simulation in a synthetic neural model' *Neuroscience* **59**:229–243.

Frith, C. (2007) *Making up the Mind: How the Brain Creates Our Mental World* (Malden: Blackwell).

Gangestad, S.W. and Simpson, J.A. (2007) *The Evolution of Mind: Fundamental Questions and Controversies* (New York: Guilford).

Geary, D.C. (2005) *The Origin of Mind: Evolution of Brain, Cognition, and General Intelligence* (Washington, DC: American Psychological Association).

Geary, D.C. (2008) 'An evolutionarily informed education science' *Educational Psychologist* 43:179–195.

Gershon, M. (1999) *The Second Brain: A Groundbreaking New Understanding of Nervous Disorders of the Stomach and Intestine* (New York: Harper Perennial).

Gigerenzer, G. (2000) *Adaptive Thinking* (Oxford: Oxford University Press).

Gigerenzer, G. and Selten, R. (2002) *Bounded Rationality: The Adaptive Toolbox* (Cambridge, Mass: MIT Press).

Gilbert, S.F. (2006) *Developmental Biology* (Sunderland: Sinauer).

Gilbert, S.F. and Epel, D. (2009) *Ecological Developmental Biology* (Sunderland: Sinauer).

Glezer, L.S., Jiang, X. and M. Riesenhuber (2009) 'Evidence for highly selective neuronal tuning to whole words in the "Visual Word Form Area"' *Neuron* 62:199–204.

Goldberg, A.E. (2016) 'Subtle implicit language facts emerge from the functions of constructions' *Frontiers in Psychology* 6:2019.

Goodman, K., Fries, P., Strauss, S. and Paulson, E. (2016) *Reading: The Grand Illusion. How and Why Readers Make Sense of Print* (New York: Routledge).

Gopnik, A. (2009) *The Philosophical Baby: What Children's Minds Tell Us About Truth, Love & the Meaning of Life* (London: Bodley Head).

Gopnik, A., Meltzoff, A.N. and Kuhl, P.K. (2000) *The Scientist in the Crib: What Early Learning Tells Us About the Mind* (New York: William Morrow Paperbacks).

Goswami, U. (2004) 'Neuroscience and education' *British Journal of Educational Psychology* 74:1–14.

Goswami, U. and Bryant, P. (2007) *Research Survey 2/1a Children's Cognitive Development and Learning.* Primary Review Interim Reports (Cambridge: Cambridge University Press).

Gottschalk, J. (2012) *The Story-Telling Animal: How Stories Make us Human* (USA: Mariner Books).

Greenspan, S. (1997) *The Growth of the Mind* (Cambridge, Mass: Perseus books).

Greenspan, S. and Shanker, S. (2004) *The First Idea: How Symbols, Language, and Intelligence Evolved from Our Primate Ancestors to Modern Humans* (Cambridge, Mass: Da Capo Press).

Grefkes, C. and Fink, G. (2005) 'The functional organization of the intraparietal sulcus in humans and monkeys' *Journal of Anatomy* 207:3–1.

Griffiths, P.E. and Stotz, K. (2000) 'How the mind grows: A developmental perspective on the biology of cognition' *Synthese* 122:29–51.

Grill-Spector, K. and Witthoft, N. (2009) 'Deos the bairn not raed ervey lteter by istlef, but the wrod as a wlohe?' *Neuron* 62:161–162.

Haidt, J. and Kesebir, S. (2010) 'Morality'. In S Fiske, D Gilbert, and G Lindzey (Eds.), *Handbook of Social Psychology* (Hoboken, NJ: Wiley).

Haith, M.M. (1998) 'Who put the cog in infant cognition? Is rich interpretation too costly?' *Infant Behavior and Development* 21:167–179.

Halliday, M.A.K. (1977) 'Text as semantic choice in social contexts.' Reprinted in full In J. J. Webster (Ed.), *Linguistic Studies of Text and Discourse.* Volume 2 in the Collected Works of M.A.K. Halliday (London and New York: Continuum): 23–81.

Halliday, M.A.K. (1993) 'Towards a language-based theory of learning' *Linguistics and Education* 5:93–116.

Halliday, M.A.K. (2003) 'Introduction: On the "architecture" of human language'. In J.J. Webster (Ed.), *On Language and Linguistics.* Volume 3 in the Collected Works of M.A.K. Halliday (London and New York: Continuum).

Halliday, M.A.K and Webster, J.J. (Eds.) (2009) *Continuum Companion to Systemic Functional Linguistics* (New York: Continuum).

Halliday, M.A.K. and Matthiessen, M.I.M. (2014) *An Introduction to Functional Grammar* 4th edition (Abingdon: Routledge).

Hannun, A, Case, C., Casper, J., Catanzaro, B., Diamos, G., Elsen, E., Prenger, R., Satheesh, S., Sengupta, S., Coates, A. and Ng., A.Y. et al. (2014) 'Deep speech: Scaling up end-to-end speech recognition' *arXiv preprint arXiv:1412.5567.*

Harford, T. (2011) *Adapt* (London: Abacus).

Harris, K.D. and Mrsic-Flogel, T.D. (2013) 'Cortical connectivity and sensory coding' *Nature* **503**:51–58.

Hartwell, L.H., Hopfield, J.J., Leibler, S. and Murray A.M. (1999) 'From molecular to modular cell biology' *Nature* **402** Suppl: C47–C52.

Hauser, M.D. (2006) *Moral Minds: How Nature Designed our Universal Sense of Right and Wrong* (New York: HarperCollins).

Hauser, M.D., Yang, C., Berwick, R.C., Tattersall, I., Ryan, M.J., Watumull, J., Chomsky, N. and Lewontin, R.C. (2014) 'The mystery of language evolution' *Frontiers in Psychology,* 07 May 2014.

Hawkins, J. (2004) *On Intelligence* (New York, NY: Holt Paperbacks).

Hebb, D. (1949) *The Organization of Behavior* (New York: Wiley & Sons).

Hoey, M. (2005) *Lexical Priming: A New Theory of Words and Language* (Routledge).

Holy, T.E. (2012) 'Reward alters specific connections' *Nature* 482:39–41.

Hruby, G.G. and Goswami, U. (2011) 'Neuroscience and reading: A review for reading education researchers' *Reading Research Quarterly* **46**:156–172.

Hudson, G. (2000) *Essential Introductory Linguistics* (Oxford: Blackwell).

Hunston, S. and Francis, G. (2000) *Pattern Grammar: A Corpus-driven Approach to the Lexical Grammar of English* (Cambridge Mass: MIT Press).

Hurford, J.R. (2001) 'Review of human language and our reptilian brain: The subcortical bases of speech, syntax, and thought' *Quarterly Review of Biology* **76**:383.

Huth, A.G., de Heer, W.A., Griffiths, T.L., Theunissen, F.E. and Gallant, J.L. (2016) 'Natural speech reveals the semantic maps that tile human cerebral cortex' *Nature* **532**:453–458.

Huybregts, M.A.C., Berwick, R.C. and Bolhuis, J.J. (2016) 'The language within' *Science* **352**:1286.

Jablonka, E. and Lamb, M.J. (2006) *Evolution in Four Dimensions* (Cambridge, Mass: MIT Press).

Jeon, H-A. (2014) 'Hierarchical processing in the prefrontal cortex in a variety of cognitive domains' *Frontiers in Systems Neuroscience* 8:223.

Johnson, K. (2004) 'Gold's theorem and cognitive science' *Philosophy of Science* **21**:571–592.

Johnson, M.H. (2007) *Developmental Cognitive Neuroscience* (Oxford: Blackwell).

Joseph, J.E., Love, N. and Taylor, T.J. (2001) *Landmarks in Linguistic Thought II: The Western Tradition in the Twentieth Century* (London: Routedge).

Junker, B.J. and Schreiber, F. (2008) *Analysis of Biological Networks* (Hoboken, NJ: Wiley-Interscience).

Kagan, J. (2009) *The Three Cultures: Natural Sciences, Human Sciences and the Humanities in the 21st Century* (New York: Basic Books).

Kahneman, D. (2011) *Thinking, Fast and Slow* (New York: Farrar, Straus and Giroux).

Kandel, E. (2005) *Psychiatry, Psychoanalysis, and the New Biology of Mind* (Washington, DC: American Psychiatric Publishing).

Kandel, E. (2006) *In Search of Memory: The Emergence of a New Science of Mind* (NewYork: W. W. Norton).

Kandel, E. (2012) *The Age of Insight: The Quest to Understand the Unconscious in Art, Mind, and Brain, from Vienna 1900 to the Present* (New York: Random House).

Kandel, E., Schwartz, J.H., Jessell, T.M., Siegelbaum, S.A and Hudspeth, A.J. (2013) *Principles of Neural Science* (New York: McGraw Hill Professional).

Kant, I. (1781) *Critique of Pure Reason* (London: Palgrave Macmillan).

Kapur, S. (2003) 'Psychosis as a state of aberrant salience: A framework linking biology, phenomenology, and pharmacology in schizophrenia' *The American Journal of Psychiatry* **160**:13–23.

Karmiloff-Smith, A. (1996) *Beyond Modularity: A Developmental Perspective on Cognitive Science* (Cambridge, Mass: MIT Press).

Kenneally, C. (2008) *The First Word: The Search for the Origins of Language* (London: Penguin).

Kingsley, R. (2000) *Concise Text of Neuroscience* (Philadelphia: Lippinscott, Williams and Wilkins).

Knott, A. (2012) *Sensorimotor Cognition and Natural Language Syntax* (Cambridge, Mass: MIT Press).

Ko, H., Cossell, L., Baragli, C., Antolik, J., Clopath, C., Hofer, S.B. and Mrsic-Floge, T.D. (2013) 'The emergence of functional microcircuits in visual cortex' *Nature* **496**:96–100.

Komarova, N.L. and Nowak, M.A. (2005) 'Language, learning, and evolution'. In M H Christiansen and S Kirby (Eds.), *Language Evolution* (Oxford: Oxford University Press): 317–337.

Kuperberg, G.R. and Jaeger, T.F. (2015) 'What do we mean by prediction in language comprehension?' *Language, Cognition and Neuroscience*, doi: 10.1080/23273798.2015.1102299.

La Cerra, P. and Bingham, R. (1998) 'The adaptive nature of the human neurocognitive architecture: An alternative model' *Proceedings of the National Academy of Sciences* **95**:11290–11294.

La Cerra, P. and Bingham, R. (2002) *The Origin of Minds* (New York: Harmony).

Lakoff, G. and Johnson, M. (1980) *Metaphors We Live By* (Chicago: University of Chicago Press).

Lakoff, G. and Johnson, M. (1980a) *Philosophy in the Flesh: The Embodied Mind and its Challenge to Western Thought* (New York: Basic Books).

Lakoff, G. and Núñez, R.E. (2000) *Where Mathematics Comes From: How the Embodied Mind Brings Mathematics into Being* (New York: Basic Books).

Laland, K.N. and Brown, G.R. (2004) *Sense and Nonsense: Evolutionary Perspectives on Human Behaviour* (Oxford: Oxford University Press).

Landauer, T.K. and Dumais, S.T. (1997) 'A solution to Plato's problem: The latent semantic analysis theory of the acquisition, induction, and representation of knowledge' *Psychological Review* 104:211–240.

Landauer, T., Foltz, P.W. and Laham, D. (1998) 'Introduction to latent semantic analysis' *Discourse Processes* 25 (2–3):259–284.

Laubichler, M.D. and Maienschein, J. (2007) 'Embryos, cells, genes, and organisms: Reflections on the history of evolutionary developmental biology'. In Sanson and Brandon (Eds.), *Integrating Evolution and Development. From Theory to Practice* (Cambridge, Mass: MIT Press): 25–92.

LeDoux, J.E. (1998) *The Emotional Brain: The Mysterious Underpinnings of Emotional Life* (New York: Simon & Schuster).

LeDoux, J. (2002) *Synaptic Self* (New York: Viking).

Lee, N., Mikesell, L., Joaquin, A.D.L., Mates, A.D.W. and Schumann, J.H. (2009) *The Interactional Instinct: The Evolution and Acquisition of Language* (Oxford: Oxford University Press).

Li, W.S. and Clifton, C. (1994) 'Semantic integration in heterogeneous databases using neural networks' *Proceedings of the 20th VLDB Conference Santiago*, Chile.

Liebenberg, L. (1990) *The Art of Tracking The Origin of Science* (Cape Town: David Philip).

Lieberman, P. (1984) *The Biology and Evolution of Language* (Cambridge, Mass: Harvard University Press).

Lieberman, P. (2000) *Human Language and Our Reptilian Brain: The Subcortical Bases of Speech, Syntax and Thought* (Cambridge, Mass: Harvard University Press).

Lieberman, P. (2006) *Toward an Evolutionary Biology of Language* (Cambridge, Mass: Harvard University Press).

Løvtrup, S. (1984) *Beyond Neo-Darwinism* (London: Academic Press).

Low, L.K. and Cheng, H-J. (2006) 'Axon pruning: An essential step underlying the developmental plasticity of neuronal connections' *Philosophical Transactions of the Royal Society B* 361:1531–1544.

MacLean, P.D. (1989) *The Triune Brain in Evolution: Role in Paleocerebral Functions* (New York: Plenum).

Maguire, E.A., Woollett, K. and Spiers, H.J. (2006) 'London taxi drivers and bus drivers: A structural MRI and neuropsychological analysis' *Hippocampus* 16:1091–1101.

Marchant, J. (2016) 'Honest fakery' *Nature* 535:S14–S15.

Marcus, G.F. (2003) *The Algebraic Mind* (Cambridge, Mass: MIT Press).

Mante, V., Sussillo, D., Shenoy, K.V. and Newsome, W.T. (2013) 'Context-dependent computation by recurrent dynamics in prefrontal cortex' *Nature* 503:78–84.

Marbach, D., Costello, J.C., Küffner, R., Vega, N.M., Prill, R.J., Camacho, D.M. (2012) 'Wisdom of crowds for robust gene network inference' *Nature Methods* 9, 796–804.

Matyja, J.R. and Dolega, K. (2015) 'Commentary: The embodied brain: Towards a radical embodied cognitive neuroscience' *Frontiers in Human Neuroscience* **9**: Article 669.

Maynard Smith, J. and Szathmáry, E. (2007) *The Major Transitions in Evolution* (Oxford: Oxford University Press).

Merker, S. (2007) 'Consciousness without a cerebral cortex: A challenge for neuroscience and medicine'. *Behavioral and Brain Sciences* **30**:63–134.

Mesulam, M.M. (2000) 'Behavioral neuroanatomy: Large-scale networks, association cortex, frontal syndromes, the limbic system and hemispheric lateralization'. In *Principles of Behavioral and Cognitive Neurology*, 2nd ed. (New York: Oxford University Press): 1–120.

Meunier, D., Lambiotte, R. and Bullmore, E.T. (2010) 'Modular and hierarchically modular organization of brain networks' *Frontiers Neuroscience*, 08 December 2010 | http://dx.doi.org/10.3389/fnins.2010.00200.

Miller, G.A. (1956) 'The magical number seven, plus or minus two: Some limits on our capacity for processing information'. *Psychological Review* **63**:81–97.

Moore, D.S. (2015) *The Developing Genome: An Introduction to Behavioural Epigenetics* (Oxford: Oxford University Press).

Mountcastle, V.B. (1997) 'The columnar organization of the neocortex' *Brain* **120**:701–722.

Myers, D.G. (2003) *Intuition: Its Powers and Perils* (New Haven: Yale University Press).

NCTE (National Council of Teachers Education) (2008) 'On Reading, Learning to Read, and Effective Reading Instruction: An Overview of What We Know and How We Know It' www.ncte.org/positions/statements/onreading.

Nichols, J. (1984). 'Functional theories of grammar' *Annual Review of Anthropology* **13**:97–117.

Nicholls, J.G., Martin, A.R., Wallace, B.G. and Fuchs, P.A. (2001) *From Neuron to Brain* (Sunderland: Sinauer).

Noble, D. (2008) *The Music of Life: Biology Beyond Genes* (Oxford: Oxford University Press).

Noble, D. (2011) 'Neo-Darwinism, the modern synthesis and selfish genes: Are they of use in physiology?' *The Journal of Physiology* **589**:1007–1015.

Noble, D. (2012) 'A theory of biological relativity: No privileged level of causation' *Interface Focus* **2**:55–64.

Noble, D. (2013) 'Physiology is rocking the foundations of evolutionary biology' *Experimental Physiology* **98**:1235–1243.

O'Reilly, R.C., Wyatte, D. and Rohrlich, J. (2014) 'Learning through time in the thalamocortical loops' http://arxiv.org/abs/1407.3432.

Osher, D.E., Saxe, R.R., Koldewyn, K., Gabrieli, J.D.E., Kanwisher, N. and Saygin, Z.M. (2015) 'Structural connectivity fingerprints predict cortical selectivity for multiple visual categories across cortex' *Cerebral Cortex* **2015**:1–16.

Oudeyer, P-Y., Kaplan, F. and Hafner, V.V. (2007) 'Intrinsic motivation systems for autonomous mental development' *IEEE Transactions On Evolutionary Computation* **11**:265–286.

Oyama, S., Griffiths, P.E. and Gray, R.D. (2001) *Cycles of Contingency: Developmental Systems and Evolution* (Cambridge, Mass: MIT Press).

Painter, C. (2004) 'The "interpersonal first" principle in child language develop-
ment'. In Geoff Williams and Annabel Lukin (Eds.), *The Development of
Language: Functional Perspectives on Species and Individuals* (London:
Continuum): 137–157.

Painter, C., Derewianka, B. and Torr, J. (2007) 'From microfunction to metaphor:
Learning language and learning through language.' In Ruqaiya Hasan, Christian
Matthiessen and Jonathan J. Webster (Eds.), *Continuing Discourse*, Vol 2
(Sheffield: Equinox): 563–588.

Panksepp, J. (1998) *Affective Neuroscience: The Foundations of Human and Animal
Emotions* (London: Oxford University Press).

Panksepp, J. and Biven, L. (2012) *The Archaeology of Mind: Neuroevolutionary
Origins of Human Emotion* (New York: W. W. Norton and Company).

Panksepp, J. and Panksepp, J.B. (2000) 'The seven sins of evolutionary psychology'
Evolution and Cognition 6:108–131.

Panksepp, J., Panksepp, J.B. and others (2001) 'Evolutionary psychology: An
exchange' *Evolution and Cognition* 7:1–80.

Panksepp, J., Lane, R., Solms, M. and Smith, R. (2017) (In Press) 'Reconciling
cognitive and affective neuroscience perspectives on the brain basis of emotional
experience' *Neuroscience and Biobehavioral Reviews*.

Peacocke, A.H. (1989) *An Introduction to the Physical Chemistry of Biological
Organisation* (Oxford: Clarendon Press).

Peperkamp, S. and Mehle, J. (1999) *Language and Speech* 42:333–346.

Perfetti, C.A. and Frishkoff, G.A. (2009) 'The neural bases of text and discourse
processing'. In B Stemmer and H A Whitaker (Eds.), *Handbook of the
Neuroscience of Language* (USA: Elsevier): 165–174.

Pessoa, L. and Engelmann, J.B. (2010) 'Embedding reward signals into perception
and cognition' *Frontiers in Neuroscience* 24:17.

Petsko, G.A. and Ringe, D. (2009) *Protein Structure and Function* (Oxford: Oxford
University Press).

Piaget, J. (1951) *Play, Dreams and Imitation in Childhood* (London: Routledge).

Pickering, M.J. and Garrod, S. (2013) 'An integrated theory of language production
and comprehension' *Behavioral and Brain Sciences* 36:329–392.

Pigliucci, M. and Müller, G.B. (2010) *Evolution – The Extended Synthesis*
(Cambridge, Mass: MIT Press).

Pinker, S. (1994) *The Language Instinct: The New Science of Language and Mind*
(London: Penguin).

Pinker, S. (2002) *The Blank Slate* (London: Penguin Books).

Poggio, Tomaso and Bizzi, Emilio (2014) 'Generalization in vision and motor
control' *Nature* 431:768–774.

Polley, D.B., Kvašňák, E. and Frostig, R.D. (2004) 'Naturalistic experience trans-
forms sensory maps in the adult cortex of caged animals' *Nature* 429:67–71.

Price, C.J. and Friston, K.J. (2007) 'Functional ontologies for cognition: The
systematic definition of structure and function' *Cognitive Neuropsychology*
22:262–275.

Pullum, G.K. and Scholz, B.C. (2002) 'Empirical assessment of stimulus poverty
arguments' *The Linguistic Review* 19:950.

Pulvermüller, F. (2002) *The Neuroscience of Language* (Cambridge: Cambridge University Press).

Purves, D. (2010) *Brains: How They Seem to Work* (Up Saddle River: FT Press Science).

Putnam, H. (1967) 'The "Innateness Hypothesis" and explanatory models in linguistics' *Synthese* 17:12–22

Raff, R.A. and Sly, B.J. (2000) 'Modularity and dissociation in the evolution of gene expression territories in development' *Evolution and Development* 2:102–113.

Ramachandran, V.S. (2011) *The Tell-Tale Brain* (London: Heinamann).

Reber, M. Burrola, P. and Lemke, G. (2004) 'A relative signalling model for the formation of a topographic neural map' *Nature* 431:847–853.

Rhoades, R. and Pflanzer, R. (1989) *Human Physiology* (Philadelphia: Saunders College Publishing).

Richerson, P.J. and Boyd, R. (2005) *Not by Genes Alone: How Culture Transformed Human Evolution* (Chicago: University of Chicago Press).

Richardson, R.C. (2007) *Evolutionary Psychology as Maladapted Psychology* (Cambridge, Mass: MIT Press).

Roe, A.W., Pallas, S.L., Kwon, Y.H. and Sur, M. (1992) 'Visual projections routed to the auditory pathway in ferrets: Receptive fields of visual neurons in primary auditory cortex' *The Journal of Neuroscience* 12:3651–3664.

Robinson, G.E. (2004) 'Beyond nature and nurture' *Science* 304:397–399.

Robinson, G.E, Fernald, R.D. and Clayton D.F. (2008) 'Genes and social behaviour' *Science* 322:896–900.

Rolls, E. (1999) *The Brain and Emotion* (Oxford: Oxford University Press).

Rosenfelder, Mark (2010) *The Language Construction Kit* (Yonagu Books).

Roux, B. (Ed.) (2011) *Molecular Machines* (New York: World Scientific).

Rozin, P., Haidt, J. and McCauley, C.R. (2008) 'Disgust: The body and soul emotion in the 21st century'. In D. McKay and O. Olatunji (Eds.), *Disgust and its Disorders* (Washington, DC: American Psychological Association): 9–29.

Ruse, M. (1999) *Mystery of Mysteries: Is Evolution a Social Construction?* (Cambridge, Mass: Harvard University Press).

Sampson, G. (2005) *The 'Language Instinct' Debate* (London and New York: Continuum).

Sapolsky, R.M. (2004) 'Social status and health in humans and other animals' *Annual Review of Anthropology* 33, 393–418.

Sapolsky, R.M. (2005) 'The influence of social hierarchy on primate health' *Science* 308:648–652.

Saygin, Z.M., Osher, D.E., Norton, E.S., Youssoufian, D.A., Beach, S.D., Feather, J., Gaab, N., Gabrieli, J.D.E. and Kanwisher, N. (2016) 'Connectivity precedes function in the development of the visual word form area' *Nature Neuroscience* 19:1250–1255.

Schaffner, K.E. (2016) *Behaving: What's Genetic, What is Not, and Why Should We Care?* (Oxford: Oxford University Press).

Schlosser, G. and Wagner, G.P. (2004) *Modularity in Evolution and Development* (Chicago: University of Chicago Press).

Schmidhuber, J. (2015) 'Deep Learning in Neural Networks: An Overview' *Neural Networks* 61:85–117.

Scott, A. (1995) *Stairway to the Mind* (New York: Springer Verlag).

Seung, S. (2012) *Connectome* (USA: Houghton Mifflin Harcourt).

Shanahan, D. (2007) *Language, Feeling, and the Brain: The Evocative Vector* (New Brunswick, NJ: Transaction Publishers).

Shanahan, D. (2008) 'A new view of language, emotion and the brain' *Integrative Psychological Behavioral* 42:6–19.

Shaywitz, S. (2003) *Overcoming Dyslexia: A New and Complete Science-Based Program for Reading Problems at any Level* (New York: Vintage).

Shaywitz, S.E. and Shaywitz, B.A. (2005) 'Dyslexia (Specific Reading Disability)' *Biological Psychiatry* 57:1301–1309.

Shaywitz, S.E. and Shaywitz, B.A. (2008) 'Paying attention to reading: The neurobiology of reading and dyslexia' *Development and Psychopathology* 20:1329–1349.

Sherman, S.M. (2016) 'Thalamus plays a central role in ongoing cortical functioning' *Nature Neuroscience* 19:S33–S41.

Simon, H.A. (1962) 'The architecture of complexity' *Proceedings of the American Philosophical Society* 106.

Simon, H.A. (1992) *The Sciences of the Artificial* (Cambridge, Mass: MIT Press).

Sirois, S., Spratling, M., Thomas, M.S.C., Westermann, G., Mareschal, D. and Johnson, M.H. (2008) 'Précis of neuroconstructivism: How the brain constructs cognition' *Behavioral and Brain Sciences* 31:321–356.

Smith, F. (2004) *Understanding Reading: A Psycholinguistic Analysis of Reading and Learning to Read* (New York: Routledge).

Sohoglu, E., Peelle, J.E., Carlyon, R.P. and Davis, M.H. (2012) 'Predictive top down integration of prior knowledge during speech perception' *The Journal of Neuroscience* 32:8443–8453.

Sole, R. (2005) 'Syntax for free' *Nature* 434:289.

Solms, M. and Panksepp, J. (2012) 'The "id" knows more than the "ego" admits: Neuropsychoanalytic and primal-consciousness perspectives on the interface between affective and cognitive neuroscience' *Brain Sciences* 2:147–175. doi:10.3390/brainsci2020147.

Schultz, W. (2016) 'Dopamine reward prediction error coding' *Dialogues in Clinical Neuroscience* 18:23–32.

Sporns, O. (2011) *Networks of the Brain* (Cambridge, Mass: MIT Press).

Squire, L.R., Cohen, N.J. and Nadel, L. (1984) 'The medial temporal region and memory consolidation: A new hypothesis'. In Weingartner H and Parker E (Eds.), *Memory Consolidation* (Hillsdale, NJ: Lawrence Erlbaum): 85–210.

Sterelny, K. (2014) *The Evolved Apprentice* (Cambridge, Mass: MIT Press).

Sternberg, E.M. (1997) 'Neural-immune interactions in health and disease' *The Journal of Clinical Investigation* 100:2641–2647.

Sternberg, E.M. (2000) *The Balance Within: The Science Connecting Health and Emotions* (New York: W H Freeman and Co).

Stone, J.V. (2015) *Information Theory: A Tutorial Introduction* (Sheffield: Sebtel Press).

Sur, M. and Rubenstein, J. (2005) 'Patterning and plasticity of the cerebral cortex' *Science* 310:805–810. doi:10.1126/science.1112070.

Stevens, A. and Price, J. (2000) *Evolutionary Psychiatry: A New Beginning* (New York: Taylor and Francis).

Stokoe, W.C. Jr (1960) *'Sign Language Structure: An Outline Of The Visual Communication Systems Of The American Deaf* (Department of Anthropology and Linguistics University of Buffalo).

Stryker, M.P., Sherk, H., Leventhal, A.G. and Hirsch, H.V.B. (1978) 'Physiological consequences for the cat's visual cortex of effectively restricting early visual experience with oriented contours' *Journal of Neurophysiology* 41:896–909.

Swisher, M. (1987) 'Similarities and differences between spoken languages and natural sign languages' *Applied Linguistics* 9:343–356.

Tabery, J. (2015) *Beyond Versus: The Struggle to Understand the Interaction of Nature and Nurture* (Cambridge, Mass: MIT Press).

Tanaka, K.Z., Pevzner, A., Hamidi, A.B., Nakazawa, Y., Graham, J. and Wiltgen, B.J. (2014) 'Cortical representations are reinstated by the hippocampus during memory retrieval' *Neuron* 84:347–354.

Thibault, P.J. (2011) 'First-order languaging dynamics and second-order language: The distributed language view' *Ecological Psychology* 23:1–36.

Tomasello, M. (1999) *The Cultural Origins of Human Cognition* (Cambridge, Mass: Harvard University Press).

Tomasello, M. (2003) *Constructing a Language: A Usage-based Theory of Language Acquisition* (Boston: Harvard University Press).

Tooby, J. and Cosmides, I. (1992) 'The psychological foundations of culture'. In J.H. Barkow, L. Cosmides, and J. Tooby (Eds.), *The Adapted Mind: Evolutionary Psychology and the Generation of Culture* (New York: Oxford University Press).

Toronchuk, J.A. and Ellis, G.F.R. (2007) 'Criteria for basic emotions: Seeking DISGUST?' *Cognition and Emotion* 21:1829–1832.

Toronchuk, J.A. and Ellis, G.F.R. (2012) 'Affective neuronal selection: The nature of the primordial emotion systems' *Frontiers in Psychology* 3:589. [www.ncbi.nlm.nih.gov/pmc/articles/PMC3540967/].

Trivers, R. (1971) 'The evolution of reciprocal altruism' *Quarterly Review of Biology* 46: 35–57.

Tsodyks, M. and Gilbert, C. (2004) 'Neural networks and perceptual learning' *Nature* 431:775–781.

Tversky, A. and Kahneman, D. (1974) 'Judgment under uncertainty: Heuristics and biases' *Science* 185:1124–1131.

van der Westhuizen, D. and Solms, M. (2014) 'Social dominance and the Affective Neuroscience Personality Scales' *Consciousness and Cognition* 33C:90–111.

Van der Westhuizenand, D. and Solms, M. (2015) 'Basic emotional foundations of social dominance in relation to Panksepp's affective taxonomy' *Neuropsychoanalysis* 17:19–37.

Volkow, N., Fowler, J., Wang, G., Baler, R. and Telang, F. (2009) 'Imaging dopamine's role in drug abuse and addiction' *Neuropharmacology* 56(Suppl 1):3–8.

von Melchner, L., Pallas, S. and Sur, M. (2000) 'Visual behaviour mediated by retinal projections directed to the auditory pathway' *Nature* 404:871–876. doi:10.1038/35009102.

Vygotsky, I.S. (1962) *Thought and Language* (Cambridge, Mass: MIT Press).

Wagner, A. (2011) *The Origins of Evolutionary Innovations* (Oxford: Oxford University Press).

Wagner, A. (2015) *Arrival of the Fittest* (New York: Penguin Random House).

Weiskrantz, L. (1997) *Consciousness Lost and Found: A Neuropsychological Exploration* (Oxford: Oxford University Press).

West-Eberhard, M.J. (1998) 'Evolution in the light of developmental and cell biology, and vice versa' *Proceedings of the National Academy of Sciences* 95:8417–8419.

West-Eberhard, M.J. (2003) *Developmental Plasticity and Evolution* (Oxford: Oxford University Press).

West-Eberhard, M.J. (2005) 'Developmental plasticity and the origin of species differences' *Proceedings of the National Academy of Sciences* 102, Suppl. 1:6543–6549.

Westermann, G., Mareschal, D., Johnson, M.H., Sirois, S., Spratling, M.W. and Thomas, M.S.C. (2007) 'Neuroconstructivism' *Developmental Science* 10:75–83.

Willis, J. (2008) 'Building a Bridge From Neuroscience to The Classroom' (Phi Delta Kappan February 2008, 424–427).

Wilson, A.D. and Golonka, S. (2013) 'Embodied cognition is not what you think it is' *Frontiers in Psychology* 4: Article 58.

Wilson, E.O. (1975) *Sociobiology: The New Synthesis* (Cambridge, Mass: Harvard University Press).

Wimsatt, W.C. (1994) 'The ontology of complex systems: Levels of organization, perspectives, and causal thickets' *Canadian Journal of Philosophy* supp. Vol 20:207–274.

Wolpert, D.M. and Flanagan, J.R. (2016) 'Computations underlying sensorimotor learning' *Current Opinion in Neurobiology* 37:7–11.

Wolpert, L. (2002) *Principles of Development* (Oxford: Oxford University Press).

INDEX

Abadzi, H., 161–163
abduction problem, innate cognitive
    modules and, 76–77
abstraction
    linguistics and, 125
    modular units and, 42–43
action grammar
    evolution of, 66–67, 126–127
    language and, 120
    spoken word recognition and, 103
action potential propagation, 40–41
activity-dependent connections, 22–23
adaptation
    brain modules theory and, 5–6
    innate cognitive models and, 7–8
    macro level functional plasticity and, 49–50
    neural Darwinism and, 113–115
    top-down effects in, 46
adaptive modular systems, 7–8
Adaptive Representational Networks
    (ARN), 7–8
Adger, P., 137
affect
    behaviour and development and, 131–133
    brain structure and, 17–18
    defined, 27–29
    development and, 2–4, 113–115
    diffuse connections and role of, 10–11
    extended taxonomy of, 99–100
    feelings and, 86–99
    function and, 13–14, 113–115
    homeostatic *vs.* emotional affects, 27–29
    law of, 144–146
    in mammals, 83–85
affective valence
    embodied mind and, 101–103

learning and, 27
aggression, RAGE system and, 92–93
Alitto, H. J., 30–32
Amodei, D., 122–124
amphetamines, seeking instinct
    and, 89
amygdala
    FEAR system and, 94–95
    memory and, 27
    RAGE system and, 92–93
    structure of, 26
Anderson, R. C., 163–165
Anderson, S., 108–109
Ansaldo, U., 137
appetitive systems, SEEKING instinct
    and, 89–91
Archangeli, D., 137
Ardrey, Robert, 100
ascending systems, 10–11
    hard-wired connections, 112–113
    hard-wired connections and, 14
    innate cognitive modules, 109–111
association cortex, 24–27
atoms, in brain modules, 40
automatization, 27–29
axons, pathfinding of, 52–57

Baldwin effect, 76
Barkow, J. H., 61–62
Barrett, Clark, 81, 109–111
Bayesian inference
    behaviour and, 80–82, 115
    categorization ability, 118
behaviour/function
    affect and, 131–133
    brain modules theory and, 5–6

behaviour/function (cont.)
  innate cognitive modules and, 6–7, 59,
    106–113
  needs and, 21–22
  unconditioned behavioural responses, 27–29
Benítez-Burraco, A., 37
Berridge, K. C., 87–91
Bickerton, D., 70
Bingham, R., 6–7, 12, 60–61, 68–69, 80–82, 105,
    172–173
biology
  evolution and innate cognition and, 138–144
  innate cognitive models and, 59, 106–113
  modules in, 43
Biven, L., 91–92
black-box abstractions, 42–43
blindsight, 23–24
Bloch, Carole, 14, 116–117, 155–156, 167
body-monitoring nuclei, 21–22
Boeckx, C., 37
Booch, G., 42–43
brain modules
  abstraction and information hiding in, 42–43
  atoms and cells in, 40
  developmental origin of, 55–58
  emotions and, 146
  evolutionary origin of, 4–6
  guiding principles concerning, 4–6
  hard- and soft-wired connections in, 8–10
  hierarchy in, 38–39
  innate knowledge and, 1–4
  interlevel relations, 44–46
  levels and emergence of, 38–41
  plasticity and development of, 50–55
brain structure and function, 12, 16–18
  affective and cognitive structures, 17–18
  connectionist view of, 46–50
  evolution and, 35–37
  extrinsic connectivity and, 34–35
  functional domains, 32–35
  hierarchy in, 48
  innate cognitive models and, 59–63
  inner and outer worlds and, 19–24
  language-ready brain model and, 37
  learning and, 24–27, 146–155
  mind and, 19–24
  periaqueductal grey (PAG) matter, 86–87
  plasticity and development in, 50–55
  spoken and written language and, 159
  triune brain structure, 16, 145–146
Broca's area, 32–35

Brown, G. R., 12, 60–61, 80–82
Bruner, J. S., 79–80
Bryant, P., 151
Buller, D. J., 7–8, 12, 80–82
Buss, D. M., 12, 13, 138–139

CARE system, 97–98
  gender and, 133–134
  LUST instinct and, 91–92
Carruthers, P., 62–63, 68–71, 122–123
Cartwright, 2–4
Cassenaer, S., 113–115
categorization ability, language acquisition
    and, 118
causality, interlevel relations and, 44–46
cells
  in brain modules, 40
  diversification in nervous system of, 52
  nerve cell generation, 52
central nervous system, 16
  development of, 38–41
  hierarchical structure of, 38–39
  induction and patterning of, 52
  innate cognitive modules, 109–111
  modular outcomes thesis concerning, 58
cerebellum, innate cognitive modules, 109–111
chain of causation, 5–6
  developmental causation, 51
cheater detection modules, 69
Chloe's Story (Bloch), 14, 116–117
cholinergic system, 10–11
Chomsky, Noam, 1–2, 12, 13, 14, 32–35, 59
  on abstract structure, 125
  on gender and language, 133–134
  innate cognitive modules and, 63–67, 74–75,
    77–79
  innate language modules, 101–103
  linguistics and, 168–172
  poverty of stimulus hypothesis and, 79–80,
    122–123
Christiansen, M. H., 76, 126–127, 137, 157–161
clauses, Systemic Functional Linguistics and,
    129–133
cocaine, SEEKING instinct and, 89
cognition
  brain structure and, 17–18, 32–35
  genome pathways to, 72–75
  language learning and, 117–119
  manipulation of abstractions and, 24–27
  neural network connectivity and weights
    and, 47

perception and, 22–23
uniformity and predictability of, 72–75
cognitive functional linguistics, 119
cognitive integration, 172–173
Cohen, L., 33–34, 160–161, 165
cold aggression, 92–93
Coles, G., 120–122
collocations, mental lexicon and, 64–65
communication, brain and evolution and, 36–37
compound objects, abstraction of, 42–43
computer programming, top-down effects in, 45–46
conditioned pattern recognition, 29
connectionist brain model, 46–50
connectivity
in neural networks, 47
pruning of connections, 53–55
'Connectome' model, 46–50
consciousness, extended reticulo-thalamic activating system, 21–22
consolidation
affective valence, 27
learning and, 25–26
consummation system, SEEKING instinct and, 89–91
context
brain development and, 52
development and, 143
innate cognitive modules and, 76–77, 106–113
pattern recognition and, 30
perception and, 34–35
social context, language learning and, 117–119
corpus linguistics research, 64–65
Language Pattern View, 127–128
Systemic Functional Linguistics and, 129–133
cortex
development and plasticity of, 53–55
functional domains in, 32–35, 74–75
gender and activation of, 133–134
hippocampus and, 26
language pre-requisites and, 78
microconnections in, 58
pattern recognition in, 22–23
physical and social interactions and development of, 80–82
primary and association areas, 21–22
semantic mapping and, 34–35
soft-wired connections in, 9–10
corticofugal feedback, 30–32
corticoid tissue, 26

corticothalamic circuitry, 30–32
Cosmides, I., 61–62, 113–115
Coulter, D., 108–109
Crespi, Bernard, 138–139
Cudeiro, J., 30–32
Culbertson, J., 137
culture
innate cognitive models and, 59
innate cognitive modules and, 76–77

Dąbrowska, E., 137
Damasio, A., 11, 12
Darwin, Terry Burnham, 138–139
Deacon, T., 14, 123–125, 169
deafness, language acquisition and, 158
deep brainstem, body-monitoring nuclei in, 21–22
Deep Learning Neural Networks, 66–67, 74–75, 123–124
degeneracy, cognitive function and, 32–35
Dehaene, S., 33–34, 160–161, 165
despair, 95–97
development
affect and, 131–133
of brain modules, 55–58
emotions and, 2–4, 145
epigenetics and, 143
evolution and, 138–144
in humans, 143–144
innate cognitive modules and, 76, 113–115
language and, 116–133
linguistics and, 126
plasticity and brain development, 50–55
primary systems for, 134–135
top-down effects in, 44–46
Developmental Systems Theory, 140–141
Devlin, J. T., 34–35, 70
de Waal, F., 71–72
diencephalic nuclei, 21–22
diffuse systems
hard-wired connections, 8–10
microconnections, 58
neuronal connections, 56–57
role of emotion and, 10–11
DISGUST system, 99–100
affect and intellect and, 113–115
distress vocalizations, 95–97
distributed functional view, language acquisition, 128–133
DNA
epigenetics and, 143

DNA (cont.)
  innate cognitive models and, 6–7, 108–109
  selection and, 140–141
Dobzhansky, T., 4, 106
Dolega, K., 32–35
domain links, neuronal connections, 56–57
domain-specific brain modules, 1–4
dopamine systems, 10–11
drive
  defined, 27–29
  language acquisition and, 78–79
Dunbar, R., 122
dyslexic students, 161–163

Edelman, G. M., 7–8, 11, 12, 22–23
education
  divide in, 167
  evolutionary theory and, 146–148
  fear of learning and, 165–167
  written and spoken language learning and,
    155–165
Ekman, P., 87
Ellis, George, 99–100, 155–156, 171, 174–177
Elman, J. L., 80–82
embodied construction grammar,
  development and learning and, 126
Embodied Construction Grammar, 14, 78,
  101–103, 116–117
embodied language, 119–120, 126, 174–177
embodied mind, 101–103
  language evolution and, 66–67
emergence
  levels in brain of, 38–41
  Systemic Functional Linguistics and, 132–133
emotions
  affects and, 27–29
  brain structure and, 17–18, 146
  development and, 2–4, 145
  diffuse connections and role of, 10–11
  evolution and, 14, 115–116, 145–146
  extended taxonomy of, 99–100
  feelings and, 86–99
  functions of, 13–14
  gender and, 133–134
  innate cognitive modules and, 11, 113–116,
    144–146
  language development and, 36–37, 116–133
  in mammals, 83–85
  primary systems for, 113–115, 134–135
  teaching and, 166–167
encapsulation, modularity and, 43

Enfield, N. J., 137
environmental context, Evo-Devo tradition
  and, 139–141
environment of evolutionary adaptedness
  (EEA), 6–7, 68–69, 146–148, 150–152
epigenetics
  development and, 143
  innate cognitive modules and, 76
ethical modules, 71–72
Evans, V., 137
Everett, D. L., 137
Evo-Devo tradition, innate modules and,
  138–144
evolution
  action grammar and, 126–127
  brain structure and, 35–37
  education and, 146–148
  emotions and, 14, 115–116, 145–146
  guiding principles of, 4–6
  innate cognitive modules and, 6–7, 72–75, 76,
    112–113, 115–116, 138–144
  multilevel selection and, 142
  primary systems for, 134–135
  top-down effects in, 46
  written and spoken language and, 156–157
evolutionarily informed education science
  (EIES), 146–155, 161–163
evolutionary educational psychology, 152–153
evolutionary psychology, 60–61
  cheater detection module, 69
  innate cognitive modules and, 74, 80–82,
    138–139
experience-dependent connections, 22–23
extended mind hypothesis, 172–173
Extended Mind hypothesis, 103
extended reticulo-thalamic activating system
  (ERTAS), 21–22
extrinsic connectivity
  brain development and, 34–35
  Visual Wordform Area and, 33–34

face recognition module, 68–69
facial attractiveness, instinct for detection of,
  68–69
Faculty Psychology, 60–61
FEAR system, 94–95
feelings, 98–99
  CARE system, 97–98
  DISGUST system, 99–100
  evolutionary value of, 100–101
  FEAR system, 94–95

instincts and, 86–99
LUST system, 91–92
PANIC/GRIEF system, 95–97
RAGE system, 92–93
RANKING/HIERARCHY/DOMINANCE
    system, 100
SEEKING system, 87–91
Feferman, S., 66
Feldman, J. A., 119–120, 174–177
fight or flight response, 94–95
filopodia, axon guidance and, 52
'fire together, wire together' principle, 106–113
fixed function networks, 49
Flanagan, J. R., 103
flexibility, innate cognitive modules and, 76–77
Fodor, J. A., 55, 62–63, 76–77, 103, 106
folk biology modules, 70, 134–135, 146–155
folk physics modules, 69, 134–135, 146–155
folk psychology modules, 34–35, 69, 134–135,
    146–155
folk sociology module, 71
foraging (SEEKING) instinct, 87–91
formal learning theory, 170–171
framing problem
    embodied language and, 119–120
    emotion, development and modules and,
        61–62
    innate cognitive modules and, 74, 82,
        106–113
Friederici, A. D., 32–35
Fries, Peter, 130–131, 132–133
Frishkoff, G. A., 159
Friston, K. J., 159
functional hierarchy, 39–40
    innate cognitive modules, 109–111
    language and, 126
'functional language system' (FLS), 66–67
Functional Linguistic Grammar, 116–117,
    128–129

Gangestad, S. W., 60–61
Garrod, S., 101–103
Geary, David, 12, 13, 34–35, 76, 115–116, 146–155,
    161–163, 165–167
gender
    CARE system and, 97–98
    language and, 133–134
    LUST instinct and, 91–92
gene/culture co-evolution, 36–37
    innate cognitive models and, 60–61
gene regulatory networks, 140–141

genetics
    cognitive innateness and, 2–4
    environmental influences and, 13
    Evo-Devo tradition and, 139–141
    gender and, 133–134
    innate cognitive modules and, 76, 107–109
    top-down effects in, 44–46
genome pathways, to cognition, 72–75
genotype, selection and, 140–141
gestalt holism, 163–165
Gigerenzer, G., 76–77
Gilbert, S. F., 51
Goldberg, A. E., 137, 169
Gold's theorem, 78–79, 170–171, 176–177
Goodman, Kenneth, 155–156
Gopnik, A., 134–135
Goswami, U., 151, 155–156, 171
grammar
    embodied language and, 119–120, 126
    innate cognitive modules and, 65–66,
        123–124
    Language Pattern View and, 127–128
Greenspan, S., 74–75, 115–117, 120–123, 169–170
Griffiths, P. E., 107–109, 144
group formation
    emotions and, 120–122
    primary emotion systems and, 113–115
    selection and, 140–141
growth cone, axon guidance and, 52
guilt, as hybrid affect, 27–29

Haidt, J., 99–100
Haith, M. M., 74–75
Halliday, M. A. K., 116–117, 122, 126, 129–133
hard-wired connections, 8–10
    affective and cognitive brain structures,
        17–18, 113–115
    in cognitive modules, 13
    development, 109
    diffuse systems, 10–11
    evolution of, 112–113
    functions, 109–111
    instinct as, 27–29
    soft-wired interaction with, 111–112
Harris, K. D., 34–35, 37
Hauser, M. D., 71–72
Hawkins, J., 171
heuristic capacity, innate cognitive modules
    and, 76–77
hierarchy
    abstraction and information hiding in, 42–43

hierarchy (cont.)
  in brain, 48
  complexity and, 38–39
  in grammar, 65–66
Hilbert, David, 176–177
hippocampus, systems consolidation
    and, 26
histamine system, 10–11
Hodgkin-Huxley law, 40–41
Hoey, M., 64–65, 127–128, 130–131
holistic processes
  gestalt holism, 163–165
  innate cognitive modules and, 74
  spoken and written language and, 157–161
  Systemic Functional Linguistics and, 132–133
homeostatic affects, 27–29
hot aggression, 92–93
Hruby, G. G., 155–156
human behavioural ecology, 60–61
human development, 143–144
human sociobiology, 60–61
Huybregts, M. A. C., 158
hypothalamus, 19–20
  LUST instinct and, 91–92

iconicity, innate cognitive modules and, 78
illusion, power of, 30
implementation hierarchy, 39–40
incompleteness theorem, 66
individuals, selection and, 140–141
inductive signaling, 52
infinity, language modules and, 78–79
information hiding, modular units and, 42–43
information processing
  hierarchy in, 48
  innate cognitive modules and, 76
  network plasticity and, 46–50
Ingroup/Outgroup detection, 71
inheritance, modularity and, 43
innate arithmetic module, 70, 79–80
innate cognitive modules
  alternative modules, 68–72
  alternatives to, 80–82
  arguments against, 75–80, 136–138
  arguments for, 72–75
  CNS modules, 27–29, 56–57
  cortical modules and, 13
  development and structures, 107–109, 113–115
  discourse of brain, behaviour and biology in,
      59–63
  education and, 146–148

emotions and, 11, 113–116, 144–146
evolution and, 6–7, 72–75, 76, 112–113, 115–116,
    138–144
evolutionary psychology and, 80–82, 138–139
function, 109–111
future research issues, 172–173
grammar and, 65–66, 123–124
greedy proposal for, 63
hard-wired modules, 109
intuition *vs.*, 148–150
language and, 63–67, 74–75, 77–79, 116–133
learning implications, 76–77, 146–155
modest proposal for, 62–63
origins of, 1–4
primary emotion systems and, 134–135
principles of, 6–8
range of, 106–113
soft-wired modules, 109
summary of discourse on, 104–106
theoretical background on, 59–63
thesis concerning, 58
innate emotional systems, 72
innate modularity, 61–62
innateness
  defined, 63
  Putnam's discussion of, 168–172
inner world, brain structure and function
    and, 19–24
instincts, 27–29
  CARE system, 97–98
  DISGUST system, 99–100
  evolutionary value of, 100–101
  for facial attractiveness detection, 68–69
  FEAR system, 94–95
  feelings and, 86–99
  LUST system, 91–92
  in mammals, 84–85
  PANIC/GRIEF system, 95–97
  periaqueductal grey (PAG) matter, 86–87
  PLAY system, 98–99
  RAGE system, 92–93
  RANKING/HIERARCHY/DOMINANCE
      system, 100
  SEEKING system, 87–91
Integrated Causal Model (ICM), 61–62
integrative view, language acquisition, 128–133
intellect, affect and, 113–115
intention-reading, language development and,
    118
interlevel relations, modular hierarchical
    structures, 44–46

intuition, 27–29
 innate modules *vs.*, 148–150

Johnson, K., 51, 53, 176–177

Kamorova, N. L., 1–2, 79–80, 174–177
Kandel, E., 48, 51, 53–55, 108–109
Kant, Immanuel, 95
Karmiloff-Smith, A., 12
Kingsley, R., 9
Kirby, S., 76, 126–127, 137, 157–161
Knott, A., 120
Ko, H., 111–112

labelling
 abstraction and, 42–43
 symbolic ability and, 118
La Cerra, P., 6–7, 12, 60–61, 68–69, 80–82, 105, 172–173
Lakoff, George, 70
Laland, K. N., 12, 60–61, 80–82
language
 action grammar and, 120
 affective and cognitive brain structures, 17–18
 alternatives to innate models of, 116–117
 ascending systems and, 14
 automatization and, 29
 brain and evolution and, 36–37
 cognitive prerequisites and social context, 117–119
 embodied language, 119–120
 embodied mind and, 101–103
 emotion link to, 116–133
 functional domains and, 32–35
 gender and, 133–134
 gestalt holism and, 163–165
 infinities, 174–177
 innate cognitive modules and, 63–67, 74–75, 77–79, 116–133, 137
 integrative view of, 128–133
 language-ready brain model and, 37
 modalities, 157–161
 origin of universals, 124–125
 poverty of stimulus and, 122–123
 rule-based systems for, 2–4
 Systemic Functional Linguistics, 129–133
 written and spoken language, 155–165
Language Acquisition Device (LAD), 79–80
language instinct, 1–2
Language Pattern View, 127–128

'language universals,' 17–18
Latent Semantic Analysis (LSA), 2–4, 66–67
Laurent, G., 113–115
learning
 basic process, 166–167
 brain structure and function and, 24–27
 evolutionarily informed education science and, 146–155
 fear of, 165–167
 innate cognitive modules and, 76–77, 146–155
 intention-reading and, 118
 linguistics and, 126
 macro level functional plasticity and, 49–50
 mathematical theory of, 176–177
 mathematics, 165
 motivation and, 153–155
 primary and secondary abilities and, 150–152
 SEEKING instinct and, 89
 Systemic Functional Linguistics and, 131–133
 written and spoken language, 155–165
LeDoux, J., 11
lexical priming studies, 64–65, 127–128
Lieberman, P., 79–82
LIKING system, 89–91
limbic system, innate cognitive modules, 109–111
linguistics
 nature of, 125–133
 Systemic Functional Linguistics, 129–133
lip reading, 160–161
Lovtrup, S., 145–146
lower-level modules, interlevel relations and, 44–46
LUST system, 91–92, 100

MacLean, P. D., 16, 145–146
macro level functional plasticity, 49–50, 171
 neural substrates, 113–115
mammals
 emotion/affect in, 83–85
 instinct in, 84–85
 values in, 85
maternal instinct, LUST instinct and, 91–92
mathematical theory of learning, 176–177
mathematics, 165
 fear of learning and, 166–167
Matthiessen, M. I. M., 116–117, 126, 129–133
Matyja, J. R., 32–35
Maynard Smith, J., 65–66, 120
McLean, 145–146
meaning, embodies theory of, 119–120

Mehle, J., 158
memory, consolidation and, 25–26
mental illness, seeking instinct and, 89
mental lexicon, 64–65
metabolic regulatory networks, 140–141
mind
  brain structure and function and, 19–24
  embodied mind, 101–103
  innate cognitive modules and modularity of,
    76–77
Modern Synthesis, 138–144
modular hierarchical structures
  brain development and plasticity and, 50–55
  complexity and, 13
  interlevel relations, 44–46
  levels and emergence of, 38–41
  modularity in, 41–44
  neural complexity and, 4–6
  thesis of CNS development and, 58
  top-down effects in, 45–46
  units in, 40
mother-child bonding
  development and learning and, 126
  language learning and, 14, 116–117
motivation, learning and, 153–155
motor system, 17
  innate cognitive modules, 109–111
  output systems, 72
Mrsic-Flogel, T. D., 34–35, 37
Müller, G. B., 139–141
multilevel selection, 142

National Council of Teachers of English, 164
nativism, 60–61, 137
natural pedagogy hypothesis, 71
natural selection, brain module evolution and,
  4–6
nature/nurture debate, current discourse on,
  1–4
'need detectors,' in hypothalamus, 19–20
needs, learning and, 27
Nelson, 4
neocortex, 16
  innate cognitive modules and, 109–111,
    136–138
  mathematics learning and, 165
nerve cell generation, 52
networks
  in brain modules, 39–40
  information processing and functional
    plasticity, 46–50

modular units and, 40
neural Darwinism, 7–8, 11, 27
  affect and intellect and, 113–115
  emotion/affect and, 13–14
  instincts and, 100–101
neural networks
  cognitive innateness and, 2–4
  connectivity and weights in, 47, 49
  cortical pre-requisites and, 78
  Deep Learning Neural Networks, 66–67,
    74–75, 123–124
  embodied language and, 126
  grammar and, 65–66
  information processing and, 46–50
  principle of, 48
neural plasticity
  brain development and, 50–55
  brain modules theory and, 5–6
  cortical modules and, 13, 53
  hard- and soft-wired interactions, 111–112
  information processing and, 46–50
  innate cognitive models and, 7–8
  innate cognitive modules and, 76–77
  at macro level, 49–50
  in neural networks, 49
  nonlocal neural connections and, 13–14
  physical and social interactions and
    development of, 80–82
neural substrates, 113–115
neuronal cell death, 53–55
neuronal connections, classification of, 56–57
Neuronal Group Selection, 113–115
neuroplasticity, sensory and motor systems in,
  17
niche construction, 140–141, 143–144
Nichols, J., 128–129
non-declarative memory, 29
noradrenaline (norepinephrine) system, 10–11
'Nothing Makes Sense Except in the Light of
  Evolution' (Dobzhansky), 4
Nowak, M. A., 1–2, 79–80, 174–177
number module, 70
  mathematics learning and, 165

ontogeny, evolution and, 145–146
opioids
  LIKING system and, 89–91
  PANIC/GRIEF system and, 95–97
Osher, D. E., 34–35
Oudeyer, P.-Y., 126
outer world

brain structure and function and, 19–24
learning and, 27
oxytocin, lust and, 91–92

Painter, C., 120–122, 131–133
panic, 95–97
PANIC/GRIEF system, 95–97, 100, 126–127
affect and intellect and, 113–115
gender and, 133–134
Panksepp, Jaak, 2–4, 11, 12, 13–14
on affect and intellect, 113–115
evolutionary psychology and, 138–139
extended taxonomy of, 99–100
on feeling and instinct, 86–99
law of affect and, 144–146
PANIC/SEPARATION system, 126–127
patterned neuronal connections, 56–57
pattern recognition
categorization ability, 118
cortical plasticity and, 53
number module and, 70
patterns of activity
instinct as, 27–29
learning and, 24–27
in nervous system, 52
Peperkamp, S., 158
perception
contextual nature of, 34–35
modalities of, 22
in tectum, 23–24
Perfetti, C. A., 159
periaqueductal grey (PAG) matter, 86–87
RAGE system and, 92–93
SEEKING system and, 89–91
peripheral nervous system, 16
phrenology, 60–61
Piaget, Jean, 120–122
Pickering, M. J., 101–103
Pigliucci, M., 139–141
Pinker, Stephen, 1–2, 12, 13, 59, 63–67, 75–80,
106, 133–134, 157–161
placebos, embodied mind and, 101–103
plastic networks, 49
PLAY system, 98–99, 100
gender and, 133–134
learning and motivation and, 153–155
pleasure
as instinct, 86–99
periaqueductal grey (PAG) matter and,
86–87
pluripotency, cognitive function and, 32–35

posterior fusiform gyrus, 34–35
poverty of stimulus hypothesis, 1–2
future research and, 172–173
innate cognitive modules and, 69–71, 74–75
language and, 78–79, 122–123
mother-child bonding and, 14
Putnam and, 169–170
Systemic Functional Linguistics and, 131–133
prediction
language learning and, 160–161
SEEKING instinct and, 89
senses and thalamus and, 29–32
Price, C. J., 159
Price, J., 12, 100, 126–127
primary emotion systems
evolution and development and, 113–115,
134–135
innate cognitive modules and, 136–138
problem-solving, intuition and, 148–150
procedural learning, non-declarative memory
and, 29
proneural region, nerve cell generation and,
52
proteins, 140–141
protest behaviour, 95–97
Pulleyblank, D., 137
Pulvermüller, F., 116–117
'purity' module, 99–100
Putnam, Hilary, 168–172

Raff, R. A., 4
RAGE system, 92–93, 100
CARE system and, 97–98
Ramachandran, V. S., 49–50
random microconnections, 58
RANKING/HIERARCHY/DOMINANCE
system, 100, 153–155
rational choice, emotions and, 144–146
reading
dyslexic students and, 161–163
evolution and, 156–157
gestalt holism and, 163–165
posterior fusiform gyrus and, 34–35
recursion
innate cognitive modules and, 76
language acquisition and, 66–67
representations
cognition and, 22–23
cortical plasticity and, 53
learning and, 24–27
reusability, modularity and, 43

Richardson, Robert, 138–139
Robinson, G. E., 108–109
Rolls, E., 87–91
Rosenfelder, Mark, 125
Rozin, P., 113–115
rule-based language systems, 2–4
  abstract structure, 125
  computational strategies and, 66–67
  innate cognitive modules and, 65–66, 77–79

sadness, 95–97
Sampson, G., 79–80
Sapolsky, R. M., 100
'second brain,' stomach as, 99–100
SEEKING system, 87–91
  affect and intellect and, 113–115
  cold aggression and, 92–93
  learning and motivation and, 153–155
  primary emotions and, 134–135
selection
  Evo-Devo tradition and, 139–141
  learning and principle of, 25–26
  multilevel selection, 142
Selten, R., 76–77
semantic mapping, cortex and, 34–35
semiotics
  language universals and, 124–125
  linguistics and, 126
sensory affects, 27–29
sensory experience
  innate cognitive modules, 109–111
  input systems, 72
  modalities of perception and, 22
  sensory motor system, 17
  synaptic tuning and, 53–55
  tectum and, 23–24
  thalamus and, 29–32
serotonin system, 10–11
sexuality, LUST instinct and, 91–92
Shanahan, D., 120–122
Shanker, S., 74–75, 115–117, 120–123, 169–170
Shaywitz, S., 156–157, 161–163
signalling
  emotions and language and, 120–122
  nerve cell generation and, 52
signal transduction networks, 140–141
sign language, 158
Sillito, A. M., 30–32
Simon, H. A., 42–43
Simpson, J. A., 60–61
*Simpson, 122–123

Sly, B. J., 4
Smith, Godfrey, 76
Social Brain Hypothesis, 138–144
social constructivism, innate cognitive models
  and, 60
social context
  language learning and, 117–119
  linguistics and, 126
Social Intelligence Hypothesis, 138–144
social needs
  brain and evolution and, 35–37
  learning and, 27
soft-wired connections, 8–10
  development, 109
  evolution of, 112–113
  functions, 109–111
  hard-wired interaction with, 111–112
Solms, M., 100
specific microconnections, 58
specific neuronal connections, 56–57
spelling, fear of learning and, 167
spoken language
  education and, 161–163
  embodied mind and, 103
  evolution and, 156–157
  learning and, 155–165
  modalities, 157–161
  Systemic Functional Linguistics, 129–133
Standard Social Science Model (SSSM), 60
Sterelny, K., 142, 143–144
Stevens, A., 12, 100, 126–127
stimulants, SEEKING instinct and, 89
Stoeger, William, 174–177
Stotz, K., 107–109, 144
structured microconnections, 58
structure/physiology
  brain modules theory and, 5–6
  innate cognitive models and, 7–8
subjective states, 21–22
  hippocampal activation and, 26
substantia innominata, 26
Sur, M., 2–4, 53–55, 160–161
survival, primary emotion systems and, 113–115
Svenonius, D., 137
Swisher, M., 158
symbolic ability
  language acquisition and, 118, 120–122
  language universals and, 124–125
synapses
  formation and generation of, 52
  hard- and soft-wired interactions, 111–112

neuron connections in, 40–41, 113–115
sensory experience and tuning of, 53–55
'Synaptic Self,' 46–50
syntax
    evolution of, 66–67
    innate cognitive modules and, 70
Systemic Functional Linguistics, 129–133
systems level brain modules, 43
Szathmáry, E., 65–66, 120

targeted hard-wired connections, 8–10, 53–55
teaching
    emotional environment and, 166–167
    of writing, 167
tectum
    language-ready brain and, 37
    structure and function of, 23–24
thalamus
    language-ready brain and, 37
    senses and prediction and, 29–32
Theory of Mind
    innate cognitive modules and modularity of, 69, 76–77
    intention-reading and, 118
Thibault, P. J., 128–129
Tomasello, M., 79–80, 116–117, 124–125, 126–127, 132–133
Tooby, J., 61–62, 113–115
tool use, folk physics module and, 69, 150–152
top-down effects
    embodied mind and, 101–103
    hard- and soft-wired interactions, 111–112
    interlevel relations and, 44–46
Toronchuk, J. A., 99–100
triune brain structure, 16, 145–146

Universal Grammar (UG) hypothesis, 66–67, 124–125, 137
    gender and, 133–134
    innate cognitive modules and, 64, 76, 78–79
universality, innate cognitive modules and, 78

universals, language and origin of, 124–125, 168–172
usage-based linguistics, 119, 126–127
Usrey, Martin, 30–32

valence, body-monitoring nuclei and, 21–22
values
    brain plasticity and, 113–115
    innate cognitive modules and, 106–113
    'liking' system and, 89–91
    in mammals, 85
Van der Westhuizen, D., 100
ventral tegmental area, SEEKING instinct and, 87–91
visual cortex, sensory experience and tuning of, 53–55
visual perception
    innate cognitive module, 68–69
    sensory experience and, 53–55
    Systemic Functional Linguistics and, 132–133
Visual Wordform Area (VWFA), 33–34

WANTING system, 89–91
weights
    in neural networks, 47
    synaptic weight adjustment, 53–55
Wernicke's area, 32–35
West-Eberhard, M. J., 12, 41–42, 46, 51
Wilson, E. O., 112–113
Wimsatt, W. C., 38–39
Wolpert, L., 51, 55, 103, 108–109
written language
    development of, 116–117
    education and, 161–163
    evolution and, 156–157
    fear of learning and, 167
    interpretation of, 30
    learning and, 155–165
    modalities, 157–161
    Systemic Functional Linguistics, 129–133
    Visual Wordform Area and, 33–34

Printed in Great Britain
by Amazon